CONFRONTING
CULTURE

CONFRONTING CULTURE

Sociological Vistas

David Inglis and John Hughson

polity

First published in 2003 by Polity Press in association with Blackwell Publishing Ltd

Editorial office:
Polity Press
65 Bridge Street
Cambridge CB2 1UR, UK

Marketing and production:
Blackwell Publishing Ltd
108 Cowley Road
Oxford OX4 1JF, UK

Distributed in the USA by
Blackwell Publishing Inc.
350 Main Street
Malden, MA 02148, USA

A catalogue record for this book is available from the British Library.

Library of Congress Cataloging-in-Publication Data
Inglis, David.
　　Confronting culture : sociological vistas / David Inglis and John Hughson.
　　　　p. cm.
　　Includes bibliographical references and index.
　　ISBN 0-7456-2561-4 — ISBN 0-7456-2562-2 (pbk.)
　　　　1. Culture.　2. Sociology.　I. Hughson, John.　II. Title.
　　HM621 .I54 2003
　　306—dc21　　　　　　　　　　　　　　　　　　　　　2002155614

Typeset in 10.5/12pt Sabon
by Graphicraft Ltd, Hong Kong
Printed and bound in Great Britain by MPG Books Ltd, Bodmin, Cornwall

For further information on Polity, visit our website: www.polity.co.uk

Contents

Acknowledgements

The writing of this book has been a long and difficult task, but the experience has also proved extremely rewarding in that it has allowed us to share a wealth of ideas with friends and colleagues. We would like to extend our gratitude to colleagues at the University of Aberdeen and the University of Wolverhampton.

At Aberdeen, I would like to offer sincere thanks to all those in the Department of Sociology who have helped in the writing of this book. Special mention in this regard should be given to Roland Robertson, Karen O'Reilly and Norman Stockman. Especial gratitude is also due to Andrew Tudor of the University of York, without whose analytic rigour my own thoughts on matters cultural would be much the poorer. Thanks also are due to my parents, who continue smilingly to tolerate the eccentricities of their verbose offspring.

David Inglis

I would like to thank my many friends, academic and otherwise, both in Australia and the UK, for their input and support over the years. During my time at Wolverhampton, I was particularly indebted to Paul Willis, both for sharing with me his long experience in the sorts of issues we were writing about, and for tolerating views that sometimes diverged from his own. Above all, I would like to thank Lisa for all the love and consideration she has always shown me, no matter what.

John Hughson

As ever, whatever strengths the book may have derive from the background presence of many other people. Its faults remain wholly our own.

Introduction:
Sociology and Culture

Culture is important

Just before we sat down to write the introduction to this book, both of the present authors were watching television news. The story dominating the news came from the Far East. Some days before, a bomb had gone off in a bar on the island of Bali, killing almost two hundred people. The majority of the dead were Western tourists and backpackers. Many of them came from Australia. This was not surprising given the popularity among Australians of Bali as a holiday destination offering cheap accommodation, sunshine and a little Far Eastern exoticism. The bomb was suspected to have been planted by an Islamic fundamentalist group, dedicated to the same kinds of aim as the people who had been responsible for the destruction of the World Trade Center in New York on 11 September 2001.

After the emotional impact that the scenes of the carnage had on us had begun to recede a little, we both began to reflect on why such an event had taken place at all. Why was it that certain people would wish to take the lives of others in such an apparently cruel and senseless fashion? It became increasingly apparent to us as we thought about this matter that what was involved was a clash of *ideas*, *values* and *emotions*.

From the point of view of most present-day Westerners, people wishing to take a holiday in some far-off clime, merely wanting to experience a little sun and fun, are doing nothing wrong. Seeking relaxation by lying on the beach, or wanting to drink, dance and party, seem from the Western point of view to be entirely innocent activities, causing no one any harm or offence. But from a strongly

religious point of view, be it Christian or Islamic, these sorts of behaviour can seem both decadent and immoral. Uncovered flesh being
exposed on the beach or by the swimming pool, large amounts of
alcohol being consumed, the types of boisterous conduct that people
can engage in when under the influence of alcohol or other drugs,
sexual opportunities being sought and taken up – all of these things
seem to certain strictly religious viewpoints as affronts to morality
and spirituality, activities to be condemned rather than condoned,
to be censored and forbidden rather than accepted, tolerated or
encouraged.

One reason for the Bali bombing, then, was a confrontation between two very different ways of thinking, believing and feeling. On
the one hand, there was a primarily secular set of attitudes, characteristic of the modern West, where individualism, consumerism and
hedonism are dominant. On the other hand, and in stark contrast to
the former, was a religious view of the world, in this case Islamic,
which regards such Western values as abominable and unacceptable,
corrupting of moral life and insulting to God. From this point of
view, the killing of people who indulge in what is seen as an immoral
lifestyle, is not in fact murder, but holy and righteous retribution
being wreaked on wicked people. In turn, from the Western point of
view, the wickedness lies with those people who planted the bomb,
and those like them, who are seen as narrow-minded zealots who
have no respect for human life in general and that of the innocents
they killed in particular.

A shorthand way of describing the situation we have just described
is that in part the Bali massacre, and other events like it, was the
outcome of a *clash of cultures*. The ideas, values and emotions of
one group, that group's 'culture', come into conflict with those of
another group, that other group's 'culture'. It takes just a moment
of reflection to realize how many instances we have in the contemporary world where different groups, each with their own sets of
thoughts, beliefs and expectations, are in opposition to each other:
Protestants and Catholics in Northern Ireland, Tamils and Sinhalese
in Sri Lanka, Jews and Palestinians in Israel, to name just a few
instances of groups of people in often bloody conflict with each other,
in large part because of cultural differences.

Although these and other conflicts like them have complex economic and political causes, at their heart they are disputes over ideas,
beliefs and values. The word 'culture' describes what different groups
of people think, believe and feel; their ways of thinking and the
values that they hold are generally deeply ingrained both within
the mind of each individual and in the texture of the collective life of

the group to which they belong. On occasion, the ingrained ways of understanding the world and the cherished beliefs and attitudes of a particular group can enter into discord with those of other groups, the result in many cases being violence and death. Culture is vastly important in human affairs, not least because every day around the world people are killed because of their cultural affiliations and dispositions. Culture is always in one way or another at the centre of disputes, controversies and conflicts. For that reason alone, it is something that urgently needs to be studied and understood. When we examine culture in any one of its many forms, we are not just engaged in a dry, academic exercise. Instead, we are embarked upon an endeavour to get to the heart of some of the most controversial and disputed issues that human beings face in their lives.

Cultural issues need not always involve situations of hostility and opposition. Culture can also be involved in the creation and operation of (relatively) harmonious and cooperative relations between human beings. It is cultural factors – ideas, beliefs, values – that give the human person an identity and a personality, by bringing him or her into the life of the group of which he or she is a part. Moreover, when culturally based disputes do occur, they do not of course always take the extreme form of events like the Bali bombing. Cultural conflicts can take place as much *within* specific groups as *between* them. Cultural disputes within groups can often occur in more subtle and insidious ways than those involving disputes between groups. For example, for sociologists inspired by Marxist thought, the cultural (rather than the explicitly political and economic) conflict between social classes within a particular society often takes place in rather indirect and roundabout ways. Cultural conflict need not result in violence, but, even so, its effects in terms of powerful groups dominating other groups can be just as, or even more, marked than if the dominant groups used physical violence against their opponents. A central theme of this book is the argument that if you want to understand how power is distributed in any society, you need to analyse the cultural factors in that society, and how they contribute towards either the maintenance or the overthrow of the status quo in that society.

Once again, the point is that the sociological study of culture is crucial, not just for understanding the relationships *between* groups or between societies, but also for comprehending what goes on, especially in terms of the wielding of power, *within* particular groups and societies. Quite simply, *culture is important*. Without a good understanding of the various things the word 'culture' indicates, your understanding of human social life will be greatly lacking.

Culture is everywhere

So far, we have said that culture involves ideas, beliefs and values. Clearly therefore 'culture' refers to a huge amount of different things, from someone's emotional responses to a particular event to the moral point of view embodied in a religion or a novel. In fact, if you begin to think about it, you will soon realize that 'culture' is everywhere.

For example, the wide array of cultural products we are faced with in contemporary Western societies is mind-boggling: books, magazines, newspapers, films, television programmes, internet sites and so on. The vast number of ways in which these are disseminated is also amazing, with huge networks of communication having come, in a very short space of time, to span the globe.

Such a tremendous diversity of objects and processes is in fact only one dimension of what 'culture' might mean. It could also mean what some people regard as the very highest achievements of the human race: the symphonies of Beethoven or the plays of Shakespeare. At the same elevated level, 'culture' could refer to the ultimate and highest values that a particular person or group or whole society adheres to – for example, a culture of democracy, freedom and brotherly (and sisterly) love. Culture might also refer to everyday practices and attitudes, the ordinary ways in which people think, and act, and feel, and into which they have been socialized from an early age.

So 'culture' does indeed seem to be everywhere. And yet it is a word that can refer to so many different things; it is a word that is notoriously difficult to pin down. How do you identify a 'culture'? How do you know it is different from another culture? How can you describe a culture, or understand what it means? Just as culture seems to be everywhere, it also seems to slip through your fingers when you try to get hold of it. It is one of the words that describes so many aspects of human life, and yet it is one of the most slippery words we have. In the early 1950s, the American anthropologists Alfred Kroeber and Clyde Kluckhohn (1963 [1952]) reviewed all the various meanings of 'culture' (and what they took as being its close verbal cousin, 'civilization') that they could find. The result was 164 definitions of what 'culture' could mean. The literary scholar Raymond Williams (1976) famously noted that 'culture' was one of the most complex words in the English language, having a whole series of meanings that had changed a great deal over time. Among contemporary meanings of 'culture' are (1) 'high culture', art, civilization; (2) personal refinement; (3) cultural objects such as books or films; (4) the 'whole way of life' of a given group of people. Thus 'culture' can refer simultaneously to 'high culture' and 'popular culture', to the ways of thinking and valuing characteristic of everyone in a given society, and to the capacities of individuals. It is clear that 'culture' can cover a huge range of related issues and ideas.

Defining culture

In order to avoid confusion, we need to be clear from the outset what we mean by 'culture'. In this book we will work with the following broad definition, which has six parts:

1 *Culture comprises the patterns of ideas, values and beliefs common to a particular group of people.* It does not matter whether the group is small or large, or whether it comprises a set of people within a particular 'society', or everyone within that society, or people from different societies related to each other in some way across national boundaries. Culture is defined as always being part of the collective life of given groups of human beings.

    Culture comprises recurring patterns of ideas, values and beliefs. A 'culture' persists to some extent over time. It has some capacities to endure over time, as well as to change and be changed.

2 *The culture of one group differentiates it from other groups, each of which has its own culture.* Different types of group can be said to have 'their own' cultures: the culture of a 'nation' (e.g. French culture), of a social class (e.g. working-class culture), of an ethnic group within a nation (e.g. Italian-American culture), of a group outside the 'mainstream' culture (e.g. a youth subculture of punks or goths). Each of these types of group can be said to have *its own* culture, its own distinctive set of ideas, values and beliefs. This is not, however, to suggest that there are no overlaps between different cultures, and no shared aspects between them (e.g. working-class culture in the United States is part of, and shares many of the features of, more general 'American' culture).

3 *Culture contains meanings. Culture is meaningful.* These meanings are the ways through which people in the group comprehend, make sense of, and respond intellectually and emotionally to, the world around them.

4 *The ideas, values and beliefs of a group are embodied in symbols and artefacts.* These symbols can be pictorial or can be part of a written language. These artefacts are physical objects which are imprinted in some way with the ideas, values and beliefs of the group.

5 *Culture is learned.* Culture is transmitted by one generation of
   people to the next generation. This learning process means that
   individuals internalize the ideas, values and beliefs of the group.
   These become habitual and taken for granted, and are generally
   experienced as 'natural' rather than learned.
6 *Culture is arbitrary.* Culture is the result of human activities,
   rather than the product of 'nature'. It is neither 'natural' nor
   inevitably the way it is. It could be different from the way it is if
   the life conditions of the group change.

In short, culture involves what different groups of people believe,
think and feel. All parts of the definition except the final one are
relatively uncontroversial. Most social scientists see human 'culture'
as somehow above or beyond 'nature', the natural environment in
which humans live, and this attitude is reflected in most of the paradigms we will investigate in the coming chapters. But as we will see
in chapter 1 and again in the overall conclusion to this book, there
is a countertrend amongst some sociologists who wish to see how
'culture' and 'nature' are interrelated.

The definition above allows us to make a start in *confronting
culture*. The subtitle of this book is 'Sociological Vistas'. In what
follows, we will examine many of the ways in which sociology and
sociologists (and others who have thought in ways rather like sociologists) have attempted to deal with the kinds of issue just described.
In essence, we are setting out and analysing what might be called *the
sociology of culture*, looking at what is involved in such an enterprise, and reflecting on whether its attitudes and findings are worth
listening to.

Sociology looks at culture

As this is a book about sociological ways of understanding culture,
and as sociology concerns itself with 'social' factors as well as cultural ones, we will also have to define 'social' and 'society'. We have
defined 'culture' in terms of what particular groups of people think,
believe and feel. We define 'social relations' as what people *do*, their
socially shaped actions and activities. 'Society' on this view comprises *the patterns of the actions of individuals, interacting with each
other*.

Society therefore comprises the patterned ways in which people act.
The patterns of recurring actions are 'social structures'. These are
reproduced over time by individuals continuing to act and interact in

similar ways. Conversely, social structures are changed by alterations in the forms taken by actions and interactions.

In a way, there is no such thing as *the* sociology of culture. After all, there are many different types of sociology: structuralist sociology, action theory, phenomenological sociology, structurationist sociology, and so on. Almost all types of sociology have something to say about 'cultural' matters, and many of them are dealt with in this book. The ways in which they deal with culture are, of course, to a great degree determined by their more general theoretical and practical orientations. Thus Marxist sociologies, which are interested in the nature of class power, conceive culture in those terms, and examine it for the purposes of saying interesting things about class power. Likewise, Weberian sociologies, which focus on the motivations of people engaged in forms of action, see cultural matters as involved in the motivation of people's actions. And so on it goes, with each type of sociology bringing its own conceptions and concerns to the definition and analysis of culture.

Nonetheless, all versions of sociology do have certain things in common with each other. The view that underpins the present book is that all persons claiming to be sociologists have to confront, whether they are fully aware of it or not, and whether they like it or not, two crucial issues:

1 'Theory' has to be informed in some way by empirical data.
2 There should be an engagement with issues of *social structure* and *social action* (or *agency*).

The first criterion is what makes sociology different from philosophy (or at least some brands of philosophy). Sociology is a way of thinking that has to be backed up by some kind of empirical reference. The 'armchair theorist', who just 'theorizes' about social life without being concerned about the lack of any evidence to back up his or her claims, is not by definition a *sociologist* but a *social philosopher*. It is entirely possible to be an 'armchair sociologist' if one makes claims that other people could submit to some kind of empirical test. But someone who makes claims without *wanting* to have them supported by empirical data does not, on this definition, qualify as a sociologist. It does not matter *how* the empirical data is gathered, or *how* it is related to the more speculative, theoretical claims. The only crucial thing is that there is some kind of connection between 'theory' and 'data'.

The second criterion is that the fundamental focus of sociological theorizing concerns the relations between 'social action' (or 'agency') and 'social structure' (Alexander, 1982: 114; Mouzelis, 1995: 60; Anderson et al., 1987: 154). Quite simply, this means looking both at what individuals do ('action') and what society compels or requires them to do ('structure'). This criterion, that sociology must look at *both* of these issues, is probably more controversial than the first, as certain brands of sociology, which fall onto one side of the divide or the other, sometimes repudiate the possibility or point of investigating the term that signifies the opposite side. Particularly prone to do this are various forms of micro-sociology, which deny the possibility of looking at so-called 'social structures', because such things are mere abstractions, the fabrications of more macro-minded sociologists. Nonetheless, just as we remained agnostic about precisely how empirical materials were to be related to theoretical contentions, we also remain agnostic here about whether sociologists should focus on one side of the divide, or attempt to bridge it in the manner, for example, of Giddens (1984). Instead, what we would say is that a distinguishing feature of all forms of thought that are identifiable as 'sociological' is that they deal *in some fashion* with the structure/action problem. They might embrace the divide or seek to transcend it or polemicize against it, but we identify as 'sociological' in nature any approach to social life that more or less explicitly deals *in whatever way* with this issue.

Our argument is that these two criteria must be met if a given approach is to be defined as 'sociological' in nature. Any approach that claims to be engaged in doing a sociological study of cultural matters would have to meet these two criteria. In addition, a form of thought that could be identified as being part of the *sociology of culture* would have to meet a further criterion, namely:

3 Attempts should be made to understand relationships that hold between 'social' factors and 'cultural' factors.

A *sociological* approach to culture is therefore defined as one that makes some kind of reference to both cultural and social factors. Once again, we are not prescribing what any particular approach *should* say about such matters. It is merely enough that it makes reference to them, and tries to think about the relationships that might hold between 'culture' on the one side and 'society' on the other. As sociology is about the investigation of the *social* dimensions of human life, the study of culture within sociology is therefore simultaneously about investigating both cultural and social factors. Without a consideration of social factors, a study is not sociological. Most of the approaches to culture we will examine in this book are concerned with understanding the relations between, as each perspective defines them, 'social' and 'cultural' factors.

It is through this dual focus that sociological contributions towards understanding cultural matters can be said to be somewhat unique, because other approaches to cultural issues – for example, by literary critics and philosophers – do not generally focus as much on the relationship of 'social' to 'cultural' factors. By bringing 'society' into the study of culture, sociology contributes a focus that other disciplines downplay or ignore.

Organization of the book

The organization of the book is as follows. The majority of the chapters are about how a particular set of themes in the sociology of culture was developed over time in one of four national contexts: Germany, France, Great Britain and the United States. The reason for this focus is simple – it was in these places that most sociological approaches to culture were first developed. On occasion, chapters are devoted to a particular type of thinking about culture that is not completely nationally located, such as is the case with postmodernism, which is mostly, but not exclusively, inspired by developments in French thought. Another case is the chapter devoted to a single figure: that of the French sociologist Pierre Bourdieu. So vast is the amount of writing that Bourdieu produced on cultural matters, and such is the influence it has had in many parts of the world, that we thought Bourdieu deserved (at the very least) a chapter to himself.

Each chapter is concerned with setting out the main contours of the topic at hand, and examining its strengths and weaknesses, especially, although not exclusively, in light of the three issues set out above: the relations of 'theory' to 'data', of 'structure' to 'action', and of 'culture' to 'society'.

We begin in chapter 1 by examining the nature of some of the assumptions of later sociological approaches to matters cultural by assessing the work of the 'classical' sociologists of the nineteenth and early twentieth centuries. We proceed in chapter 2 to appraise the ideas of one of the first systematic attempts in the mid-twentieth century to analyse cultural matters from a sociological perspective: this is the work of the Frankfurt School. In chapter 3, we analyse the work of American thinkers of the same period on the nature of 'mass culture'. Chapter 4 involves developments in the English context away from a form of cultural analysis that privileged notions of 'high culture', towards one which defended the notion that culture should be seen as the 'way of life' of a given group of people. Chapter 5 crosses the Channel to France, to investigate the nature of structuralist ideas about the semiotic study of culture. Chapter 6 remains to a certain degree in France, constituting as it does an explication and critique of the ideas associated with the intellectual and artistic movement known as 'postmodernism'. Chapter 7 looks at the contribution made by Pierre Bourdieu to understanding the nature of social and cultural power. The theme of how culture is actually produced has been primarily developed by certain American scholars, and their work is the subject of chapter 8. The final conclusion deals with some of the issues now facing sociological approaches to culture in the early twenty-first century.

1

Setting Up the Terrain: Classical Sociology and Culture

Introduction

Contemporary issues, debates and controversies in the sociology of culture would scarcely be understandable if one did not take account of the contributions of the sociologists of the nineteenth and early twentieth centuries. Most of the themes that have been dealt with by later thinkers were first identified and pursued by the early sociological pioneers. In fact, much of the later writings in the sociology of culture have involved extensions, refinements, reworkings and rejections of the assumptions and ways of thinking first forged by the classical sociologists.

Writing in 1988, the American social theorist Jeffrey C. Alexander (1988: 1) stated that, at that point in time, there was 'as yet, scarcely any cultural analysis' in sociology. Such a statement barely describes the actual state of affairs. Even a passing glance at the works of the nineteenth- and early twentieth-century sociologists shows that they were almost all engaged in ways of understanding culture. An important part of early sociology is a series of reflections upon culture. From the very beginning, sociology was not just an investigation of *social* life, but of *cultural* life too.

Examining the ideas of classical sociology is therefore not just an exercise in archaeology. It is an absolutely necessary way of understanding how sociology operates today. In this chapter we will examine the different schools of thought in classical sociology, and look at two key issues that informed the classical sociologists' efforts to understand cultural matters. The first issue is a theoretical one: what are 'culture' and 'society', and how do the two relate to each other?

The second issue is a more substantive one: in the classical sociologists' opinions, what was the nature of *modern* culture, and what were its strengths and weaknesses? Was the culture of modern society a 'healthy' one, or one that was corrupt and harmful for the well-being of modern social life? The various answers that the classical sociologists gave to these questions are at the root both of what they offered later sociologists, and of what they might bequeath to us today.

We begin this chapter by examining the crucial intellectual split that informs much of later sociology, namely the divide between Enlightenment and Romanticism. We will examine this division in terms of how it led both to very different conceptions of culture and to divergent kinds of sociologies. We then turn to the ideas of Karl Marx, and the legacy of Marxist understandings of culture. We continue by examining the contributions made to later German sociological studies of culture by, among others, Alfred Weber, Max Weber and Georg Simmel. We then consider the tradition set up by Emile Durkheim, a mode of understanding culture developed further by two of his twentieth-century inheritors, Karl Mannheim and Talcott Parsons. We conclude by considering the ways in which classical sociology continues to inform thinking about culture today.

Enlightenment and Romanticism

The term 'classical sociology' is a relatively recent invention. The sociologists of the nineteenth century and before, to whom the term refers, did not of course see their own endeavours in such a light, because 'classical' is a description that can only ever be used after the events it refers to have passed. The very word 'classical' suggests something out of a museum, rather than a living, breathing thing. But in their time, the people we now call 'classical sociologists' were engaged in some of the greatest intellectual controversies of their day. Generally, they felt that what they were doing was not just a dry academic exercise, but was of pressing importance not only for understanding the society in which they lived, but also in changing it for the better (or, at the very least, in complaining about how bad things were becoming). There were always, in one way or another, *political* motives behind the sometimes apparently 'neutral' views put forward by sociologists, a situation that continues today. These political dispositions were shaped in turn by the social backgrounds of the people involved in creating knowledge about society, a fact they were sometimes very aware of and sometimes not. The main point is that the early sociologists studied culture in ways that were profoundly formed by *who they were* and *what they believed in*. So in order fully to understand what their various opinions were as to cultural matters, we have to grasp the social and intellectual contexts out of which they and their ideas arose.

The terrain that we now call 'classical sociology' is a very complex one, for it is made up of a whole series of ideas and positions that are in some ways often very different from each other, but in other ways also often bear striking resemblances. A good way of making sense of this complicated field is to divide it up into two major trends. This is inevitably a simplification of a convoluted situation, but it does help us see more clearly the issues we are dealing with. The two main tendencies we can identify are those of Enlightenment and Romanticism. Enlightenment thinking came to prominence, particularly in France, in the later eighteenth century. The themes pursued by Enlightenment thinkers, such as the philosophers Voltaire and Diderot, included an emphasis on scientific thinking as being superior to other types of thought, especially the more imaginative and poetic types (Frankel, 1969). The form of thought known as Romanticism arose in the early nineteenth century as a critical response to Enlightenment's focus on, and celebration of, rational thought and the natural sciences. While Enlightenment thought glorified the scientist, Romantic ideas were primarily produced by, and eulogized, artists and poets. Such ideas were especially important in Germany and England. Romanticism defended against the scientific mentality of Enlightenment such values as individualism, poetic expression and artistic imagination (Berlin, 2000).

The divide between 'scientific' and 'poetic' thinking was therefore an expression of the social and political divisions between rationalist scientists on the one side, and anti-rationalist poets, literary figures and artists on the other. The cleavage between these two broad camps also expressed a national divide: between the French who tended to advocate an Enlightenment view of the virtues of natural science, and the Germans who were more inclined towards a defence of the benefits of a poetic, 'spiritual' and 'imaginative' approach to life. In Britain, Enlightenment and Romanticist thought took hold of different sections of the intellectual community, with Romanticist ideas being particularly important for the development of the specifically English approach to culture known as 'culturalism' (see chapter 4).

The division between Enlightenment and Romanticism wrought profound effects on the nature of the various different types of sociology that developed in the later eighteenth and early nineteenth centuries (Dawe, 1970). This was true both in terms of the methods of study that were developed, and in terms of the political views of the early sociologists. In terms of the methods by which sociology was to be carried out, Enlightenment thinking emphasized that sociology should be a project based on the model of the natural sciences. This meant, amongst other things, a search for the 'laws' of social life, a collection of empirical 'data', and attempts at working out rigorous ways of collecting that data. This style of sociology was particularly influential in France, with figures from Auguste Comte (1798–1857) through to Emile Durkheim (1858–1917) and beyond all stressing the virtues of 'positivist' science, which had the characteristics just described. This position argued for an approach to the study of society based on 'hard' scientific evidence.

While Enlightenment-influenced positivist sociologists looked to the natural sciences to provide a model for the newly emerging social sciences, those influenced by Romanticist ideas argued for a non-'scientific', more interpretative and imagination-driven approach, characteristic of humanities disciplines like literary criticism (Hawthorn, 1976). As was the case with Romanticist thinking more generally, this kind of approach within sociology specifically was most dominant in Germany. Particularly influential in this context were the ideas of Johann Gottfried Herder (1744–1803; see Barnard, 1965). Herder argued that a particular 'culture' was comprised of the typical mental patterns, attitudes, emotions and ways of doing things characteristic of a certain group or nation. Each nation had a unique culture that could not be compared with any other nation's culture. The analyst should see a particular culture as an 'organic' whole, woven out of the various different elements that make up the life of a nation, such as religious beliefs, moral ideas and ways of speaking. It is important to note that, on this view, 'culture' is not just the 'high culture' of that society – the 'great' works of art, philosophy and so on – but *everything*, including the tiniest details of everyday life.

At a later date, but still in the same line of thinking, the German philosopher Wilhelm Dilthey (1833–1911) formulated a distinction which subsequently came to be very influential in German sociology (Makkreel, 1975). He argued that the natural sciences (*Naturwissenschaften*) and the human (or 'cultural') sciences (*Geisteswissenschaften*) were wholly different, not just in terms of the objects they examined but also in terms of approaching and studying those objects. The natural sciences study natural objects, which are either inert (e.g. rock formations) or living but subhuman (plants and animals). But the objects of the human sciences are living, breathing human beings, invested with 'spirit' (*Geist*) and who are alive, creative and endowed with consciousness. In line with Herder, Dilthey asserted that this 'spirit' does not derive from individuals but from socio-cultural groups (*Volk*), whose collective cultural life (*Kultur*) is thoroughly permeated with spiritual values that are unique to that group. Thus the human ('cultural') sciences (*Geisteswissenschaften*) are literally the study of the human 'spirit', this spirit taking on unique cultural forms at different times and in different places. Herder had already argued that each culture arises 'spontaneously' from the life of each nation. As a result, it is not susceptible to supposedly 'scientific' investigation, as positivist science alleged. Instead, the analyst must sympathetically imagine what it is like to be a member of that culture. He or she must seek to reconstruct by interpretation how the typical individual brought up in that culture thinks and feels. The study of 'culture' meant *interpretation* of the spiritual values and the forms of consciousness of a given group of people (Rickman, 1988). This idea of 'interpretative understanding' (*Verstehen*) came to be central not only in German sociology, but also in anthropology in various national contexts (Kuper, 1999).

As a result of these different dispositions in France and Germany, there grew up what were in some ways very different attitudes towards what sociology was supposed to be examining. In the French context, sociology was pre-eminently the study of *social* factors, those elements of human life involving the *structured patterns of interaction* between people. In Germany, however, sociology was generally regarded as an exercise in the study of *culture*, where the term was understood to refer to the aspects of human life involving ideas and spiritual values.

These two distinct sets of disposition towards what sociology should look like were also connected to divergent political views about what the *purpose* of sociology should be. Herder and other German thinkers influenced by Romanticism rejected the Enlightenment view that there was a hierarchy of cultures, with less sophisticated ones at the bottom and more complex ones at the top. For Herder, each culture is to be valorized for its own sake, and not subjected to false comparisons with other cultures that are designed to make it look 'inferior' to them. Sociology, which was in effect synonymous with the study of culture, sometimes came to figure in Germany as a celebration of particular cultures (especially ones that no longer existed) rather than as a critique of them.

The reason for this lay in the highly critical attitudes German Romanticism had towards present-day society. Modern society was regarded as being highly 'mechanical' and 'impersonal', in stark contrast to how the medieval past was imagined to be: a society which possessed a truly 'organic' culture, that had sprung from 'the people' and so was utterly 'authentic', unlike the highly 'artificial' and 'inauthentic' culture of the present. This assessment of the relative merits of present and past cultures lay at the base of the ideas of the important early German sociologist Alfred Tönnies (1855–1936). Tönnies's (1955 [1877]) key analytic distinction was between the type of society characteristic of pre-modernity, including the medieval period (*Gemeinschaft*) and the type of society characteristic of modernity (*Gesselschaft*). The older type of society had been organic in the way it had functioned, and had bound individuals together into a community characterized by a common culture. By contrast, the new type of society was mechanical in its functioning, and the atomized individuals that lived within it had no sense of being bound to the people around them. In this line of thought, shared by Tönnies and many others influenced by Romantic ideas, 'culture' (*Kultur*) was understood as involving the superior, 'spiritual' qualities of traditional German ways of life. It was morally and aesthetically superior to 'civilization' (*Zivilisation*), the modern-day society characterized by material progress in the economy, the rise of scientific thought in the intellectual sphere, and an increasing level of triviality in thought and feeling (Elias, 1995 [1939]). In this German tradition, 'culture' was seen as something not only removed from and (partly or wholly) autonomous of the social, political and economic spheres, but also as something vastly superior to them.

For French Enlightenment thought, the exactly opposite opinion was the dominant one. Here, the idea of 'civilization' was generally regarded in a very positive light, for it suggested material and intellectual progress. Present-day society was felt to be more sophisticated than, and so superior to, the medieval past. This previous society was felt to be riven with superstition and brutality, elements that would or could be erased from human life now that history was moving in a direction of constant improvements in all spheres of life (Febvre, 1998). What was valorized in France (science, material progress) was denigrated in Germany, and what was celebrated in Germany (traditional ways of thinking and acting, the 'organic' culture of the past) was despised in France. This situation had profound effects on the nature of French social science. Enlightenment-derived sociology in France tended to see culture as mystificatory ways of thinking, propagated by particular powerful groups such as priests and aristocrats in order to muddle the thinking of other groups, and so keep themselves in a position of power. Culture on this view is like a fog that is draped over society at the instigation of the powerful. It hides from the view of the powerless what the society is really like. The purpose of sociology becomes to reveal to the powerless how the powerful have duped them through the means of culture. While Romanticist thinking tends to see 'social' and 'cultural' factors as very closely related, if not actually completely synonymous, Enlightenment-inspired thought separates them, with culture being shown to be in the service of particular types of *social power*. This way of thinking was particularly powerful in the French context, where it was part of the sentiments associated with the French Revolution of 1789. But it is also from this form of Enlightenment thinking that Karl Marx, rebelling against the tendencies of his German upbringing, derived his claim that culture is *ideological*, the view that culture often has the social role of hiding sources of social power and aiding them to operate more effectively (Eagleton, 1991).

'Culture' and 'Nature'

Enlightenment-derived sociology, especially prominent in France, therefore was generally more crucially concerned with issues of social power than was German sociology (although, as we will see shortly, the German Max Weber put issues of power at the centre of his sociology). Sociology derived from Enlightenment principles also tended to give much more attention than did Romanticist thought to the relations between social and cultural factors on the one hand, and those of 'nature' on the other. The influential position of Dilthey, which drove a wedge between the social/cultural sciences and the natural sciences, meant that the former were regarded in the German situation as not being concerned with the roles that physical nature plays within the social or cultural realms.

But, arguably, this position closes down an important aspect of the study of culture: finding out how and why culture may be different from 'nature'. Regardless of how unsatisfactory their attempts might now look, Enlightenment-inspired sociologists in France and elsewhere at least tried to grapple with this problem. For example, the Englishman Herbert Spencer (1820–1903), a leading light in the study of social development as an *evolutionary* process, regarded *cultural* development as a result of *social* evolution, which was in its turn a result of transformations of the 'natural' factors of matter and energy. Spencer refers to the cultural realm as the 'super-organic environment'. By this he means that culture is something beyond nature, yet produced by it. In very primitive societies, he argues, humans are affected mostly only by the 'organic environment', that is, the natural world. But as human societies develop and become more complex, so too does the 'super-organic environment' of culture.

Spencer, in like fashion to other evolutionary scientists of the time, sees the development of culture in terms of an evolution from simplicity to complexity, such that

> the once few and simple customs, becom[e] . . . more numerous, definite, and fixed . . . [a]nd then there slowly evolve also the products we call aesthetic . . . [f]rom necklaces of fishbones we advance to dresses elaborate, gorgeous, and infinitely varied; out of discordant war-chants come symphonies and operas . . . in place of caves with rude markings there arise at length galleries of paintings; and the recital of a chief's deeds with mimetic accompaniment gives origin to epics, dramas, lyrics, and the vast mass of poetry, fiction, biography, and history. (1961 [1897]: 1022–3)

There are two important things to notice here. First, Spencer's argument goes against German Romantic viewpoints in that *cultural* developments are not treated as resulting only for *cultural* reasons, but for *social* and *material* reasons too, the latter rooted in the development of human life on earth. However, Spencer does not just reduce cultural factors to these other elements. He argues that at the most evolved levels of human society, culture constitutes 'an immensely-voluminous, immensely-complicated, and immensely-powerful set of influences' on social life (ibid. 1023). Thus, while society initially creates culture, culture itself comes to have effects on society.

Second, Spencer sees increasing complexity as characteristic of social and cultural development, with modern Western society being the most complex of all. Society moves from being an entity made up of a few simple parts, to one made up of a multiplicity of distinct components. This is a process of *structural differentiation*, whereby over time new social spheres emerge that are separate from other spheres. This is a result of an increasing complexity in the *division of labour*. For example, where there initially was one sphere called 'religion' in a less complex society, in a more complex society, of which Western modernity is the most developed example, out of this sphere arises a series of separate realms. As law, morality, art and so on become distinct social institutions, they get decoupled from religion, the sphere that initially encompassed them all. As a result, the religious sphere itself shrinks to encompass only narrowly 'sacred' matters (e.g. beliefs in 'God'), and loses much of its previous social importance. As society becomes more differentiated into autonomous spheres, so too does culture, with separate spheres of culture – the art sphere, the legal sphere, the academic sphere – being characteristic of the complex society of modernity. At the level of the division of labour – that is, at the level of different types of job – the religious sphere initially was operated by people called priests, who also had legal, moral, intellectual and artistic functions. But as these areas become separate spheres in their own right, priests are replaced by specialists who operate each field – professionals such as lawyers, moralists, academics and artists.

Spencer's views on the nature of social evolution are today generally regarded as being far too Eurocentric, as they over-privilege Western modernity by claiming it to be the most 'developed' form of society (Sztompka, 1993). Nonetheless, Spencer's views remain useful for two reasons. First, he attempts to face an issue his German counterparts generally ducked out of: relating society and culture to 'nature'. Second, his theme of structural differentiation and his focus on the emergence in the modern West of separate spheres of culture have both remained important in later sociological studies of culture.

Karl Marx: culture as ideology

Karl Marx (1818–83) stands as one of the most important of the early sociologists, although he did not describe himself as a 'sociologist'. Marx's ideas have been hugely influential upon later sociological studies of culture. Thus it is necessary to understand the full importance of what he was attempting to do. Most of those we now term the 'classical sociologists' examined the nature of modern society in light of the increasing complexity of the division of labour and processes of structural differentiation, and Marx was no exception. As a communist revolutionary whose political aim was the overthrow of capitalist society, he had a particular perspective on these issues. He developed an approach that was highly critical of such developments, in contrast to what he saw as the blandly optimistic views held by people such as Spencer. In this regard, Marx was like many other Germans who held Romanticist ideas about the less than ideal nature of modern society. For Marx, as for the German Romantics, modern society was a cold and mechanical, if not in fact a wholly brutal, form of society, that isolated individuals from each other and exhibited vast amounts of socially induced misery. The cultural state of this society was such that, in Marx's view, far from being welcome, it was one that people should actively strive to abolish, by helping to foment working-class revolution. The theme of human emancipation was crucial for both Romantic and Enlightenment ways of thinking, but the latter located human freedom in the further pursuit of scientific knowledge, whereas the former often emphasized individual rebellions against the ordered, bureaucratic nature of modern life. Marx retained this Romantic strain in his thinking, but shifted the focus to *collective* revolutionary activity by the working class against their capitalist masters.

Conversely, Marx's actual method of social and cultural analysis owed less to any German ideas about 'cultural science', and more to Enlightenment ideals of natural science methodology, orientations particularly strong in France and Britain. In fact, much of Marx's intellectual attention was given over to rebelling against the highly 'spiritual' tendencies dominant in German thought, and to providing an alternative way of understanding human life that took account of 'material' factors too. These latter included relations of social power, the theme of Enlightenment social science, and the connections between society, culture and nature – the focus of evolutionary thinkers contemporary with Marx such as Spencer. Marx's (1991 [1845–6]) particular target was the philosopher G. W. F. Hegel (1770–1831), whose highly spiritualistic philosophy was at that time a dominant force in German thought.

Hegel was part of the *idealist* movement in German philosophy, which argued that human life was best understood as involving ideas and mental representations (1975; see also Taylor, 1975). The world that humans confront is not to be understood as a material world that imposes itself on how human subjects view it. Instead, the world is a product of how it is viewed by those subjects. Thus the social world itself is composed of ideas. In more modern terms, we can say Hegel, rather like Herder, sees a particular society as the product of its characteristic and unique 'culture'. Culture (like ideas) is the primary factor in the life of a society, political and economic factors being downplayed in Hegel's account, if actually mentioned at all. Marx did find some of Hegel's thought useful, especially on how society and culture change by means of conflicts between antagonistic forces. Nonetheless, Marx insisted that the direction of Hegel's thinking would have to be reversed, and that the point was to 'turn Hegel on his head'. The resultant approach was called *historical materialism*, the fundamental focus of which is 'real individuals, their activity and the material conditions under which they live, both those which they find already existing and those produced by their activity' (Marx, 1991 [1845–6]: 42). Whereas Hegel, and idealist philosophy generally, claimed that it was ideas that produced the social world, Marx turned this proposition upside down, and argued that it was in fact the case that it was the social world that created ideas. *Instead of culture creating society, society is seen to create culture.* Marx expresses the position in the following way: 'It is not the consciousness of men that determines their existence, but their social existence that determines their consciousness' (1977 [1859]: 21).

Thus Marx insists on an approach that sees not how 'culture' and other 'ideal' factors create social factors, but one that shows how social factors generate cultural phenomena. Actually, 'social' factors is rather a misnomer, for Marx actually refers to 'socio-economic' factors as being at the root of everything else, culture included. How the economic realm is socially organized in a particular society shapes very fundamentally the nature of that society's culture. He developed this position in some of his earlier writings, ideas that were further expanded in his more mature phase. In the later writings, the image that he utilized to describe the relationship between socio-economic and cultural factors has perhaps been the most controversial element of his sociological study of culture. This is the famous idea of 'base' and 'superstructure':

> In the social relations of their existence, men [sic] inevitably enter into definite relations, which are independent of their will, namely relations of production appropriate to a given stage in the development of the material forces of production. The totality of these relations of production constitutes the economic structure of society, the real foundation, on which arises a legal and political superstructure, and to which correspond definite forms of social consciousness. The mode of production of material life conditions the general process of social, political and intellectual life. (1977 [1859]: 21)

This passage illustrates the notion of 'mode of production', which is central to the work of the mature Marx. Two related aspects of human production of material objects are being described. The first is how economic production is socially organized. The term used to identify such organization is *relations of production*. These relations involve how the work process is organized in terms of who controls it. The division of labour is based upon the division of people into property-owning and propertyless classes. The class that controls production is the ruling class. Their control is dependent upon the ownership of the tools and raw materials involved in the production of goods. These latter factors constitute the *forces of production*, and comprise the second aspect of human production of objects identified by Marx. The relations of production are the mechanisms whereby the forces of production are organized and controlled. Taken together, the forces and relations of production constitute the *material* (or 'socio-economic') *base* of a particular mode of production.

Marx's analysis of culture is dependent upon his claim that a mode of production consists of a *material base* and a *cultural superstructure*.

He phrased this point in terminology that derives from architecture. The base or foundation of the overall edifice (the overall mode of production) is made up of economic production, both its forces and relations. The *superstructure* of the edifice comprises 'forms of social consciousness', such as ideas, values and beliefs: that is to say, the stuff of culture. Moreover, legal and governmental apparatuses are also part of the superstructure. The superstructure *arises* on the basis of the material foundation. In other words, the base comes first, and the superstructure follows. Material factors are primary; cultural factors secondary. The essential thrust of Marx's argument is that if we want to understand a society, we should examine the nature of its material base. The base expresses itself in the nature of the superstructure. Thus a particular type of base will produce a particular form of cultural superstructure.

For example, the base of the modern capitalist economy generates a superstructure which is made up of a series of institutions and cultural forms that are characteristic of capitalist society. Marx tends towards a form of functionalist argument in outlining the roles of these institutions and cultural forms. The state is regarded as having the role of securing the interests of the ruling, capitalist class. The legal system is a mechanism which enforces the rights of the capitalist class to control production. Ways of thinking ('forms of consciousness') are ideologies, which operate in the service of masking the true, class-based and exploitative nature of the society. The general sense of Marx's argument is that the capitalist economic base both produces these things and relies for its continuance over time on their effective operation.

In a class-based society such as that of modern capitalism, part of the cultural superstructure is comprised of *dominant ideologies* which disguise the nature of the power held by dominant, elite groups by representing the social order as operating in the interests of all, not just elites. As Marx famously expressed this point:

> The ideas of the ruling class are in every epoch the ruling ideas: i.e. the class which is the ruling *material* force of society, is at the same time its ruling *intellectual* force. . . . The ruling ideas are nothing more than the ideal expression of the dominant material relationships, the dominant material relationships grasped as ideas. (In McLellan, 1984: 184)

Marx's claims about the nature of this dominant ideology involve the conditions of both its *production* and its *consumption*. As concerns the latter, the classes lacking in power *materially* will also lack power *culturally*. As a result, they will generally not be in a position to ascertain that the dominant ideology is a *misrepresentation* of the actual social situation, operating in the interests of the dominant class. Furthermore, they will generally be accepting of the status quo. In this model, *culture* is understood as being *ideological*, where the latter term means a misrepresentation of social (and economic and political) reality in the service of the powerful. Thus, culture helps to reproduce society by means of cloaking the true nature of that society in the eyes of those who live within it. In terms of the *production* of ideologies, these are created and disseminated by particular groups within the dominant class of a society, such as intellectuals, artists, philosophers and priests. It is their role to produce and spread the ideological ways of thinking taken on and accepted in other sectors of the society. It is important to note that Marx is not here subscribing to a conspiratorial kind of argument. These ideological producers are not setting out deliberately to mislead or distort. Generally, they believe what they are saying and writing. The production of a dominant ideology is the result of generally unintentional activities on their part.

The *unintended consequences* of particular actions was a key theme that Marx took from Hegel. Hegel had identified a condition of *alienation*, whereby a human subject creates an object which then seems to take on a life of its own and as a result takes control over the subject that created it. This is rather like the story of Frankenstein's monster, written about the same time as Hegel penned his philosophy. A human subject (Baron Frankenstein) creates an object (the Monster), which takes on a life of its own, and runs amok, causing great misery to its creator. For Marx and for other thinkers influenced by German Romantic ideas, this was exactly the condition of modern culture. People created ideas – cultural forms – that then came to enslave them, because the original creators could not recognize that they had themselves created such things initially – a situation of utter alienation (Marx, 1981 [1844]: 63).

In his later work, Marx (1988 [1867]: 163–77) emphasized the ways in which the capitalist economy – the socio-economic base of capitalist society – created a cultural superstructure that was alienated from, and out of the control of, the people who operated within it. He described this situation as the *fetishism of commodities*. Under a capitalist economy, the products – commodities – made by workers seem to have a life all of their own. This life is called 'market forces', whereupon the 'economy' appears to be an independent entity, rather than what it actually is: the result of human productive activity. The people who have made the commodities come to believe that the commodities have ultimate power over them, and come to accept this alienated situation as inevitable and unavoidable. A later Marxist, Georg Lukács (1971 [1923]), termed this predicament *reification*, a process whereby, in a class-based society such as capitalism, humans come to perceive the reality around them through a distorted cultural lens, such that the true nature of the society remains systematically hidden from view. For Marx and for other German thinkers influenced by Romantic ideas, modern society seemed to be like an out-of-control juggernaut which no one could take charge of. But unlike these others, who often blamed the debased nature of modern culture for this calamity, Marx and the Marxist tradition laid the blame squarely at the door of the capitalist economy, which is seen to disempower the people who actually make things – the working class – and to ensure continued power of the dominant elite – the class of capitalist owners. Cultural malaise is seen to be the result of imbalances in power in the socio-economic realm.

The passage cited above that outlines Marx's 'base' and 'superstructure' model has been the subject of more controversy and dispute than perhaps any other part of Marx's writing. This has been in large part due to its apparent downgrading of culture as a mere 'superstructural' offshoot of the socio-economic base. On this model, culture becomes a mere appendage or afterthought to an allegedly more fundamental set of material, socio-economic factors. What critics from both inside and outside Marxism have claimed is that this model simply does not grasp the true nature of culture. Different critics have different opinions on this matter, but their objections to the base and superstructure paradigm boil down to this series of possible objections:

1   Culture is not actually derivative or secondary to 'material factors'. It is either as important as or more important than material factors in the operation of actual human societies.
2   Not all societies exhibit such a preponderance of 'economics' over 'culture' as does modern Western capitalism. Marx's model might hold for that society, but it does not apply universally. Other societies are much more based around cultural matters than modern capitalism is.
3   There is never a complete or absolute division between 'material' and 'cultural' factors. They are always mixed up together in concrete instances. Culture has 'material' aspects, and 'material factors' possess cultural elements.
4   It is false to say that material (socio-economic) factors are 'real' and cultural factors merely 'ideal'. The latter are just as 'real' as the former.

5   Strangely enough, Marx's hostility to idealist views leads to a
    situation where he understands 'culture' as being somehow 'above'
    society, in the 'superstructure'. This unintentionally recreates one
    of the problems that Marx identified in idealism: that it cannot
    understand how 'society' and 'culture' are related to each other.
    The critic of idealism has fallen into the same trap into which he
    himself alleged the idealists fell.
6   Culture cannot be reduced just to 'ideology' and the interests of a
    ruling class. There is more to culture than Marx admits.
7   Culture should not be seen as being wholly tied to the material
    base. It should be seen either as autonomous – independent of
    material factors – or at least as semi-autonomous.

This last criticism, that culture is more autonomous than Marx allows,
was actually an issue that Marx and his collaborator Friedrich Engels
[1820–95] wrestled with between themselves. In a letter written towards the end of his life, Engels responded to what he saw as mis-
interpretations of Marx's position, which claimed that it was a form
of *economic determinism*, a method of analysis which ruthlessly reduced everything else, especially cultural factors, to the primacy of the
economic base. Engels characterized what he saw as Marx's actual
position in this way:

> the *ultimately* determining element in history is the production and
> reproduction of real life. More than this neither Marx nor I have ever
> asserted. Hence if somebody twists this into saying that the economic
> element is the *only* determining one, he transforms that proposition
> into a meaningless, abstract, senseless phrase. The economic situation
> is the basis, but the various elements of the superstructure . . . also
> exercise their influence upon the course of the historical struggles and
> in many cases preponderate in determining their *form*. There is an
> interaction of all these elements in which . . . the economic movement
> finally asserts itself as necessary. (1968 [1890]: 692)

Here Engels formulated what has subsequently become known as the
thesis of 'determination in the last instance'. This is the notion that
cultural factors *can* play a significant role in social life. In particular,
they can shape the forms that struggles between the classes take, with
class being viewed by Marx and Engels as the central aspect of human
life up until the present day. For example, classes may come into
conflict over the details of a cultural phenomenon such as a religious
doctrine. But this class conflict, which in this case takes on religious
form, is *ultimately* traceable to the antagonism between classes at the

material, socio-economic level. Thus cultural factors are important, but *ultimately not as important* as material factors. Thus Engels is arguing that Marx's schema gives a certain degree of autonomy to cultural factors. But in the last instance, the 'real' (rather than 'ideal') socio-economic factors in a situation determine its fundamental character. Economic factors are, says Engels, 'ultimately decisive'.

German sociology's responses to Marx

Although it was intended as a final statement on these matters, Engels' position here has created almost as much controversy as have the base/superstructure statements of Marx himself. It has often been alleged that what Engels (and Marx) give with one hand – an admittance of the importance of cultural factors in social life – they take away with the other, through the assertion that despite the importance of cultural phenomena, they are ultimately both products of, and also therefore less 'decisive' than, the material factors in the economic base. The degree to which cultural factors are regarded as having an autonomous role in social life beyond the constraints of the economic base has become one of the foci of conflicts within later Marxism. The question later Marxists have struggled with is this: if cultural factors are *partly independent* of the material base, to what extent are they actually autonomous? A great deal or just a little? And the apparent *economic reductionism* of Marx and Engels has been the main charge that critics outside Marxism have brought to bear on the historical materialist approach to the study of culture and society.

German sociologists in the period after Marx's death debated long and hard about these issues. The debate was set up in terms of whether 'material' (socio-economic and 'natural') factors were more important in human life than 'ideal' (cultural) factors, such as ideas and values. Marx's critics accused him of having gone too far in the 'materialist' direction when he rejected the 'idealist' ideas of Hegel. These critics asserted that cultural factors are not just simply the products of social and economic factors. What Marx's materialist position missed was that cultural processes and artefacts are *meaningful* and therefore need to be *interpreted*. This echoed the ideas of Herder from the beginning of the nineteenth century. But by the end of that century and on into the early twentieth century, German sociologists generally concurred that a completely idealist position was as unsatisfactory as a wholly materialist one. Therefore the problem became one of finding a way of taking account of both materialist

and idealist forms of analysis, and thus of seeking some way of dealing with both 'society' and 'economy' on the one side, and 'culture'
on the other.

Max Scheler (1874–1928), for example, argued that the task of
sociology was to examine a particular concrete situation and to *meas-
ure* how influential both 'material' and 'ideal' factors were within it
(1980 [1924]). The benefit of this position was that it forced sociologists to carefully consider the *empirical evidence* pertaining to a particular situation. The drawback is that it assumes that the evidence
will somehow speak for itself, and let the analyst know whether
material or ideal factors were more important within the situation.
This does not take account of the possibility that such decisions are
made not just on the basis of evidence, but also rely upon the previously existing commitments by the analyst to a more materialist or
more idealist way of analysing issues. The raw data do not contain
any answers in themselves, because they have to be interpreted in
light of a particular type of analysis.

Another attempt to strike some kind of balance between 'idealism'
and 'materialism' was put forward by Alfred Weber (1868–1958).
He rejected the division of 'material' and 'ideal' factors, arguing there
were actually three elements involved in human life rather than just
two. Weber (1998 [1920–1]) identified the first element as the *social
process*. This was comprised of the 'material' aspects of social organization: the division of labour, economic activities, forms of political
power, kinship organization and so on. The second element was the
civilizational process, which involved the development of rational
knowledge, scientific thought and, on these bases, the development
of technology. The third element was the *cultural process*, which
referred to the idea of Herder that each particular nation's 'culture' is
unique and unlike any other. Each 'culture' is the embodiment of the
'soul' of a given set of people, their innermost strivings to represent to
themselves the nature of the universe. What Weber was trying to do
was twofold. First, he wanted to show that other thinkers had mixed
up these three elements, or had downplayed one at the expense of the
others. Thus Marx had overemphasized the social and civilizational
processes at the expense of the cultural process, whereas Herder and
the German Romantics had overemphasized the latter at the expense
of the other two. Second, Weber argued that while the social process
involved material factors, and the cultural process ideal factors, the
civilizational process actually was made up of *both* material and ideal
features. This was because it comprised both rational thought (ideas)
and technological advances (material factors such as machines). It
remains unclear in Weber's analysis precisely how the three processes

relate to each other. Nonetheless his is a sophisticated attempt to think of a way out of the simple divide between 'materialism' and 'idealism', and to take sociology in a less dogmatically materialist or idealistic direction.

The same may be said of Alfred Weber's brother, Max (1864– 1920). On the face of it, Max Weber seems to belong more in the 'idealist' than the 'materialist' camp. His definition of culture as 'a finite segment of the meaningless infinity of the world process, a segment on which human beings confer meaning and significance' (cited in Turner, 1996: 5) follows the typically German Romantic and idealist tradition of stressing the *meaningfulness* of culture. Likewise, his definition of sociology as 'the interpretive understanding of social action' (cited in Alexander, 1983: 30) is close to the view of Dilthey and others that sociology should not be like a natural science, but should involve an interpretative approach to the study of how cultural meanings motivate social actors to act in particular ways. The understanding of social action involves the reconstruction of the meaning-laden cultural contexts in which the actions in question take place.

Some later commentators have seen Weber's sociology as being in deliberate opposition to Marx's approach (Parsons, 1937). Many of Marx's earlier works were unavailable to Weber because they were as yet unpublished, and thus Marx's work probably did seem to him rather crudely materialist in parts. Even so, Weber's approach to sociology can also be seen as an attempt to *refine* the ideas of Marx, especially those involving culture, rather than as a rejection of them. As Weber said at the end of his most famous work – his study of the 'Protestant ethic' (often taken as his most 'idealist' contribution to sociology):

> it is, of course, not my aim to substitute for a one-sided materialistic an equally one-sided spiritualistic causal interpretation of culture and of history. Each is equally possible, but each, if it does not serve as the preparation, but as the conclusion of an investigation, accomplishes equally little in the interest of historical truth. (1930 [1905–6]: 183)

Like Scheler, then, Weber is a *sociological agnostic*, for he wishes to claim that one cannot assume that either 'cultural' or 'ideal' factors on the one side, and 'material' or 'economic' factors on the other, *must* be the most important in explaining any given situation. Instead, one must look carefully at the empirical data, and then make a decision as to what side of the coin one will emphasize. The main difference between Marx and Weber in this regard is that Marx *always* assumes the priority of 'material' and 'economic' factors, whereas Weber will admit this is sometimes a useful assumption, but that it can also sometimes be misleading. For Weber, the reality of any situation is complex and messy, and all the sociologist can do is to build models to make some sense out of the chaos. But these models must be sensitive to the situation under study, so forcing a 'material-ist' or 'idealist' model onto a situation where it is not warranted must be avoided. Weber is not interested in *mono-causal* explanations, but *poly-causal* ones, which attempt to model the complexities of the actual situation under study, as far as empirical evidence will allow (Bendix, 1966; Roth, 1979).

This much was hinted at by Scheler, but arguably Max Weber went further in fleshing these ideas out. He did this in a variety of ways. First, Weber (1982) denied what he took to be Marx's conten-tion that membership of a class is the primary way an individual in a class-based society will think about themselves. There are other cul-turally mediated identities people may have, such as the pride in being a member of a particular group such as a sports club. Sports club membership and the feelings it provokes will be related to class issues (e.g. most of the members may be middle class), but this is an *indirect* relationship, and it is this possibility of other identities being more crucial than class membership that Marx does not allow for.

Second, Weber rejects what he thinks is Marx's position that socio-economic factors are always primary, while cultural factors are secondary. This makes too wide a division between cultural factors such as religion and what happens in the socio-economic realm. Weber's (e.g. 1966) studies of the main world religions attempted to show that economic actions were in fact motivated, at least ini-tially, by religious beliefs. For example, he argued that the 'mindset' associated with Chinese Confucianism encouraged forms of social action oriented towards traditionalism and a desire to preserve the status quo. Christianity, by contrast, has inherently within it a 'world-transformative' capacity, which is oriented towards changing social conditions. Thus one of the reasons why modern capitalism developed in the West and nowhere else was *partly* because of the inherently dynamic nature of the religious-cultural factors associated with Chris-tianity (Schroeder, 1992). In the same vein, Weber's study of the 'Protestant ethic' (1930 [1905–6]) was an attempt to show how Pro-testantism's religion of self-denial and hard work helped to shape the cultural context of early capitalist entrepreneurs, who in like fashion denied themselves pleasure and reinvested the profits they made in order to make even more profits. Protestant culture was, argued Weber, a significant – but not the only – feature of the development of capitalism, a fact that Marx's obsession with material factors had made him blind to. Against Marx, Weber argued that a cultural phenomenon like a religious doctrine could be an important factor in its own right in stimulating 'material', economic developments.

Third, Weber not only argued that a cultural factor such as religion could be important in shaping the 'material' socio-economic realm; he also contended that, vice versa, material factors could influence the nature of religion too. He put forward the idea of 'elective affinity' (*Wahlverwandtschaft*), which points to situations where certain 'material' and 'ideal' factors can have a special relationship with one another, each exerting influence on the other. For example, certain religious ethics (ideal factors) tended to be adopted by particular social groups because of the material interests of those groups in maintaining or improving their power and wealth. Aristocratic groups maintain their power in part by adopting elaborate rituals as ways of excluding lower prestige groups. As a result, aristocracies tend to be attracted to and adopt types of religion that are very formal and have highly elaborate rituals, leaving more 'enthusiastic' and emotional forms of worship to groups lower in the social hierarchy (Collins, 1986: 136). (The notion of a particular group being oriented to specific types of cultural products is a key idea in later sociological studies of cultural consumption – see chapter 7.) Overall, then, Weber attempted to show that material and ideal factors are constantly affecting each other, and that a balance must be struck between the more materialist position of Marx and the more idealist positions prevalent amongst German thinkers.

This sophisticated position informs Weber's diagnosis of the social and cultural ills of modernity. At the beginning of the twentieth century, an air of pessimism was dominant amongst German intellectuals about contemporary cultural conditions. Standards in cultural life, and therefore in the quality of life per se, were felt to be rapidly in decline, due to the rise of a mass culture characterized by a lack of subtlety and feeling (Liebersohn, 1988). Weber's contemporary, Georg Simmel (1858–1918), referred to this situation as the 'tragedy of culture' (Frisby and Featherstone, 1997). Like Marx, Simmel drew on Hegel's idea of alienation to depict a scenario whereby the products made by a certain group of people came to take on a life of their own and dominate the original creators. In this case, Simmel saw the mass culture then arising – which involved newspapers, magazines and popular novels – as an increasingly powerful force in life, over which individuals had less and less control. Partly, these ideas were stimulated by the fear of German intellectuals like Simmel, and of the German educated middle classes (*Bildungsburgertum*) more generally, that these new cultural forms threatened their own hold on cultural power, and their ability to adjudicate for the wider public as to what was 'good' and 'bad' culture.

Max Weber too was one of those intellectuals who distrusted and disliked the new mass culture that was beginning to transform Western societies. But he did not, like Simmel, see these issues as purely the result of modern culture itself, nor did he, like Marx, locate the source of the problems of the modern world solely in the economic base of the capitalist economy. Instead, his famous diagnosis of modernity as an 'iron cage' of bureaucratic control stresses that this problem has both 'material' and 'ideal' aspects. The former are to be located in the material organization of modern society through the means of bureaucracies, both in the economic sphere of capitalist big business, and in the political sphere of state administration. At the more 'ideal' level, there is a mentality centred on a calculating form of rationality, oriented towards regulating and controlling ever more areas of life, and eliminating older religious and spiritual values in favour of what he and other German thinkers saw as a sterile scientific mindset. The people who live within such a cultural context are, in the words of the poet Goethe, 'specialists without spirit, sensualists without heart' (Weber, 1930 [1905–6]: 182). Weber is not claiming that this problem is only 'cultural' in aspect, as it is as much to do with the material organization of society through bureaucratic means as it is a result of a change in mentalities in the cultural sphere. Once again, Weber refused to submit to what he saw as the oversimplified explanations, either 'materialist' or 'idealist', that had plagued sociology up until then.

Durkheimian studies of culture

The tension between materialist and idealist approaches to the study of culture and society informs the work of another foundational figure of sociology, Emile Durkheim (1858–1917). While his earlier work was more 'materialist' in orientation, his later ideas were much more 'idealist' in nature. In one sense, Durkheim's (1982 [1895]) ideas about how sociology should operate are very much part of the French Enlightenment tradition that argued that sociology should be based on the methods of the natural sciences. Nonetheless, throughout his career he gave serious attention to cultural phenomena, and in his later writings he switched the typical Enlightenment emphasis on how *society* produces and shapes *culture*, to how the latter shapes the operation of the former.

The continuity between Durkheim's early (e.g. 1984 [1893]) and late (2001 [1912]) works is the functionalist assumptions with which he always worked, cultural phenomena being seen to contribute to the generally harmonious functioning of the 'whole' society. This emphasis derived from Durkheim's desire to utilize sociology as a way of identifying and solving social problems, with a functionalist model of society and culture being used to highlight how particular factors could be engineered to be useful for the smooth operation of a society as a whole. In particular, Durkheim diagnosed as a central problem of modernity a condition of alienation he refers to as 'anomie' – 'norm-lessness'. Without strongly held beliefs, reinforced by cultural norms, modern individuals would feel dislocated from the society of which they were part. Durkheim stresses the part that culture has to play in reducing anomie and in maintaining social order. Culture's 'role' is to ensure that social patterns are maintained. Marx had argued much the same thing, but Durkheim's 'culture' is more beneficent than Marx's ideology, because 'culture' operates in the service of maintaining the *whole society*, whereas Marx saw ideology as upholding the interests of an elite.

In his early work, *The Division of Labour in Society* (1984 [1893]), Durkheim holds the view that it is *social structural* factors that shape the forms that *cultural* factors take. More specifically, it is the form taken by the *division of labour* that dictates the nature of that society's corresponding culture. In *Suicide* (1952 [1897]), Durkheim argued:

> Given a people, consisting of a certain number of individuals arranged in a certain way, there results a determinate set of collective ideas and practices . . . [.] [A]ccording to whether the parts composing it are more or less numerous and structured in this or that way, the nature of collective life necessarily varies and, in consequence, so do its ways of thinking and acting. (Cited in Lukes, 1973: 231)

In other words, the *shape* of a particular society (its particular form of division of labour) determines the nature of the corresponding culture. For Durkheim and his collaborator Marcel Mauss (1872–1950), a society's culture is made up of a set of *collective representations* (1969 [1903]). These are the ways in which reality is made sense of collectively by the members of a society. The sense they have of their world derives from the ways in which their minds have been culturally shaped in the socialization process that begins at birth and which makes each person truly a 'member' of a certain society. Collective representations (or 'classifications') are the socially created lenses through which people make sense of reality and the world around them, the frameworks through which they think and the bases on which they act. Culture, in the form of collective representations, transforms the world as perceived by the human senses into a realm mediated by and centred on symbols. In this way, the phenomena of 'nature' are transformed into objects of 'culture' (Lukes, 1973: 424). Humans have no direct access to 'reality'; instead, their reality is socially shaped by culture, which consists of the symbolism deployed in the collective representations. Culture on this view is a means of *processing* natural phenomena, giving them sense and meaning for human beings. Culture is a way of *dealing with* nature, bringing it into the grasp of the human mind.

All the collective representations of a given society taken together constitute that society's *cosmology* – its overall worldview. The assumption made by Durkheim and Mauss here is that the various elements of that cosmology are congruent and fit together. They do not contradict or clash with each other, but in sum create a seamless whole, the organizing principle of all thought and action within that society. The moulding of the mind by cultural forms in turn depends on the 'shape' of the society itself, because a particular type of society produces a corresponding set of *collective representations*. For example, the sense a given society has of time, and how it classifies time into a calendar with important events marked on it, is a product of the rhythms of collective life, such as when harvests occur. The collective representation (cultural understanding) of time is therefore a product of patterns of social organization. On this view, social patterns are expressed in cultural patterns, and the latter are generated by the former. This is an idea somewhat similar to Marx's base and superstructure model. Durkheim's particular version of this way of thinking argues that a simple division of labour produces a simple form of culture, made up of the religious beliefs of that society. A complex division of labour, by contrast, produces a complex culture, made up of a series of partly or fully autonomous spheres. For example, it is only when a certain level of social structural complexity has been reached that there can exist within culture a separate realm of 'art' that is not religious in aspect. This is because it is only when there is a sufficiently complex division of labour, which allows a group of secular artists to exist who are not directly connected to religious institutions, that secular art, rather than artworks used for religious purposes, can be created. This is Durkheim's take on the idea of the *structural differentiation* of society and culture which we remarked upon in relation to Spencer.

The idea that *society* produces *culture* is central to Durkheim's earlier works. But from the beginning he also argued that 'one would form an entirely false idea of economic development if one neglected the moral causes which play a part in it' (1972: 92). In other words, rather like Max Weber, Durkheim refused to separate cultural factors like morality and religious beliefs from more 'material', socio-economic factors like the division of labour. In his later work, he moved towards a viewpoint that has some affinities with the German Romantic outlook, namely that culture constitutes society rather than the other way around.

In making this argument, Durkheim turned to 'primitive' societies with a low level of division of labour, in particular focusing on the religious-cultural aspects of Australian aboriginal societies. From analysis of such a 'simple' type of society, the most general and basic aspects of *all* societies could be deduced. Durkheim's central claim in *The Elementary Forms of the Religious Life* (2001 [1912]) is that the main 'building blocks' of all societies are religious ideas, morals and values. It is these that are the crucial elements of any social order, not 'material' factors like the division of labour. The implications of this position are threefold. First, all cultures, regardless of the complexity of the society, have the same social function as religion: they bind people together through the sharing of common norms and values. Second, cultures, like religion, divide the world into two realms, that of the 'sacred' and that of the 'profane'. By identifying things that are morally 'bad', culture identifies what things are morally good and so can illustrate to members of the society the key values they must not only accept but also cherish. Third, such attachments to the wider society are periodically reinforced via the means of rituals. Rituals create a sense of common bonds between the members of a society, and render afresh their commitments to the society's central cultural values. In these various ways, norms and beliefs are instilled into the consciousness of individuals, compelling them to act in socially desirable fashions. This holds for modern societies as for any others. Grand ritualistic celebrations, such as the inauguration of a president, are ritualistic reinforcements of key values (e.g. the 'sanctity' of democracy). In this way, citizens' faith in those norms is reconfirmed, and the patterns of the society are maintained (Alexander, 1988).

After Durkheim: into the twentieth century

We have seen that Durkheim's earlier writings were more 'materialist' in character, whereas the later work was somewhat more 'idealist'. These alternatives were each taken up by later sociologists inspired by Durkheim. The more 'materialist' strain was developed by Karl

Mannheim (1887–1947), who was influenced not just by Durkheim but also by Marx. Mannheim is generally regarded as one of the main twentieth-century founders of the 'sociology of knowledge'. This project is defined by Mannheim as 'a theory of the social . . . determination of actual thinking' (1985 [1936]: 267). Mannheim sought to relate certain *styles of thought* to the shape of the social conditions that produced them. He (ibid. 4) argues that if a group of people is to realize its aims, it has to struggle with its environment, both the natural environment of physical nature and the social environment that comprises other groups of people. The particular way in which those struggles occur determines the ways in which the group conceives the world around it, the 'worldview' (*Weltanschauung*) characteristic of that group. It is therefore collective activity, oriented towards the survival of the group, which produces the particular worldview which characterizes the group's culture. In other words, the way a group or society *acts* is the basis and generator of how it *thinks*. Mannheim's particular innovation is to apply Durkheim's views on the social generation of culture away from the level of a whole society, to the study of particular groups *within* a society. Mannheim generally agrees with Marx that such groups are classes. Thus the social conditions of each class are regarded as producing the particular worldview of that class. Each class in a society, therefore, 'sees' the world somewhat differently from the others. The implication of this view is that each class in a society has its 'own' culture – that is, its own distinctive set of tastes and preferences, its own particular types of beliefs and values, and its own specific ways of understanding the world.

An important ramification for later sociology follows from this. Mannheim (1956: 184) argues that in societies where 'the political and social order basically rests upon the distinction between "higher" and "lower" human types, an analogous distinction is also made between "higher" and "lower" objects of knowledge or aesthetic enjoyment'. In other words, where there is a class division between rulers and ruled, culture will be divided upon those lines. There will be a culture of the ruling classes that is defined as 'high', and a culture of the lower class(es) that will be defined as 'low'. There is nothing intrinsically superior about the products of the 'high' culture. They are only regarded as 'high' because the ruling class has defined them that way. There is also nothing intrinsically inferior about the cultural objects used or enjoyed by the lower classes. Their inferiority is only a result of them having been defined as inferior by the ruling class. Such ideas as to the *relativity of cultural value* will be central in later sociologies of culture, as we will see.

The more 'idealist' strain of the sociology of culture coming out of Durkheim is that associated with the work of Talcott Parsons. In his book *The Social System* (1951) and elsewhere, Parsons argues that sociology should focus on the relations between the *social system*, the *cultural system* and the *personality system*. In particular, the sociological study of culture is defined as 'the analysis of the inter-dependence and interpenetration of social and cultural systems' (1961: 991). In other words, sociology looks at the relationships between *culture* and *society*, where the former means *values* (i.e. norms, beliefs and ideas) and the latter means *patterns of social interaction*. The cultural system contains the most general and abstract values of a society (e.g. a belief in God or democracy). From these values are derived more concrete *norms*, which guide interactions in the social system. The relation between cultural and social systems is therefore characterized by the former guiding the latter.

Moreover, the cultural system patterns the *personality system*, that is, the ways in which people in a society think and feel. Echoing Weber as much as Durkheim, Parsons argues that it is culture that motivates people to act, by constructing their ideas as to what they want and how to get it. From this viewpoint, it is 'the structure of cultural meanings [that] constitutes the "ground" of any system of action' (Parsons, 1961: 963). In other words, it is values, rather than the 'material' factors emphasized by Marx, that drive action. Over-all, Parsons is arguing for a sociology which treats cultural values as the primary basis of any society. How any society works is absolutely dependent on a cultural context characterized by *value consensus*: all (or at least most) people in the same society must share the same values and act in regular ways on the basis of them. In this way social order is maintained over time. One of the usual criticisms of this position, obviously enough, is that it seems to make actors out to be 'cultural dopes', obeying the 'instructions' of culture in somewhat automatic ways (Wrong, 1980 [1961]). As a result, claim some crit-ics, Parsons sets up the polar opposite of Marx's alleged economic determinism, namely a *cultural* determinism. In this sense, it is often argued that the Durkheimian focus on a commonly shared culture smothers out both individual scope for action and the conflicts which Marxist and Weberian sociologies emphasize as being at the heart of social life (Dahrendorf, 1959).

Conclusion

The purpose of this chapter has been to examine some of the debates that characterized sociological approaches to culture in the nineteenth and early twentieth centuries. Classical sociologies of culture sought to explicate the relations between 'culture' on the one hand and 'society' (and politics and economics) on the other. Some forms of classical sociology tried to think through the relations between 'culture' and 'nature', while others ignored it completely. A particular source of contention was whether to adopt a more 'materialist' or 'idealist' approach, or whether to combine the two in some kind of attempted synthesis. The early sociologists also often attempted to diagnose the social ills of modernity by identifying the cultural dilemmas of such a society.

Classical sociology's responses to cultural matters cannot be seen as a set of eternal truths. In fact, most of the classical sociologists were primarily concerned to expose the apparent flaws in the ideas of their adversaries. But the classical sociologists can be seen as asking important questions about the nature of culture and how it relates to society. The various types of sociology of culture we have examined, whether they are more influenced by Enlightenment or Romanticist ways of thinking, are all open to criticism and contestation. But they do provide ways of thinking about culture and society that have inspired later generations of sociological thinkers. Throughout this book, the voices of the classical sociologists will sometimes be heard loud and clear, and sometimes only as dim echoes. But in each and every way of looking sociologically at culture that we will examine, the legacy of the pioneers is evident.

2

High German Seriousness:
The Frankfurt School
on Culture

Introduction

The thinkers associated with the Frankfurt School were some of the first scholars seriously and systematically to engage with the new cultural conditions of the twentieth century. The classical theorists of the nineteenth century had witnessed the beginnings of mass markets in newspapers and book publishing. But the appearance of radio and cinema, as well as the extension of the production of cultural goods based around the written word, were twentieth-century innovations. The approach of the Frankfurt School thinkers to these matters remains of interest to us today for two main reasons. First, they drew upon the ideas concerning cultural matters of the classical sociologists, most notably Marx and Weber, and reworked these in often highly novel ways in order to understand the nature of twentieth-century culture. Second, their views as to the nature of 'mass culture' remain some of the most controversial and bitterly debated amongst all the various positions that make up the sociological study of culture. Critics have denounced their apparently utterly pessimistic and wholly elitist views on modern culture, whilst their defenders have been equally forceful in arguing for the continuing relevance of the distinctive 'Frankfurt' approach today.

In this chapter we will examine the arguments and ideas that emerged from the Frankfurt School, look at how defensible these are and see whether they may be of any use for us in the present day. We begin by setting out the historical context in which the Frankfurt School's ideas were produced, and the novel uses they made of classical sociology. We will then turn to the analyses they gave of mass culture, before turning to some of the dilemmas involved in these understandings. There were differences of emphasis among the individual members of the School over how society and culture should be studied, and towards the end of the chapter we will focus on some of the individual contributions which depart somewhat from the mainstream of Critical Theory. Throughout the chapter, we will be particularly concerned to draw attention to the often fraught relationship between theory and empirical data.

The Frankfurt School in context

In this chapter, we will deal with what is sometimes referred to as the *early* Frankfurt School. This comprises the group of scholars associated, directly or indirectly, with the Institute for Social Research, a partly autonomous research centre established within the University of Frankfurt in 1923 (Wiggershaus, 1995). The 'early' version of this School refers to the personnel associated with it from the 1920s to the 1960s. The 'later' Frankfurt School, which we will deal with briefly towards the end of the chapter, refers to the group centred around Jürgen Habermas (b. 1929), who took over the reins of the Institute in the late 1960s. In its early phase the Institute was profoundly interdisciplinary in character, involving at different times specialists in the fields of sociology (Theodor Adorno (1903–69), Leo Lowenthal (1900–93)), philosophy (Adorno, Max Horkheimer (1895–1973), Herbert Marcuse (1898–1979), Walter Benjamin (1892–1940)), Freudian psychology (Erich Fromm (1900–80), Marcuse), literary, musical and cultural studies (Lowenthal, Benjamin, Adorno), and political economy (Friedrich Pollock (1894–1970), Franz Neumann (1900–54), Otto Kirchheimer (1905–65)) Most of the above scholars had family backgrounds in the educated upper middle class (*Bildungsburgertum*), just as had the previous generation of thinkers such as Max and Alfred Weber, and Georg Simmel. In what follows we will concentrate primarily on the work of Adorno and Horkheimer, with some reference to Benjamin and Lowenthal, as it is their work which constitutes the most extensive contributions to the study of culture out of all the Frankfurt scholars. To a large degree Adorno and Horkheimer shared the pessimistic view of modern culture that the previous generation of German thinkers had held, and, indeed, they took some of their ideas from figures such as Simmel and Max Weber. As we will see below, their elite social backgrounds have often been held against them by critics charging them with an elitist view of cultural matters.

Although dealing with different fields of study, and despite certain divergences in opinion, the work of the individual members of the Frankfurt School generally cohered around certain common principles (Held, 1980). The overall intellectual project of the Institute was the development of new forms of Marxist thought, which could grasp the new social and cultural conditions of the twentieth century that Marx and the other classical sociologists had only witnessed the beginnings of. This was not merely an academic exercise, for the Frankfurt thinkers regarded the need for a rejuvenated Marxism as absolutely crucial both for understanding the times they lived in and for finding some way of combating their worst aspects. It is fair to say that the period in which the early Frankfurt theorists lived and worked was a very turbulent one, especially for left-wing intellectuals such as they were. The rise to power of Hitler and the Nazi Party in the early 1930s cast a great shadow over Europe in general and Germany in particular. Marxist thought had not predicted such developments, so a new type of Marxist theory seemed to be required to understand why such a social and political disaster had occurred. The 'official' forms of Marxism propounded by Communist parties in Western countries at the time were more or less dictated by bureaucrats and ideologues in the Soviet Union, at that period under the control of Stalin's dictatorial regime. In Germany, Marx's hope of a working-class revolution had seemed to be crushed, as the working class had turned towards Fascism. In the Soviet Union, apparently a 'worker's state', the working class were kept in line by harsh authoritarian rule. As a result, then, something seemed to have gone very wrong in the twentieth century with Marxist politics. This problem was compounded at the theoretical level. From the viewpoint of the Frankfurt thinkers, the type of Marxism promulgated in the Soviet Union was highly rigid and extremely economically reductionist, and did not seem to be able to deal with either the growth of Fascism or the rise of mass culture. The central claim of this new kind of Marxist thought about cultural matters, as developed by the Frankfurt thinkers, was that there were very intimate connections between the rise of totalitarian regimes (both Fascist and Communist) and the development of mass culture.

From the beginning, then, the theoretical outlook of the Frankfurt thinkers was thoroughly bound up with both the social context in which they were forced to live and their political responses to it. Their position on social and cultural matters is not a 'neutral' one and nor did it claim to be. They themselves were Marxist opponents of the Nazi regime, whilst also being often fierce critics of Communism in the Soviet Union, seeking a new, more supple and independently minded form of Marxist analysis of society and culture than was offered by Communism. In fact, given the terrible circumstances in which they lived, which included the rise of Nazism and the death and destruction involved in the Holocaust and World War II, it is difficult to see how any thinkers living at the time could have claimed, or would have wanted to claim, that their ideas were 'neutral' in regard to contemporary events. This was particularly true for the Frankfurt thinkers, most of whom were of Jewish extraction. Forced to leave Germany after the Nazis had taken power, most of them made their way to the safer environment of the United States. The sad exception here is that of Walter Benjamin, who killed himself while trying to escape from German-controlled France into Spain in 1940.

Both the rise of Nazism and the shock of arriving in the New World created a profound impression on the Institute's members. The United States was known as 'the land of the free', its brand of free market capitalism apparently allowing high levels of individual freedom of choice and social mobility. But to these European émigrés, America bore worrying similarities to the situation they had left behind in Germany, and for which they had criticized the Soviet Union. As they saw it, the mass media of both dictatorships and (apparent) democracies were powerful agencies of social control. As a result, in both the 'free' world and the worlds of Fascism and Communism, the individual was increasingly being regulated, controlled and stupefied. It is a very negative appreciation of mass culture in general, and that to be found in America in particular, which especially underpinned the cultural analysis of Adorno and Horkheimer, a way of thinking that stayed with them when they returned to Germany after the war.

Rethinking Marxism

Before, during and after World War II, Adorno and Horkheimer in particular were engaged in the project of producing a new form of Marxism that they dubbed 'Critical Theory'. This was intended to be an agile form of thought that would provide a vehicle for fundamental critique of contemporary capitalist society, but which would not degenerate into dogmas as Marxism had in its communist version. The great enemy of Critical Theory was the positivist attitude towards science, an attitude that Adorno and Horkheimer felt infected both official forms of Marxism and the empirically based, often highly statistical, sociology that was dominant in the United States after the war. For a positivist, social science must model itself on the natural sciences and should search for general 'laws' of social life through impeccably neutral means of investigation, leading to the collection of pure 'facts' (Halfpenny, 1982). The main problem with such an approach, according to the Frankfurt position, is that it is not in fact neutral but ends up being a close ally of the powerful in society (Horkheimer, 1972d: 222). By collecting superficial data that only tell one about the *surface* aspects of a society, positivist social science cannot penetrate to the *essence* of that society, and thus cannot discern what is really happening. Far from being enlightening, it is a form of mystification. From this view follow three important characteristics of Critical Theory.

First, it does not claim to be neutral, because apparently 'neutral' positions are always politically biased in one way or another. Critical Theory explicitly allies itself with certain values. These involve what Adorno and Horkheimer saw as the human desire for *happiness*, which they understood to be the desire for a society free of domination. This is a value that 'requires no justification' (Horkheimer, 1972b: 44). Critical Theory is meant as a liberatory way of thinking, based on the hope for freedom from oppression. Thus, while Adorno and Horkheimer repudiated the positivist strand in Enlightenment thinking, they nonetheless drew upon the Enlightenment ideal of social science as a way of demystifying society and allowing the powerless to realize their own true social position (see chapter 1). Through 'criticism of what is prevalent' (Horkheimer, 1972c: 264), Critical Theory attempts to demonstrate how things could be different from how they are at present. It thus has a definite *utopian* element to it, looking towards a better future just as Marx had done.

Second, if Critical Theory is to reject a society's self-image, it must, in order to penetrate to the true core of that society, reject the ways of thinking that are common in that society. It must be utterly sceptical of *everything*, getting back to Marx's original intention that the study of society involves 'the ruthless criticism of everything existing' (Maier, 1984: 31). The common-sense ideas of the social actors under study must be discarded too, for they were deeply informed by dominant ideologies and reflected only the surface of social life. As Horkheimer put it, for most people, 'the world . . . seems quite different than it really is' (1972d: 214). Analysis should focus not so much on actors' versions of events, but on the 'deep causes' of those events, the 'essence' of society that only Critical Theory itself can discern. This position has been the source of some very important criticisms of Critical Theory, as we will see later.

Third, the Frankfurt view of positivism entailed a rethinking of the relationship within social science between theory and methods. Positivism is seen to fetishize 'facts' that do not actually reveal what is going on in society, but which only reflect its superficial aspects. Thus Critical Theory cannot search for 'facts', nor can it seek to prove its own contentions with reference to 'facts' (Adorno, 1976a; 1976b). This resulted in an interesting ambivalence in the Critical Theoretical perspective on issues of data collection and proof. On the one hand, as Marxist sociologists, the Critical Theorists were very critical of what they saw as purely speculative, philosophical approaches to the study of culture and society. The Institute was set up not for the purely philosophical study of such matters, but to bring empirically informed analysis to bear on them (Brunkhorst, 1999: 33). On the other hand, empirical data was seen to be, by its very nature, superficial and unable to identify actual social and cultural dynamics, and thus could not be the basis for analysis. Only Critical Theory itself can 'see' what is really happening. Thus from the very beginning there was a contradiction at the heart of Critical Theory: was it a philosophical or an empirical study of culture? This ambivalence, plus the apparent arrogance of Critical Theorists, who claimed to know 'reality' better than social actors themselves, led to further dilemmas, as will shortly become apparent.

Towards totality

One of the central claims made for Critical Theory by its originators was that it dealt with cultural matters in a much more satisfying way than did the type of Marxism advocated by the Communist parties. This latter relied heavily on a literal interpretation of Marx: that the parts of the cultural 'superstructure' were completely determined in their nature by the socio-economic 'base' (Adorno, 1967a: 28). Culture was regarded as being nothing more than a mere offshoot of the economy. This viewpoint downgraded the importance of cultural factors in general, as they appeared in all human societies. The problem stemmed from Marx's overemphasis on the importance of material production as lying at the heart of all societies (Adorno, 1973: 177–8), to the extent that he had mistakenly seen the world as a 'giant workhouse' (Jay, 1974: 57). Material production was of course important, but so too were cultural, social and political factors. The point was to see how in each society all these were related to each other in different ways at different times (Horkheimer, 1972b; 1972d: 234–8). Such an approach was particularly crucial in understanding the contemporary state of the capitalist mode of production. The base-superstructure model could not grasp how important culture was becoming *within* the capitalist economic base itself. Marx's assumption that economic factors were prior to others only applied to the nineteenth-century phase of capitalism, a phase characterized by *competition* between entrepreneurs. In the twentieth century, capitalism had entered a *monopoly* phase, with competition being replaced by economic control exercised by vast conglomerates. In this situation, political factors (especially the rise of Fascism) and cultural factors, in particular the appearance of mass entertainment, were becoming ever more crucial to capitalism's operation. Conversely, culture was more than ever at the service of the capitalist economy, as the two realms were now one. The socio-economic 'base' and the cultural 'superstructure' were increasingly merging. There was a process of *de-differentiation* going on, with the previously separate realms of economy, politics and culture all being joined together into one large conglomerate entity.

Adorno and Horkheimer conceived this situation through an idea they adopted from the work of the Hungarian Marxist Georg Lukács (1971 [1923]): the notion of *social totality*. In this way of thinking, every single part of a specific society – institutions, cultural patterns such as ways of thinking, and particular individuals – was regarded as being interrelated (Jay, 1974). Changes in one part of the totality would have ramifications for all the other parts, but these effects would be indirect rather than direct. This is because it is the totality, made up of all the parts, which shapes the nature of each individual part. There are therefore no direct relationships of shaping or determination by one part over another (e.g. the 'base' shaping the 'superstructure'). Thus 'culture' is shaped not by the economic base, but by the totality of the society in question, which is made up of all the parts. Likewise, the 'economy' is shaped by the totality too (Kolakowski, 1978: 267–9).

This focus on totality fitted well with Critical Theory's rejection of positivism. So-called 'facts' about one particular aspect of society only really meant anything if they were interpreted in light of the totality of which that aspect was but a part. For example, information about the behaviour of mass media audiences cannot be taken at face value and seen as providing information about a completely separate part of society called the 'mass media'. Rather, the mass media must be viewed as part of a totality that also includes the capitalist economy and governmental apparatuses. Information on the mass media, likewise, must be interpreted in light of data about the other elements of the totality. Quite simply, one must look at every particular part of society, such as the mass media, in the context of how this part 'fits' with all the other parts, especially political and economic factors. This position too has been the source of much controversy, because in rejecting the base-superstructure model's implication that culture is a separate sphere from the socio-economic 'base', the Frankfurt view ties cultural matters very tightly to economic and political factors, arguably leading to an inability to see ways in which culture might sometimes work *against* the interests of the economically and politically powerful.

Nonetheless, the idea of totality was felt by the Critical Theorists to be a distinct improvement on the base-superstructure model. Another failing of this model, they argued, was that it provided no account of psychological processes, and did not show how the minds of social actors worked. The Frankfurt theorists turned to Sigmund Freud for help. They took from him the idea that the human psyche is shaped by the demands of society, and that society moulds the unconscious level of the individual's mind as much as it does the conscious part. One of the members of the Institute in its early days, Erich Fromm (1971 [1932]), brought together Marxist and Freudian views by arguing that the demands of capitalist society, such as the requirement that individuals buy consumer goods to keep the wheels of the economy turning, were instilled into the unconscious of every person in that society. The mind was therefore moulded in socially prescribed ways. The assumption of this way of thinking, which was taken on in one way or another by Adorno and Horkheimer, is that the individual's mind is wholly open to manipulation and control by social forces. This was the notion that underpinned, for example, Adorno's (1996c) studies in the 1940s of how susceptible different types of people are to propaganda. The idea of 'ego weakness' was developed, describing a susceptibility to messages produced from without, and a felt need for reassurance from other people, leading to high levels of social conformity. This kind of Freudian notion of manipulation of the unconscious informs Adorno's and Horkheimer's studies of mass culture, where it is asserted that the mass of the population have a spell cast over them by the means of mass communication, whether these are controlled by Nazi propaganda chiefs or mass media magnates. Again, this is a very controversial assumption to make, and has been subject to serious criticism.

The Culture Industry

The chapter entitled 'The Culture Industry: Enlightenment as Mass Deception' in Adorno and Horkheimer's book *Dialectic of Enlightenment* (1992 [1944]) is the cornerstone of their study of mass culture. It describes their basic orientation towards understanding both the nature of mass culture and its role within modern society. The Culture Industry is the conglomeration of huge corporations which produce the films, radio programmes, newspapers and magazines for consumption by the majority of the population. The Culture Industry is regarded by Adorno and Horkheimer as exercising a monopoly over cultural life, with other forms of culture and other types of cultural production, such as authentic folk culture, having been squeezed out of the picture by its financial and organizational might. The reason for this emphasis on cultural regulation lies in the fact that *Dialectic of Enlightenment* was written during World War II, and bears the imprint of its authors' fear of the Fascist war machine then dominating most of Europe. This can be seen in terms of the overall argument of the book. It tells a highly speculative, philosophical story about how, since the beginnings of human life on Earth, there has been a tendency for ever more powerful and invasive forms of rational control to be developed. Echoing the classical sociological theme of alienation, Adorno and Horkheimer claim that these forms of control come to take on a life of their own and to dominate the very human beings who created them. Modernity takes this process to an extreme, creating a situation of very high levels of social control over the individual, the problem Max Weber had referred to as the 'iron cage'. Life becomes increasingly characterized by administration and control from above – by the powers-that-be (Adorno and Horkheimer, 1992 [1944]: 38). This was as true within 'totalitarian' Germany and Russia as it was within 'democratic' America and other Western countries.

The Culture Industry is part of the repressive totality that is modern capitalist society (Adorno and Horkheimer, 1992 [1944]: 34). By the twentieth century, culture had become part of a wholly integrated totality, and it is now almost completely fused with the capitalist economy. This meant two things. First, that culture was now a mechanism that worked solely in the service of the status quo, in ways we will see shortly. Second, culture had now been thoroughly *commodified*. Drawing on Marx's account of *commodity fetishism*, Adorno and Horkheimer argued that in the nineteenth century, cultural products such as books, paintings and musical performances had not yet been wholly subjected to capitalism's dictates of making profits. But by the twentieth century, the profit principle had thoroughly colonized cultural production. Cultural products now existed to be *consumed* rather than thoughtfully read or viewed or listened to. Their sole value was not their artistic merit – for that they wholly lacked – but their *exchange value*, their monetary worth on the market (ibid. 158). Because 'the entire practice of the Culture Industry transfers the profit motive naked onto cultural forms' (Adorno, 1996a: 86), culture was now blatantly a large-scale financial operation, rather than a realm relatively free of the economy. It was thus no longer a harbour for the socially critical thoughts of artists and intellectuals as it had been previously. Instead, cultural production comes more and more to be oriented towards making money. For example, referring to the contemporary use of the styles of certain Renaissance painters in cinema cartoons, Horkheimer (1972a: 281) ruefully notes that for 'a long time now, Raphael's blue horizons have been quite properly a part of [Walt] Disney's landscapes. The sunbeams almost beg to have the name of a soap or toothpaste emblazoned on them; they have no meaning except as a background for such advertising.' The Culture Industry, especially its advertising wing, appropriates artistic styles of the past, and deploys them for its own commercial ends. Here, nothing is sacred and everything is open to exploitation.

Those who run the Culture Industry – film producers, newspaper editors, media barons and so on – justify themselves by claiming all that they are doing is carrying out business operations (Adorno and Horkheimer, 1992 [1944]: 121). In this way they absolve themselves from any responsibility as to what they are in fact doing, which is destroying the Western cultural tradition in general and killing off its capacity for generating socially critical thought in particular. The very nature of the Culture Industry's products achieved this, because instead of being made by individual artists, they are now made as if on a *production line*. Just as the Ford company could produce thousands of cars all just the same by making them out of prefabricated parts put together on an assembly-line, so too the Culture Industry made its wares. All genuine creativity had leaked out of the process of cultural production, leaving it as a soulless, wholly rationalized process. This form of assembly of culture was based around making *standardized* products without any real individuality.

The horror of films

It is the ways in which modern cinema films are made that Adorno and Horkheimer particularly have in mind when talking about the standardized production of cultural goods. Looking at the Hollywood system of the 1940s, they discerned that a whole series of specialists are involved in putting a movie together, each specialist, such as actors, scriptwriters, camera operators, set designers and lighting operatives, having a particular role within the film-making division of labour. The film's director is not an individual 'artist' but, rather, is a manager concerned with coordinating the activities of all these different people. Each of the specialists provides his or her particular part of the product – say the music, or the sets – and all of the parts are put together to make the overall product, just as a car is made out of various components. Each specialist is constrained to produce stereotypical parts that can easily be fitted with each other. The composer Hanns Eisler, who worked in the Hollywood studio system in the 1940s, and who wrote a book with Adorno on the subject (Adorno and Eisler, 1994 [1947]), argued that the composer was reduced to being a mere musical technician. Studio bosses did not want any genuinely creative music, because it could not be easily fitted with the other standardized products that went into making a particular film. Instead, standardized music had to be composed that would fit with the other stereotypical components. Thus conventionally 'creepy' music would have to be written to accompany the equally clichéd scenes of Frankenstein's monster on the rampage, or recognizably 'stirring' music would have to be produced to go along with a film of the cowboy hero rescuing the heroine from the black-hatted villain.

Each new film was sold to the public as being 'new', 'better', 'bigger'. But each film of a given type was in fact the same as every other of that type that had come before it. To disguise its repetitive nature, the Culture Industry coated its products in an aura of individuality. Advertising and hype – which increasingly had come to resemble Fascist propaganda (Adorno and Horkheimer, 1992 [1944]: 156, 159) – loudly proclaimed that the new film had fascinating new stars, and that the story was more exciting and the settings more magnificent than anything that had ever been seen before. But story, setting and stars all came from a standardized template that had been used before. The Culture Industry therefore depended on *pseudo-individuality*. Each new product was claimed as being distinctive and novel, when actually it was just the same as all the others. The only novelties were cosmetic, with some of the parts being dressed up to look novel. The 'new' film star's apparent charisma derived wholly from the fact that she had a different hairstyle from all the other stars (ibid. 154). In the world of the Culture Industry, novelty is actually a constant repetition of the same (Adorno, 1996a: 87). Endless cycles of production produce identical products, which are sold as new and consumed enthusiastically by a public hungry for novelty, precisely because it is starved of any genuine novelty.

Given that the Culture Industry's methods of assembling products were so rationally efficient, so too were its means of distribution. Large media corporations' monopoly on cultural life was made possible through bureaucratically organized means of distribution, which ensured that the products on sale reached everyone in a given popu-lation. For example, in America there were nation-wide networks of cinemas owned by the Hollywood studios, this situation ensuring that their products would be guaranteed to reach potentially vast audiences. The system of distribution and advertising was a total one, in that each network was concerned to sell the goods of the others. Thus adverts for consumer goods would appear on TV and radio programmes, while films would be promoted on cereal packets (Adorno and Horkheimer, 1992 [1944]: 156). Just as in Hitler's Germany all the means of communication had been under the con-trol of certain powerful interest groups, so too were the airwaves and film-houses of democratic America under the rule of the powerful.

The mass audience

Now that we have looked at the Culture Industry's *production* of commodities, let us see how Adorno and Horkheimer understood these commodities to have been *consumed*. In the totality that is modern capitalism, the role of the Culture Industry is to pacify the mass of the population with consumer goods and mass entertain-ments. In the vast machine that is modernity:

> [T]hough the individual disappears before the apparatus which [s]he serves, that apparatus provides for him [or her] as never before . . . the impotence and pliability of the masses grow with the quantitat-ive increase in commodities allowed them . . . candy-floss entertain-ment simultaneously instructs and stultifies mankind. (Adorno and Horkheimer, 1992 [1944]: xiv–xv)

In backing up this claim, Adorno and Horkheimer make a funda-mental assumption about the nature of cultural consumption: there is a more or less direct 'fit' between the nature of the Culture Industry's products, and the way in which audience members consume that product. This is so in two ways.

First, unlike genuine works of art (see below), Culture Industry products have simplistic meanings, and so evoke simplistic responses in the audience. This is assumed to reduce the audience's capacity for critical discrimination and subtle thinking. Listening to a pop song, with its simple messages and simplistic musical structure, promotes a lack of thought, whereas listening to the complex musical structures of a Beethoven symphony, and understanding the nuances they con-vey, promotes a much more thoughtful response not just to art but to life in general.

Second, a Culture Industry product has built into it very conformist attitudes. For example, in his study of American television after the war, Adorno (1996d) identified in programmes such as *I Love Lucy* the promotion of attitudes that were completely accepting of the status quo, in terms of an acceptance of capitalism, of 'family values', and of obedience to the agencies of the state such as the police. Since Culture Industry products promote conformity, Adorno and Horkheimer argue that they will be consumed in a conformist fashion. 'The stunting of the mass-media consumer's powers of imagination and spontaneity . . . [is due to] the objective nature of the products themselves', with the result that 'no scope is left for the imagination' (Adorno and Horkheimer, 1992 [1944]: 126–7). Viewing or reading or listening are therefore fundamentally *passive* processes. Within the terms set by the Culture Industry, 'pleasure always means not to think about anything' (ibid. 144). And the erosion of thinking is the factor that keeps the populace pliant and submissive in face of the powers that dominate them (see e.g. Adorno, 1994a).

The 'fit' between Culture Industry product and the consciousness of each consumer happens because the consciousness of individuals is part of the overall totality of modern capitalist society. Individuals' minds are as much part of the overall system as are the products they consume (Adorno and Horkheimer, 1992 [1944]: 122). Each person's mind, and the set of attitudes contained within it, is increasingly like everyone else's. Each person is but one cog in the overall mechanism, identical and interchangeable with everyone else (ibid. 145). Modern America, land of mass entertainment, was far from being the 'land of the free' in this sense. The majority of people enjoyed a higher standard of material life than ever before, yet this was being bought at the cost of the degradation of their mental and emotional responses. Their most profound feelings and beliefs were being moulded by the Culture Industry. The very desire to buy ever more new goods, or to watch new movies and so on, had been instilled into the unconsciousness of consumers by the Culture Industry, rather than being an authentic expression of what people might truly desire if they had a genuine choice in the matter. 'What today is called popular entertainment is actually demands evoked . . . [and] manipulated . . . by the cultural industries', as Horkheimer (1972a: 288) put it. The Culture Industry guarantees its own continued existence by ensuring that the needs it has created – for satisfaction and enjoyment – are only ever met briefly, thus necessitating consumers to come back once again for more of the same. The Culture Industry 'perpetually cheats its consumers of what it perpetually promises' (Adorno and Horkheimer,

1992 [1944]: 139). Desires are stimulated that are never fully met, and so the system continues to run on forever.

This situation radically affects the nature of leisure time for most people (Adorno, 1996b). In the totality that is modern capitalist society, private life and leisure time are undermined. In the nineteenth century, the division of labour was such that the domestic family environment was – at least for the middle classes – a haven from the public world of work. Free time was time spent away from work concerns on genuine leisure pursuits. In the twentieth century, however, the distinction between public and private spheres became eroded, as the domestic arena was more fully integrated into the social totality. As a result, private life merges into public life, and leisure time becomes more and more implicated with the world of work. This leads to a paradoxical situation. The Culture Industry provides people with distractions from the jobs they have, making life more bearable by providing entertainment through the cinema or the radio. But at the same time, the Culture Industry prepares those people for returning to work, by refreshing them enough so that they have sufficient energy to return to their jobs, and so that they do not feel so discontented with their lot in life that they become troublesome to the authorities. In essence, the Culture Industry operates as a safety-valve mechanism, keeping the drones who work in boring occupations sufficiently satisfied that the overall system keeps operating. When today office workers stream out of work on a Friday night to head to the nearest bar, or when young people in ill-paid or unsatisfying jobs expend so much of their energy on clubbing, the bars, clubs and other providers of release and temporary freedom may be seen as means of keeping those people in line and of maintaining the power of the overall system under which they are constrained to live.

Yet, according to Adorno and Horkheimer, this manipulation of the mass of the population is not carried out *consciously* by elite groups. More and more, the system operates automatically, without active human intervention. In this way, 'the stultification of the oppressed' comes to affect 'the oppressors themselves, and they in turn become victims of the superior power of self-propelled wheels' (Adorno, 1996c: 41–2). Just as certain of the classical sociologists such as Max Weber had viewed modern life as a profound condition of alienation, whereby bureaucratic structures came to dictate the actions of those who thought they were in control of such structures, Adorno and Horkheimer see the Culture Industry as a vast leviathan, trundling along unstoppably by the weight of its own power, and coming to dictate the actions of those who believed themselves to be its masters.

Art as compensation

On the view set out above, the products of the Culture Industry and the consciousness of the masses are fused together, the former creating and reproducing the latter. This is an indication of Adorno's more general belief, produced by the rise of Fascism before World War II, and the triumph of capitalism in Western countries after it, that any hopes of working-class revolution had been defused once and for all. There was now no audience that would be stirred on to revolutionary action by the knowledge of capitalism as revealed by Critical Theory. As a result, the Frankfurt thinkers – with the exception of Marcuse (see below) – came in the 1950s and after to see Critical Theory as a lone and increasingly lonely protest against the inhuman nature of the contemporary social system and its culture. The tone of Adorno's work darkened even more after the war, its gloomy outlook being informed by the apparent lack of any possibility of social change. The continuation of the system seemed secured, especially given the rapid and massive spread of television, which potentially provided even more blanket-coverage of whole nations by Culture Industry products.

As Adorno (1997) saw it, the only other protest against the current system still possible in the modern world was embodied in the most advanced products of avant-garde art. Only a very few, exceptionally 'difficult' works, such as music by Schoenberg or paintings by Picasso, fell into this category. As Horkheimer (1972a: 275) had once phrased it, under capitalist conditions, art 'has preserved the utopia that evaporated from religion'. That is, the utopian hopes of a better world that were represented in mystified form in religion (e.g. the Christian promise of going to Heaven) had migrated into certain artworks. Such art was relatively independent of society, for it was still as yet not wholly commodified. Adorno referred to such artworks as 'autonomous art', because they were still produced by great artists with personal vision. The division of labour that had emerged in the nineteenth century had meant that artists had been freed up from the direct control of patrons. Art could be created in enclaves somewhat removed from the influence of power. The division of labour in the twentieth century, characterized by the Culture Industry, had not as yet completely eradicated these little pockets of artistic freedom and integrity. Autonomous art produced in this way contained utopian traces. But these traces were not directly expressed intimations of a better society. Instead, according to Adorno, autonomous art created feelings of disharmony and discomfort in the viewer or listener. In this way, they avoided the easy, comfortable, standardized responses evoked in audiences by the Culture Industry products. By creating feelings of disharmony, autonomous art indicated to its audience that all was in fact not well in contemporary society, unsettling them out of the passive and conformist mentalities nurtured by the Culture Industry.

This emphasis on the protest made by autonomous art against contemporary society leads to three important points about Adorno's approach to the sociology of culture. First, although autonomous art is the only form of culture left that is in any way socially critical, it is nonetheless relatively powerless to change things. This is because its very freedom from society was due to its being produced outside of the capitalist market, and for a small bourgeois elite. As a result, autonomous art was 'difficult' and beyond the grasp of the masses (Adorno and Horkheimer, 1992 [1944]: 135). Thus it cannot speak to them, but can only be understood by an educated minority, and that minority (of whom Adorno and the other Frankfurt theorists felt themselves to be members) is disappearing fast under the sway of the Culture Industry. As a result, autonomous art may contain a protest against current social conditions, but it expresses that protest in a way most people cannot understand. Second, while autonomous art retains its capacity to resist modern social conditions, it is the only form of dissent that exists in modern society, now that the proletariat have been brought into the system and lost their revolutionary capacities. In this sense, in Adorno's scheme, art replaces the working classes as the source of dissent against society. But such dissent is very weak and hardly registered by anyone. Art takes on the dissenting role of the powerless, but its complaints against society are increasingly impotent. Third, Adorno's whole analysis of Culture Industry products is based on his contrasting them with the qualities of autonomous art. Such art is the yardstick against which Culture Industry commodities are judged. Whereas autonomous art at least potentially fosters critical thinking, Adorno finds that Culture Industry products, with their standardization and stereotyping, promote the opposite. Thus Adorno's whole analysis is based on what Culture Industry products are said to *lack*. Autonomous art is held up as the instance of what culture *could be like* if the social conditions in which it was produced were better. Culture Industry culture is, by contrast, what culture is like in the present day, produced by a social context of exploitation, domination and misery. Whether this distinction between 'good' and 'bad' art can be justified is a source of much controversy, as we will see shortly.

Evaluating the Frankfurt School

As has been hinted at above, the ideas of the Frankfurt thinkers are often highly controversial. This is why many commentators intensely dislike the Frankfurt approach in general, and Adorno's analyses in particular, alleging that they are characterized by both condescension towards popular culture (Fiske, 1989a: 183) and a 'narcotic pessimism' (Andrews and Loy, 1993: 257). In this section, we will deal with some of the objections that have been raised against the Frankfurt account of culture.

Hooray for Hollywood?

The central question that has to be asked as to the possible relevance of the Frankfurt approach to 'mass culture' is whether it is more than an account of its prime target, the Hollywood studio system of the 1940s. Hollywood movie production of that period lies at the heart of the theory of the Culture Industry. If cultural production and consumption today do not fit this model, then the contemporary usefulness of the theory is severely called into question. It could be argued that the situation today is much more diverse than was the case in 1940s America. The term 'Culture Industry' may be misleading, because it suggests that there is just one vast mega-industry that is involved in cultural production. But the nature of cultural production in capitalist society is actually based around competition between rival companies of producers. They each seek to maximize their own profits at the expense of their competitors. It therefore might make more sense to talk of a series of *culture industries* in the plural rather than a mammoth and uniform Culture Industry in the singular. This would take the emphasis away from the *propagandistic* characteristics of the latter towards the *profit-seeking* nature of the former. On this view, the culture industries (plural) do not each seek to instil the minds of consumers with socially conformist attitudes, but instead merely attempt to make products that are attractive to customers. This view sees cultural production as much more like the usual business practices of the capitalist economy, rather than being akin to the propaganda machine of totalitarian regimes (see chapter 8 for further discussion of this issue).

It could be said that in assessing the United States in the 1940s, Adorno and Horkheimer wrongly viewed it in light of a model that made more sense if applied to Nazi Germany or Stalinist Russia. They thus perhaps missed out the important possibility that the United

States (and other Western countries, then as now) are certainly *capitalist* societies, but not totalitarian ones. There is more scope for individual dissent and less power of propagandistic institutions in the context of a capitalist society than in one that is truly rigidly regulated. If this is so, then it would be wrong to liken a television programme made today to a Nazi propaganda broadcast, because each of them is a product of, and operates within, a very different social and political context. By not differentiating enough between fully fledged totalitarian societies and those based around a capitalist market, it might be said that Adorno and Horkheimer were insufficiently *sociological* about how they characterized the United States.

It could also be argued that today many more cultural products are on offer to the contemporary consumer than the relatively restricted market of movies and radio programmes available in the 1940s. Arguably, there are nowadays far more sources of cinema production than under the situation where the big Hollywood studios controlled almost all aspects of cinema viewing. Moreover, there exist today small companies geared towards providing entertainment for particular groups with idiosyncratic tastes far removed from the mainstream of 'mass' culture. For example, there are record companies that service only one area of music, such as reggae.

This situation of increased diversity of both products and audiences has, arguably, resulted in increasing levels of *risk* for companies producing cultural goods. Even if the latest film or album is designed to appeal to what the marketing people think is the taste of a large section of the buying public, the particular product might not sell as well as expected. The careers of stars in the music and film industries rise and fall like stock-market shares, dependent on the money-making performance of the last few albums or films they have made. The history of Hollywood film is littered with expensive 'flops' that the marketing experts thought would be sure-fire successes. There does not seem to be any magic formula that can be stuck to in order always to make profitable cultural goods. This is a far cry from the apparently automatic and always successful functioning of the Culture Industry as it was identified by Adorno and Horkheimer. Audiences may be more discerning, or more fickle, than they assumed.

Nor did Adorno and Horkheimer give any real attention to types of cultural production and consumption that exist *outside* the world of the Culture Industry. There are perhaps more possibilities today than ever before for 'unofficial' types of cultural production by ordinary people, such as utilizing relatively low-cost equipment to record their own music, or using copying equipment to 'burn' CDs or 'pirate' video tapes, thus reducing the profitability of the media conglomerates which released these products. The appearance of the internet and the development of on-line 'communities' of users might also be seen as a way in which ordinary people now have the opportunity to use communications technology for their own purposes, rather than have it used by powerful institutions over and against them.

In all these various ways, then, empirical evidence can be brought to bear on the Culture Industry theory, and it can be argued on that basis that the real state of affairs is far more complicated than Adorno and Horkheimer admitted. Conversely, empirical evidence can be found that supports the continuing relevance of the Culture Industry position for understanding our own times. To a very large degree, most of the cultural products we are accustomed to consuming, from newspapers and magazines to cinema films and DVDs, are made by large media corporations (Stallabrass, 1996). Huge conglomerates such as Sony and Time-Warner have interests in practically every area of cultural production. Their reach across national and international markets is greater than ever. Hollywood films were exported all over the world from the very beginnings of the American film industry in the early twentieth century, and American movies – not to mention TV programmes and pop music – are now to be found showing practically everywhere in the world. The reach of US-based companies producing culture is now global in scope, and is arguably an important facet of a process whereby the whole world becomes increasingly 'Westernized' (Latouche, 1996). It would probably not surprise Adorno and Horkheimer very much to hear about the transplantation in very many different countries of the highly rationalized types of food production associated with the McDonald's corporation (Ritzer, 1992).

As the distribution networks of these and other companies have spread ever further across the world, their marketing machines have become increasingly sophisticated in identifying 'niche markets' that can be exploited. Adorno and Horkheimer had already in the 1940s anticipated the increasing importance of market research in fine-tuning the methods whereby companies could sell their wares: 'something is provided for all so that none may escape. . . . Everybody must behave (as if spontaneously) in accordance with his [or her] previously determined and indexed level, and choose the category of mass product turned out for his [or her] type' (1992 [1944]: 123). The point being made here is that on the surface it looks as if there are many different types of audience, each with different tastes. But on closer scrutiny, it can be seen that since all of these audiences are catered for by the same companies providing standardized goods 'tweaked' to fit particular tastes, the apparently heterogeneous audiences (plural) should actually be seen as part of a *mass* audience (singular) (Adorno, 1996g). Whether this claim is convincing or not is a matter for debate. But it does show that Adorno and Horkheimer did not simply disregard completely the issue of diversity of tastes within what they saw as a mass audience.

Biases or values?

Adorno and Horkheimer are often criticized for being utterly unbalanced in their analysis of modern cultural conditions, being not only pessimistic in their outlook but insensitive towards any types of culture other than the 'autonomous art' championed in particular by Adorno. There are indeed many objections that can be raised about the chasm he erects between the products of the Culture Industry and the types of art he privileges. It might be argued that there is a complete unawareness of what can be achieved artistically within the confines of the Culture Industry. Even in the 1940s, film directors such as Alfred Hitchcock and John Ford produced films that bore their distinctive imprints, despite being made within Hollywood studios seeking to make money out of standardized thrillers and Westerns. In today's situation, there still seems to be room in Hollywood for directors such as David Lynch and Terry Gilliam, who are regarded as 'mavericks' and who deliberately do not produce films that could be called standardized. Such directors are esteemed by Hollywood moguls for the artistic prestige that they bring with them to the studio that funds them, rather than in the anticipation of huge profits. This prestige element was ignored by Adorno and Horkheimer, who only saw film directors as managers of an assembly-line production process, rather than as 'artists' in their own right.

There is probably some truth in the charge that Adorno in particular just could not see any value in cultural products that had been seemingly manufactured. In his notorious writings on jazz (1967b; 1996e), for example, there is a systematic downgrading of this musical form as something that has been assembled in a machine-like way, without the thought or care that went into the composition of an 'autonomous' artwork, such as a Beethoven symphony. But just because a cultural form like a film or a record is released by a big company for distribution does not mean to say it necessarily must lack thought or imagination. Adorno's viewpoint prevents him from seeing what some take to be the great skill of popular jazz musicians of that time such as Louis Armstrong, or of popular performers of later periods such as Frank Sinatra and Michael Jackson. Complex questions of what might be 'good' or 'bad' *within* mass-produced culture are forgone in favour of a claim that only very few works are 'truly artistic'. This position prevents analysis of why certain groups of people regard certain cultural producers as 'artists' and other producers as mere 'hacks'. The French sociologist Pierre Bourdieu (see chapter 7) argued that the power to decide what is culturally good or bad, true 'art' or mere 'mass' culture, rests in modern societies with the educated middle class, a group that uses this power to retain its own privileged social status. From that viewpoint, when Adorno bases his whole account of the Culture Industry on how it makes products vastly inferior to 'real' art, he is actually unwittingly exercising the cultural power of the class into which he was born. So blinkered was he by his own upbringing amongst classical music and other 'approved' forms of art that he could not see that his views prevented him from carrying out a sociological analysis of 'art' itself, questioning its uses by those with high levels of legitimate cultural power. On this view, Adorno is again insufficiently 'sociological' in his outlook, regarding his own values as innately superior to others, and remaining wedded to the highly elitist and pessimistic assumptions of his forebears in the German upper middle classes (McGuigan, 1992: 48). Quite simply, he is not reflexive enough about his own biases and dispositions.

This would seem to make him a particularly poor candidate for understanding the nature of life in the twentieth century and after. After World War II, Adorno seemed to shut himself off from new developments in social and cultural life, unlike his Frankfurt colleague Herbert Marcuse (1974 [1964]), who tried to ally Critical Theory to emerging social movements such as the anti-Vietnam War peace demonstrations in North America and Europe. Marcuse therefore demonstrated that Critical Theory could embrace new developments rather than be utterly hostile to them, and that Adorno's dislike of much of the world around him was more to do with his own upbringing and personality than with Critical Theory itself. Jürgen Habermas's (1984) later reworking of Critical Theory has similarly been oriented towards providing forms of critical knowledge of society for use by groups such as the Green movement, a possibility that Adorno failed to countenance.

Another figure associated with the Frankfurt School, Walter Benjamin, also illustrated how someone brought up in a highly educated milieu could escape the assumptions into which he had been socialized. His article 'The Work of Art in the Age of Mechanical Reproduction' (1970 [1936]) contains the assertion that far from making audiences more passive, the medium of film makes them more active, because it demands new forms of attentiveness and comprehension. Although, in like fashion to Adorno, Benjamin's philosophical account of such matters lacks empirical evidence, it nonetheless showed much more openness to the possibility that audiences were more than just passive dupes. Moreover, in the same article, Benjamin claimed that in the modern world, works of art were losing their 'aura' – that is, that people were not so inclined to fetishize them as if they were holy objects. But it is precisely this kind of fetishization of so-called true 'art' that cripples Adorno's ability to see anything positive in other types of culture.

Nonetheless, it would be wrong to see Adorno as a simple-minded elitist and pessimist. Although he lost faith in the possibility of a working-class revolution in Western countries, he nonetheless remained a Marxist. One strain of Marxist thought sees human creativity as the great potential that is unleashed in a socialist society. Adorno believed that such a better future, where everyone could create freely and without hindrance, was indicated by great works of art. Only under capitalist society does 'art' remain the privilege of an elite. Adorno's hope was that one day the creativity of the 'artist' would be shared and cultivated by everyone. In that sense, he is not an elitist but a utopian.

To accuse Adorno of 'bias' also misses the point that Critical Theory *admits* it is biased, in favour of what it sees as a better future for everyone. The utopian spirit arguably never left Adorno, even in his writings that are apparently most despairing about the nature of contemporary life (e.g. 1996f). What must be remembered is that Adorno *deliberately* adopted a highly negative writing style. He was of the opinion that *how* a theory of society and culture is written is as important as *what* is actually being said. His writing was deliberately ironic and overstated (1997b; see also Buck-Morss, 1977; Rose, 1978: 11), for it was designed as a 'shock tactic' (Adorno, 1997a: 319) to force the reader to see reality in a different light from which he or she was accustomed. The usual ways of understanding things are created by modern society itself, and so disguise what is truly going on. Therefore, to encourage his readers truly to understand how things work, Adorno (1990) quite purposely says the most outrageous things, in order to get his audience *thinking* and to make them look at the world in a new way. Only then would they start to think about how things might be both *different* and *better* in a future, non-capitalist society. Adorno felt that a more 'balanced' and distanced style of writing, as demanded by positivism and as favoured by many American social scientists of the time, only shallowly reflected the surface of society, and did not actually penetrate to its core. As a result, you are *meant* to be shocked, disgusted and outraged by reading what he has to say. Only in that way might you be startled out of accepted ideas, such as that popular culture is chosen freely by those who consume it, rather than recognizing the possibility that it is imposed from above in the same fashion as in totalitarian societies. Anyone who took Adorno to task for being 'overstated', or who argued he was a wholly pessimistic thinker, would be guilty of misreading his works.

Theoretical and methodological problems

The final set of issues we will look at concerns how studies of culture should be carried out, in terms of how forms of empirical evidence are to be related to theory. Although Adorno (e.g. 1950) occasionally drew upon empirical research methods, most of his work on culture, and the Culture Industry thesis especially, was not based directly on empirical data. This was not an oversight but a deliberate strategy. The main enemy of Critical Theory was positivism, which in the social sciences advocated the privileging of 'data' over 'theory'. From Adorno and Horkheimer's anti-positivist viewpoint, data alone is never enough to reveal anything about a particular situation. Instead, the data must be interpreted in light of the special insights of Critical Theory. This assumes that the Critical Theorist him/herself already knows the true nature of the situation in question, and this knowledge cannot be challenged by data that seems to suggest a contrary attitude towards the situation. This leads to a whole series of problems.

In the first place, is it not very arrogant to *assume* that the Critical Theorist *must* know more about the situation than anyone else, and that data cannot challenge that understanding? This seems to suggest that the views put forward by Critical Theorists can never be subjected to testing, perhaps indicating that the position might actually be called *un*-Critical Theory (Lazarsfeld, 1984; Kolakowski, 1978; Popper, 1966). The problem of making huge assumptions and putting forward sweeping claims, but never testing them, arises in its most extreme form in the idea that there *must* be a direct 'fit' between the apparently conformist nature of cultural products, and the supposedly utterly passive nature of people in the audience (Swingewood, 1977). The Freudian assumption that individuals' minds are thoroughly open to manipulation is never challenged, because empirical evidence about how audiences actually think and feel is never allowed into court, a reliance on such data being seen as unacceptably positivist.

Some have argued that despite the Institute for Social Research being set up to pursue interdisciplinary research that would be both philosophically and empirically informed, the actual trajectory of

Frankfurt thinking became ever more 'philosophical' and ever less empirically sociological over time. The result of its obsessional anti-positivism was that Critical Theory eventually ended up not as a *sociology* but as a *philosophy* of culture, and as a purely theoretical viewpoint that refused to befoul itself with empirical data (Bourdieu, 1990a: 19). When forms of evidence were dealt with, they were invariably interpreted in ways that fitted the overall argument. This was partly a result of the emphasis on seeing every part of society as part of a *totality* (Adorno, 1967b). Every phenomenon was regarded as being of a piece with everything else. Therefore it was assumed that how individuals think, or how people view movies and TV, *must* completely 'fit' with the interests of the Culture Industry and the whole system of power in modern society. But are all the different elements of modern society really so tightly integrated with each other? This view seems to downgrade the possibility of struggles occurring between different groups, and the social sphere being riven with contradictions and clashes. The idea of totality was developed by the Frankfurt thinkers to get away from Marx's base-superstructure model. But by having a view of the totality of modern society as being completely tightly closed, by seeing it in light of the particular *totalitarian* circumstances of Nazi Germany and Stalin's Russia, they relinquished Marx's original insight that societies are characterized more by conflicts between groups than the total power of elites. Facing this problem, Habermas (1984) attempts to place conflictual relations back at the heart of a Critical Theoretical diagnosis of the nature of modernity.

In fairness to Adorno, many of his critics make the assumption that empirical data about social and cultural matters seem to 'speak for themselves' rather than being in need of theoretical interpretation. In contrast to a mentality that thinks everything can be revealed by quantitative surveys and data-sets, Adorno may well have a point when he argues that culture is not something that can be simply measured (McCann, 1994: xxii). Adorno would answer some of his critics by pointing out that their views are based on a naive form of empiricism which assumes that empirical data directly reveal 'the truth' to those who collect them. From Adorno's (2000: 125; 1976a; 1976b) perspective, it is fundamentally wrong to think that empirical sociology on its own can provide knowledge about any particular situation. For example, a survey of audience views might 'reveal' that the people surveyed believe there to be a great choice of programmes on television. But to accept that kind of judgement at face value might be very naive on the part of the analyst. The definition of what constitutes a 'great choice' cannot be taken at face value. The data need to be *interpreted* and, Adorno would no doubt argue, that interpretation needs to be through the means of a Critical Theory that does not just mindlessly reproduce the surface of things as these are caught by empirical research methods. The very idea of a 'great choice' of television programming is partly an idea propagated by media corporations in order to convince consumers to keep watching a certain channel. The danger with empirically based research is that it can reflect the surface of things rather than see into processes that are more hidden.

A useful attempt to deal with some of these issues was put forward by Leo Lowenthal, one of the original members of the Frankfurt School whose ideas have generally been overshadowed by those of the more well-known Adorno. Data, he argued, must be collected if the study of culture is to be *sociological* rather than purely *philosophical*. However, data only make sense within a theoretical framework. That framework must have a moral component within it – a belief in fundamental values, such as the idea of a better future society. Otherwise, the sociologist is merely a passive observer of surface phenomena, rather than a critic who can get to the heart of social relations – the underlying reality that is not immediately obvious from merely reading the data collected (Lowenthal, 1961: xi). There must be a dialectical relationship between theory and data, the one informing the other, although with theory ultimately the senior partner. But for Lowenthal, perhaps unlike for Adorno and Horkheimer, theory was not a set of unquestionable truths. As long ago as 1932, Lowenthal (1984: 249) was arguing that as 'long as a theory does not consider itself finite but rather continuously sustained and possibly altered by new and different experiences', it will not become a mere dogma. This echoes the original programme for Critical Theory as a way of thinking that took nothing for granted, formulated by Horkheimer around the same time. The main difference between Horkheimer and Adorno on the one side, and Lowenthal on the other, was that Lowenthal was less fanatically anti-positivist and so never lost sight of the need for an empirical check on theory. His empirically informed Critical Theoretical explorations of cultural issues (e.g. 1957, 1961) are worth seeking out as an alternative to the overly theoretical pronouncements of his colleagues.

Conclusion

The contributions of the thinkers of the early Frankfurt School towards the sociological study of culture constitute what might be taken as some very sharp insights and some very serious flaws. On the credit side, Adorno and Horkheimer were among the first theorists to come to terms with the new forms that culture took in the twentieth century, with the mass fabrication of cultural products coming to figure as an ever more fundamental part of life in Western modernity. They homed in on some of the crucial issues that a sociology of culture now had to deal with, including the mass production of newspapers, magazines, films, music albums, television programmes and so on, and the consumption of these by vast numbers of people. On the debit side, the ways in which Adorno and Horkheimer reacted to these developments were often too rooted in their own personal circumstances and backgrounds. In particular, their general inability to welcome any new social and cultural developments does indeed throw a shadow over their analyses. However, we must bear in mind that they were of the first generation of people really to have to confront the massive – and often seemingly frightening – social, political and cultural developments characteristic of the twentieth century. A rather nostalgic hankering after the apparent certainties of previous ages is perhaps an understandable response on the part of the Frankfurt thinkers.

Although there are large problems pertaining to how Adorno and Horkheimer understood certain matters, and the ways in which they thought the study of culture should operate, nonetheless much remains in their contributions that is of interest to us today. At the very least they provide a provocative analysis of issues that other sociologies of culture fail to engage with fully, such as the fate of the individual person under the conditions of a society where he or she might count for very little. Whatever one may think of their ideas, one has to admit that they are based not just on a sour pessimism but also on a more hopeful utopianism that dreams of a better life for all. The strong affinities that their ideas share with later postmodernist ideas about the alienating effects of modern culture are explored in chapter 6, as are the criticisms of postmodern culture forwarded by thinkers indebted to the Frankfurt vision. Moreover, the alternative lines of development of Critical Theory, pursued in the work of Marcuse, Benjamin, Lowenthal and Habermas, show that the Frankfurt enterprise need not run aground due to the personal idiosyncrasies of its founders. As a result, the works of the early Frankfurt School remain, with certain reservations, still well worth reading for those seeking inspiration as to how to understand culture today.

3

An American Tragedy?
Mass Culture in the USA

Introduction

The United States is an endless source of fascination, both for foreigners and its own citizens. For those from abroad, it signifies a whole host of feelings, from admiration for its dynamism to a loathing of its apparently imperialistic ambitions. America has been interpreted both as the template for the way the rest of the world is or should be going, and as illustrating precisely how a society should *not* be organized. For those living in the United States, their country's multiplicity and diversity compels reflection as to just what America 'is', what it stands for, and what it is to be an American citizen.

The many ways in which America can be understood are the topic of this chapter. The particular focus is on the controversial issue of 'mass culture'. Are American culture and society to be regarded as 'mass', as fundamentally impersonal and potentially highly alienating? Or should they be seen in a more positive light that stresses the community-based aspects of American life? These questions lie at the heart of attempts to define America and to say what makes it so distinctive a society. Whether a more positive or negative response has been offered to these questions has depended on who is offering it. Artistic and literary critics have tended to side with the view that sees modern American culture as almost wholly and disastrously 'mass' in nature, this culture being seen to have very negative effects on society. Sociologists, by contrast, have tended to have a much more upbeat viewpoint on how American life operates. They start from what they see as the great multiplicity of social life in the United States, and argue from this basis that American culture is not 'mass' in character but highly diverse, flexible and open. Thus the interpretation afforded of American life depends on both the intellectual backgrounds of the interpreters, and what factor they see as being the primary one, either 'culture' or 'society'. As we will see, both sides have interesting insights to contribute to how natives and foreigners alike understand the nature of America.

We begin by outlining the source of many of the later debates and controversies as to 'Americanness', namely the report on American life given by the nineteenth-century French aristocrat Alexis de Tocqueville. We then consider how literary critics and others from the 1930s onwards described and condemned American culture as a 'mass' phenomenon. Next we examine the various ways in which sociologists have sought to look at these issues in somewhat different terms and in a generally more positive light. Finally we consider how these debates are playing out today, in terms of often rather acrimonious disputes over the nature of 'multiculturalism' in contemporary America.

Defining America

The United States has long been a topic of fascination for foreigners. One of the first, and most influential, outsiders to observe the American scene was the French aristocrat Alexis de Tocqueville (1805–59), who conducted a tour of the United States in the early 1830s. His book, which reports the findings of his observations, *Democracy in America*, was intended as embodying 'a new science of politics' for 'a new world' (1952 [1835]: 7). It has come to be one of the major literary sources not only for later foreign interpreters of American life, but for Americans themselves, wishing to comprehend the 'spirit' of their society. The ideas that Tocqueville put forward contain the seeds of many later foreign observations and native self-understandings of what it is to be an American.

The background to Tocqueville's famous analysis is the social, cultural and, above all, *political* conditions that he encountered in early nineteenth-century America. As part of the 'New World' colonized by Europeans (at the expense of the original inhabitants), America was in some senses a society built from scratch. Although its inhabitants owed certain cultural traditions to their (mainly Anglo-Saxon) forebears, they were living a form of life that was in many ways distinct from that which characterized European societies. Above all, social hierarchies were much less pronounced and static than they were back in the 'Old World'. This was partly for expressly political reasons. In the Revolution of 1776, the inhabitants of the colony of America broke away from the power of the English government and established a new political order based around a democratic constitution. This Constitution enshrined the rights of the individual against intrusion by others, making freedom of speech and of religious belief central pillars of American life. Unlike in Europe, where the rule of kings over their subjects still held sway, in democratic America each man (women as yet still being viewed as second-class citizens) was free to do as he liked, as long as this did not impinge negatively on the lives of others. The principle of *liberty* was therefore a crucial component of American democratic life. Moreover, in the eyes of the law, every man was equal with and not to be treated differently from any other. The principle of *equality* was therefore as crucial as that of liberty, both as to how American law operated and how Americans understood their own social conditions. Tocqueville saw as the primary fact of American life that most people tended to be equal with each other, in terms of both wealth and status, and all other aspects of American life flowed from this fact. It was also Tocqueville's contention that the political principles of the Constitution were the underpinnings of *all* aspects of American social and cultural life. He termed these latter factors 'the ordinary practices of life' and 'the manners of the country' (1952 [1835]: 1, 15).

Tocqueville saw himself as a neutral observer of life in the United States, his views being derived from the 'mass of evidence' he had collected on his travels (ibid. 18). But this did not prevent him from making some assessments of the contradictions he discerned in American life. The main ambivalence was that there was a distinct tension between the principles of *equality* and *liberty*. While liberty stressed the freedom of the individual, equality emphasized the individual's responsibilities to the group, both that made up of the people immediately around the individual, and that constituted of the society as a whole. Too much individual liberty and the fabric of social life would be torn apart by self-interest and selfishness. On the other hand, too much equality and the individual would be trapped in a web of conformity and oppression. The two poles of social and political activity that Americans had to mediate between, therefore, were a socially irresponsible selfishness and a stifling *tyranny of the majority*. The main mediating factors that helped to avoid such extremes were individuals actively participating in political life and getting involved in community associations such as churches. Through these institutions of *civil society*, both individual needs for self-expression *and* the community's requirement that individuals cooperate with each other could be met.

Tocqueville's diagnosis of American cultural life was also based around his identification of ambiguities. On the one hand he felt that democratic societies in general, not just the United States, tended to promote a higher level of cultural appreciation in individuals of all classes than did non-democratic societies, which kept people in the lower classes in a state of ignorance through lack of education. Pursuit of 'high culture', of 'the spiritual and the beautiful', amongst the higher classes would trickle down to the lower classes, raising everyone to a certain minimal level of refinement (1952 [1835]: 315). Therefore, Tocqueville argued that democratic societies were not in themselves hostile to 'high culture', for people in such societies follow artistic pursuits 'after their own fashion' (ibid. 316). On the other hand, there were certain factors peculiar to America that militated against this process. The fact that most of its inhabitants had Puritan leanings meant that they regarded making money as more important than contemplating more spiritual matters, with the result that, much more than Europeans, their minds were diverted 'from the pursuit of science, literature and the arts' (ibid. 314). Even members of the educated elite in America seemed much less interested in these pursuits than their European counterparts, leading Tocqueville to comment that 'I know of no country . . . where the love of money has taken stronger hold' (ibid. 45). The outcome of this situation was that American culture, in the sense of 'high culture', seemed to be very mediocre, weakened by the materialist dispositions of most Americans. What artistic activities there were seemed to Tocqueville to be very trivial in comparison to what European countries had to offer. His overall argument therefore was that while democratic society per se is not antagonistic to 'high culture', the American version of it to a large degree was inimical to the flowering of anything other than the ordinary and the commonplace.

Cultural disaster

The main differences between the America of the early nineteenth century that Tocqueville had commented upon and the America of the twentieth century were fourfold. First, in the course of the later nineteenth century, the shift to an industrialized economy had created vast amounts of wealth, both for people in general and, in particular, for the capitalist class which owned the factories, railroads and the other industries which became the backbone of the United States economy. In this way, the standard of living increased for most people, but so too did social divisions, with there being a consequent diminution of conditions of equality in favour of ever greater disparities between groups in terms of wealth and status. Second, industrialization was concomitant with urbanization, and huge metropolises with vast populations such as New York and Chicago sprang up. These great cities seemed to be replacing the small-town America that Tocqueville had witnessed and which he had regarded as the typical locales in which Americans lived. Third, due to increases in population, politics became less about each person directly participating in political life, and more about citizens voting for representatives to defend their political interests. Politics, especially at the national level, became more and more a pursuit of an elite group of elected representatives, the members of which were often drawn from the richer families. Fourth, the relatively homogeneous Anglo-Saxon population was increasingly diversified by waves of immigrants, especially from Eastern and Southern Europe. In addition, Black Americans, who had been in America as long as the first white, Anglo-Saxon settlers, would come to develop a more powerful collective political voice in the 1960s.

Thus, if Tocqueville had visited the United States in the *1930s* rather than the 1830s, he would have witnessed a wealthy, urban, industrial, economically stratified and socially diverse society that in some senses would have borne little correspondence to the country he had written of a hundred years before. For many writers of the first half of the twentieth century, the negative aspects of American life first identified by Tocqueville had been made much worse by urbanization and industrialization. From this point of view, America was now a *mass society*, a social order that exhibited many of the more negative aspects of modernity, such as had been identified in a European context by Tönnies (see chapter 1). A decline in community feeling, leaving selfish individuals isolated and alone, was a central theme of this strand of thinking. The problems of a mass society were key issues for intellectuals of this time in countries other than the USA, notably Germany and England (see chapters 2 and 4 respectively). A typical, and very influential, contribution to such ideas was that offered by the Spanish philosopher Ortega y Gasset. His book, *Revolt of the Masses*, first published in 1930, divided modern society on the basis of two types of person. On the one hand, there was the especially talented, educated person who was a unique individual and a member of a small intellectual elite. Everyone else was characterized as the 'mass man', a person who resembled everyone else in the 'mass'. The vast majority of people in modern society are of this type, according to Ortega. While the elite people 'make great demands of themselves' in terms of learning, thinking and creating, the people in the 'mass' are only able to do all these things in mediocre ways, if they do them at all (Ortega, 1993 [1930]: 15). It was the United States in particular that Ortega was thinking about when he argued that modern, democratic societies promote amongst most people mediocrity and triviality over true thought and creative effort.

These kinds of idea were very influential amongst American thinkers, of both left- and right-wing views, in the period up until the 1960s. Many of these writers were literary and artistic intellectuals. Born into affluent and highly educated backgrounds, they felt very uneasy about the kind of 'mass society' they felt they were living in (Ross, 1989). It was the 'mass culture' of such a society that particularly offended them. Hollywood films, cheap novels, popular newspapers and magazines – all of these seemed to embody values that were tawdry, tacky and of no lasting worth. A much-cited contribution to the study of mass culture was an article entitled 'Avant-garde and Kitsch', by the art critic Clement Greenberg, first published in 1939. Just as Ortega had separated social life into 'elite' and 'mass' types of people, so Greenberg divided the world of cultural objects and tastes into two antagonistic parts. On the one side was the true, pioneering and difficult art of avant-garde artists. (This is conceived of in a way very similar to Adorno's conception of 'autonomous art' – see previous chapter.) On the other side, there is 'kitsch', which derives from the German word for wasted energy. It describes for Greenberg all mass-produced, mass-marketed popular culture, including 'magazine covers, illustrations, ads . . . pulp fiction, comics . . . tap dancing, Hollywood movies and so on' (Greenberg, 1986 [1939]: 11). Not only was this kind of culture easily understood – if it had any meaning at all – it was also wholly a factory-produced kind of culture. In terms both of how it was made and how it was consumed, kitsch culture lacked all the virtues of avant-garde art, which required effort and training both to make and to comprehend. 'Kitsch is mechanical and operates by formulas. Kitsch is vicarious experience and faked sensations. Kitsch changes according to style, but remains always the same. Kitsch is the epitome of all that is spurious in the life of our times' (Greenberg, 1986 [1939]: 12). It keeps the masses of people, those dwelling in the huge American cities, entertained and in so doing pacifies them and renders them ever more uncritical and complacent.

Greenberg's main complaint is not that avant-garde art has to co-exist with kitsch, but rather that the latter leeches off the former. Kitsch is based on devices and ideas stolen from avant-garde artworks, which are watered down and used for the purposes of making money rather than stimulating critical thought. An example here would be atonal styles of music, developed by avant-garde composers, being taken up and used as background music to provide 'atmosphere' in Hollywood films. Kitsch culture is vampiric on the 'true' art that Greenberg defends, and in so doing it threatens not only to sap the vitality of art, but, because producing kitsch for a mass market pays well, it also lures artists away from genuine forms of cultural production with the promise of large wage-packets. Greenberg is often taken to be arguing simply that 'high culture' is better than 'popular culture'. Clearly this is the main thrust of his argument, but he also argues that certain cultural goods *look as if* they are avant-garde even though they are in fact kitsch masquerading as higher culture. He singles out for attack the *New Yorker* magazine, which seems highbrow with its reviews of new books and discussions of art exhibitions, but which 'waters down a great deal of avant-garde material for its own uses' (Greenberg, 1986 [1939]: 13). Thus Greenberg is not arguing that it is only cultural products prepared for working- and lower-middle-class audiences that are kitsch; products aimed at an elite audience, drawn from the upper-middle class, can be highly kitsch in nature too. This identification of *different levels* of kitsch actually subverts the idea that there is just such a thing as 'mass culture'. While Greenberg did not intend it, this view opens up the way for arguing that there are different *types* of mass culture, aimed by their makers at different audiences, rather than just one set of products aimed indiscriminately at everyone.

Such a slippage was not noticed by many other authors who took up these ideas after World War II (e.g. Fiedler, 1957; Rosenberg, 1957). Another key article in this line of thought is 'A Theory of Mass Culture', penned by another literary intellectual, Dwight Macdonald, and published in 1953. Macdonald (1978 [1953]) follows the general viewpoint put forward by Greenberg, and makes favourable reference to the position on mass culture offered by Adorno (see chapter 2). Macdonald agrees with the latter that contemporary mass culture is wholly fabricated by Culture Industries, the employees of which have no freedom in making cultural forms, but who have to follow very strict templates oriented towards standardized production. The 'distinctive mark' of their cultural products is that they are 'solely and directly an article for mass consumption, like chewing gum' (1978 [1953]: 167). Macdonald argues that mass culture is 'homogenized' for 'it mixes and scrambles everything together', elements of high and low culture being merged into one easy-to-digest mixture. In so doing, this type of culture 'destroys all values, since value-judgments imply discrimination'. In this regard, mass culture was 'very, very democratic: it absolutely refuses to discriminate against, or between, anything or anybody' (ibid.). While the resultant cultural stew was unpalatable for those who were aware of higher levels of culture, the 'mass audience', according to Macdonald, gobbled this kind of thing up all too eagerly. In so doing, they become more and more infantile, passive dupes of a system aimed at keeping them in their place. Moreover, the culture of the elite comes under increasing threat too. Even the more educated are increasingly turning to mass culture rather than defending the artistic avant-garde. From Macdonald's point of view, mass culture is 'a dynamic, revolutionary force, breaking down the old barriers of class, tradition, taste, and dissolving all cultural distinctions' (ibid.). As a result, 'high culture' seems to be doomed because when 'serious ideas compete with commercialised formulae', the advantage lies with the latter, for mass culture is easily understood and requires no effort. In cultural terms, the 'bad stuff drives out the good', leaving a barren wasteland of a mass culture furthering the development of a mediocre and passive mass society (ibid. 170).

In the Cold War climate in which Macdonald was writing, it comes as no surprise that he and other authors tended to think that mass culture was an important force in destroying American democracy in favour of what they saw as the epitome of all mass societies, the Communist Soviet Union. There, all culture seemed to be produced at the directive of a political elite for the purposes of pacifying the mass of the population. It is at this point that Macdonald's argument becomes contradictory. On the one hand, he sees the totalitarian Soviet Union as embodying the most developed forms of mass culture. On the other hand, he describes mass culture as 'very, very democratic'. So is it democratic or totalitarian? Macdonald seems unable to see the possibility that mass culture in the United States might be organized differently than in the Soviet Union, in ways that might make it more compatible with the country's democratic traditions. The idea that America may have a mass *culture*, but that it exists within the context of a democratic and diverse *society*, is at the root of sociological approaches to these issues, as we will see shortly.

National culture and deviance

The assumptions made by artistic and literary critics such as Macdonald are very different from those made by American sociologists of the same period. Sociologists saw the arguments of the literary intellectuals as fundamentally flawed. In particular, sociologists argued that such ideas about mass culture tended to be based more on personal opinion and speculation than on empirical investigation. How could one prove that the effects of mass culture were to pacify 'the masses' if one had never gone out into the social world to try to investigate this issue? What evidence was there to suggest that everyone in American cities was socially atomized, isolated and alone? These are the same sorts of question that critics put to those other critics of mass culture, Adorno and Horkheimer (see previous chapter). From a sociological point of view, the ideas of the mass culture critics were seen as relying upon all sorts of invalid assumptions. For example, an unacknowledged ambivalence underlies Greenberg's views on the differing values of avant-garde and kitsch. His position is that avant-garde art, and the 'high culture' produced in Western history more generally, are *objectively* better than other types of culture. This was a position he maintained all his life (Greenberg, 1999). But at one point in his discussion he is compelled to admit that '[a]ll values are human values, in art as well as elsewhere' (Greenberg, 1986 [1939]: 15). If the worth of a cultural object is not God-given, but a result of how a particular society – or a specific group within it – *defines* its worth, then different objects will mean different things to different people. As a consequence, it could be argued that no type of culture is *objectively* better than another type, but rather that designations of value are always a product of social situations. This is the standard sociological position on cultural value, and it is the diametric opposite of the kind of view held by literary intellectuals like Greenberg and Macdonald.

This is not to say that sociologists do not often import their own value-judgements into apparently 'neutral' analyses of culture. But it does show that sociologists generally define 'culture' not in the more narrow sense of art and aesthetics as do cultural critics, but, rather, in the more 'anthropological' sense as the collection of ideas and feelings expressed in symbols that are characteristic of a given society. Perhaps the most influential American sociologist of the post-war period, Talcott Parsons, provided a definition of culture in this direction. As we saw in chapter 1, Parsons defines the *cultural system* of a given society as involving *values*, the most general and abstract beliefs and ideas current in that society. It is from these values that more concrete *norms* derive. Norms guide the actions of people in that society. Culture, therefore, is the basis for the activities of all individuals. This is a much broader, more 'anthropological', definition of culture than the mass culture being attacked by critics. It deals with the culture of a 'nation' as a whole, rather than dividing culture into the opposing camps of 'mass culture' and 'art'. It is also a much more benevolent view of cultural life in America than that held by the cultural critics. The tendentious aspect of Parsons's sociology is that he affirms rather than criticizes the values on which he sees American society being based. In his analysis of twentieth-century American national culture, Parsons (1977) sees the most general values as involving beliefs in the validity of both Christianity and democracy. It is these that underpin American social life. From this point of view, such values are not as under threat as some thinkers make out, because they exist at a taken-for-granted level, and are relatively untouched by specific developments such as the rise of the mass media. The implication is that American national culture is both irreducible to mass culture and relatively little affected by it. This idea finds an echo in later sociological work on American culture as it exists outside the big cities, such as in the research of Robert Bellah (see below).

Parsons's ideas are open to many criticisms, from the charge that he sees individuals as merely the passive carriers of dominant cultural values (Wrong, 1980 [1961]) to the notion that he is an uncritical apologist for an old-fashioned, highly conservative view of American culture which expresses a very middle-class bias (Mills, 1959). Nonetheless, he opens up the possibility of seeing culture in America as involving more than just a titanic conflict between 'high' and 'low' culture. His position is also useful in that the ways that other sociologists have reacted towards it have also opened up further perspectives on culture beyond that presented by the mass culture critics. Analysis of groups of people who have rejected, or have failed to live up to, the standards and values of middle-class America, is a very important aspect of American sociology. For example, Robert Merton (1965 [1938]) identified the possibility that certain groups – especially young, working-class males living in large cities – may have a somewhat different set of values from those of the dominant culture, that of the relatively affluent middle classes. This perspective was taken up in the 1950s by analysts of subcultures such as Albert Cohen (1955). His empirical study of 'delinquent' youths put forward the view that this group have different norms and values than those that make up America's national culture according to sociologists such as Parsons. The desire for excitement and the need to display an aggressive masculinity provokes deviant, often illegal, behaviour, which is condemned by middle-class society.

The implication of this kind of study is that American society has not one culture but many, the cultural fabric being made up of a patchwork of different sets of values, each adhered to by different social groups. Some of these groups are alienated from the 'national culture', in part because the success-driven path of social advancement embodied in the 'American Dream' is barred to them because of social disadvantage. Greenberg, Macdonald and other writers like them understood 'alienation' to involve the stultifying effects of mass culture on the population at large. By contrast, sociologists such as Cohen regarded alienation as involving certain groups, especially lower-class males, being prevented from participating in the social life open to others further up the hierarchy. Individuals in these groups felt resentful at this forcible exclusion from wider society, and as a result experienced great feelings of disenchantment with the lives bestowed upon them. While the critics of mass culture saw everyone as alienated in mass society, sociologists tended to focus in on the resentments and animosities of particular disenfranchised groups.

Another way of looking at the relationship between 'mainstream' and 'deviant' cultures is offered by the sociologists of deviance, Matza and Sykes. They reject Cohen's view that the values held by subcultural groups are completely separate from the values held by middle-class Americans. Instead, 'deviant' activities are an expression of 'subterranean values'. According to Matza and Sykes, subterranean values exist below, but not apart from, the socially legitimate value system of any society. In fact, subterranean values are not exclusive to 'delinquent' youths, but reside within all people, irrespective of age and social background. Subterranean values involve the 'search for adventure, excitement and thrills' (Matza and Sykes, 1961: 716). The problem for the youths is that they lack both the institutional leisure opportunities and the maturity of adults to express their subterranean values in ways that are socially acceptable. Although youths are under more pressure (especially from peer groups) to engage in deviant activities, even the most 'respectable' citizens are sometimes prone to express subterranean values (for example, destroying property when under the influence of alcohol). Both this hidden level of culture and the idea that America has many cultures rather than one form part of the sociological challenge to the idea that America is characterized by one single, unitary, homogeneous mass culture.

Cultures of class and ethnicity

The idea that an examination of *social diversity* undermines any simple claims about *cultural homogeneity* informs other sociological investigations of life in large American cities. In particular, sociologists were alive to the fact that big cities like New York were made up of an array of different groups, separated from each other by reason of class position and ethnic ties. Such a view sometimes went together with a more positive assessment of the nature of mass society. Talcott Parsons's sometime collaborator Edward Shils was one of the first sociologists to take on the critics of mass culture head-on. He did so on the basis of an upbeat assessment of the nature of so-called 'mass society'. Shils argued that, far from being a social context marked by individual isolation and cultural degradation, the true meaning of the mass society was that it was more socially inclusive than previous forms of social organization (1978 [1961]). Whereas before, the vast majority of people (in European countries especially) had been left out of political decision-making and artistic activities, both hitherto preserves of an elite, now they were involved in both. Democratic America furnished the *majority* of the population – the true meaning of the word 'mass' – with new means of self-expression, both politically and artistically. The mass media were important facilitators of the latter, engendering 'new experiences of sensation, conviviality, and introspection' (ibid. 204–5) among the working and lower-middle classes. This meant that the capacities of ordinary people for thought and reflection had been improved, as had the overall society's respect for the dignity of the individual. Thus, far from degrading thought and personal autonomy, mass culture actually was an expression of, and basis for, their further development. The situation of everyone in such a society was improving and continued to do so. The working and lower-middle classes were gaining new experiences, some culled from 'high culture', through exposure to television and other mass media. It was only people at the very bottom of the pile, the most disadvantaged, who still lived in a 'vegetative torpor', as Shils (ibid. 205) put it, rather than the majority of individuals in the mass society, as the cultural critics had argued.

Clearly this was a very optimistic account of modern America, and it could be accused of betraying a naive – or politically motivated – set of assumptions about how good life supposedly was. However, it did open up the possibility of looking at the issue of mass culture in different terms from those set up by the likes of Greenberg. Shils (ibid. 206n.) rejected such a use of the idea of mass culture because it conflated three separate things: the nature of cultural products, the media by which they were transmitted and the nature of the audience. The latter could not be deduced from the first two, but had to be investigated empirically. In particular, one had to investigate the social contexts in which mass media products were received. Even amongst the working class, the group that mass culture critics might have suspected was most susceptible to the blandishments of media agencies, the situation was complicated by other factors. The religious beliefs of different groups had to be taken into account when assessing how they lived their lives. In addition, much 'regional and class culture, maintained by family, by colleagues, neighbors, and friends, and by local institutions, survives and is unlikely to be supplanted' by mass cultural goods (ibid. 213). Thus, both everyday relationships and the sorts of civil society groupings such as clubs and religious affiliations mentioned by Tocqueville meant that mass cultural products were never received in a vacuum. From this Shils concluded that it was entirely 'fruitless . . . to diagnose the dispositions and outlook of a . . . [group] by analysing [only] what is presented to them' (ibid. 213n.).

In fact, argued Shils, cultural goods themselves were heterogeneous in content, because their makers had to reach out to as wide an audience as possible. For example, within a newspaper there could be aspects of 'highbrow' culture (e.g. book reviews) and 'low culture' (e.g. sports reporting). Television networks and film companies produced cultural forms for all sorts of different tastes, not the uniform 'mass audience' the mass culture critics had imagined.

This kind of analysis was taken up in the later 1960s by Herbert Gans. His background was in community studies, examining the different cultural enclaves that exist in large American cities. He was therefore an inheritor of a long tradition in American sociology that stretched back to the pioneering ethnographic studies of urban communities carried out by sociologists at the University of Chicago from the beginning of the twentieth century (Bulmer, 1985). This tradition, which included studies of particular urban milieux by figures such as Robert Park (1952), had for a long time recognized the ethnic diversity of cities such as Chicago and New York. One classic work in this area was *The Polish Peasant in Europe and America*, by W. I. Thomas and Florian Znaniecki (1984 [1918–20]). This investigation of the lives of Polish immigrants in their new environment of big city America utilized all sorts of empirical research methods and data, including autobiographies and letters written by the people under investigation, to piece together a comprehensive picture of the ties that bound a particular ethnic group together when it had been transplanted to the new world. Gans's work on such issues in the 1950s and 1960s was part of this empirically oriented, community studies tradition. The title of his study of an Italian community in Boston, *The Urban Villagers* (1962), gives a good idea of what the argument of the book consists of. In social terms, members of this community were not the 'isolated individuals' of mass society theory, but were part of networks of ethnically based community association. They had relationships not only with their own families but also with friends and other people in the neighbourhood. As a result, in cultural terms, they exercised 'selective acceptance' of the offerings of the mass media (Gans, 1962: 181). They were interested in certain products and dis-interested in others. The implication of Gans's argument was that each ethnic community – be it Italian, Chinese, Greek or whatever – had its own 'taste culture', which was oriented towards certain types of cultural goods and repulsed by others. Each such culture was a 'subculture' of tastes and preferences. From this point of view, Ameri-can 'national culture' was always fragmented on the lines of ethnic group affiliation. Nor, he argued, were there grounds to believe that 'mass culture' was ever blindly or uncritically accepted. Ethnically based criteria of what was good and bad, interesting and uninterest-ing, were always in play amongst members of the group.

Gans applied this idea of distinct 'taste cultures' to the study of social classes in the large American cities. Shils had already argued that there was not in fact one single mass culture, but 'high', 'middle' and 'low' cultures, the mass media producing these – roughly speak-ing – for elite, (lower) middle-class and working-class audiences respectively. Gans took this idea further by dividing 'mass culture' into six different class-based categories, each of which appealed to a certain class group (1978 [1966]: 277; see also Gans, 1974).

1 *Creator-oriented high culture* (products such as art magazines aimed at people who are involved in the production and dissemin-ation of high culture, such as artists and art gallery owners);
2 *Consumer-oriented high culture* (products aimed at upper-middle-class groups who are the audiences for high culture e.g. book review magazines).
3 *Upper-middle culture* (products for or used by middle-class people who have not quite got the cultural skills of the elite e.g. 'art' films that are reasonably easy to understand).
4 *Lower-middle culture* (products involving simplified versions of the products of higher cultural levels e.g. novels that have some artistic pretensions).
5 *Lower culture* (products aimed at the lowest ranks of the middle class and the higher levels of the working class, such as standard Hollywood films).
6 *Lower-lower culture* (products for lower-working-class consump-tion, such as 'simple action films', tabloid newspapers and comic books.

Gans's point is not only that there are different types of 'mass cul-ture', but also that each of them corresponds to a particular public which is interested in and enjoys them. This is an argument remarkably similar to, but produced before, that of the French sociologist Pierre Bourdieu (see chapter 7). It is Gans's contention that one cannot just look at cultural products without examining the nature of the people for whom they are made and who use them for entertainment purposes. Each of the types of culture above has its own 'taste public'. Thus, for example, lower-middle culture is enjoyed by the middle-ranking members of the middle class. Each class grouping has its own 'aesthetic standards' that 'reflect their cultural backgrounds and their needs' (Gans, 1978 [1966]: 282). Which types of culture a group enjoys will depend on numerous variables, including ethnic background, but above all the level of education that individuals possess will orient them towards occupying not only a certain position in the class structure, but also towards liking certain types of culture and disliking others. Tastes, then, are a matter of social position rather than of aesthetic failing.

The central sociological thrust of Gans's argument is that we should not see any of the levels of culture as being better or worse than the others. Instead, a 'sociological analysis of "high" and "popular" cultures must begin not with judgments about their quality but with a perspective that sees each of them as social facts that exist because they satisfy the needs and wishes of some people, even if they dissatisfy those of other people' (1978 [1966]: 263). The mass culture critics had committed five main errors. First, they had divided all cultural products up into a simplistic divide between 'high' and 'mass' cultures. Second, they had not entertained the possibility that there may be different levels *within* mass culture. Third, they had failed to account for the fact that each cultural level corresponds to a social level in the class structure. Fourth, and following on from the previous point, each level of culture was in some senses an expression of different class-based cultures, even if the goods involved were made by the Culture Industry rather than by the consumers themselves. Fifth, cultural products are always selected and used on the basis of criteria generated by the group's taste culture. In sum, mass culture was heterogeneous rather than homogeneous, as was the social arena of the great American cities in which cultural goods were made and viewed.

Gans put the gaps in the cultural critics' understanding of these processes down to their own taste culture and the biases it embodied towards liking certain forms of culture and disliking others. So wrapped up were these critics in the tastes of their class – i.e. the educated elite, which favoured producer- and consumer-oriented high culture and despised everything else – that they had been quite unable to see how people in other classes might gain enjoyment from types of culture the critics themselves loathed. Greenberg, Macdonald and others could not relinquish their own prejudices in favour of a more distanced analysis of the reasons why certain people like certain things, and what pleasure they may get from them. In other words, Gans was arguing that the theorists of mass culture were not doing sociology at all but were merely expressing class-based forms of resentment towards people they disliked. A true sociological analysis of culture, by contrast, set aside the prejudices of the group that the sociologist him- or herself came from, in favour of a more relativistic view, which sought not to *condemn* but to *understand*, to *analyse* and not *moralize*. In carrying out such an investigation, which would be empirically based rather than speculative, a more accurate picture of cultural life in contemporary America could be gained, one which swept away the myths propagated by the mass culture theorists.

Investigating Middle America

Both the critics of mass culture and the sociologists described above had concentrated their gaze on large American cities. It was these that provided the stimulus for arguing both that there existed a mass society with its own distinctive mass culture, and, conversely, that, far from being a context of cultural uniformity, modern America constituted a multiplicity of different social groups, each with their own distinctive forms of cultural taste. What both arguments failed to account for is that the large cities are but one aspect of modern America. Outside them lie a vast diversity of other communities: smaller cities, small and medium-sized towns, and rural hamlets. Moreover, there are also great regional differences in culture, differences that are in some ways consciously upheld by people in different areas. The self-conception of New Englanders, for example, is rather different from that of Texans, Tennesseeans or southern Californians, yet all are American citizens. Another current running through American sociology, beyond those we have already looked at, seeks to find out about the cultural habits and attitudes of people who live beyond the great cities, in what is often referred to as 'Middle America'.

This project is in some ways an updated version of Tocqueville's original analysis of the dispositions of Americans in the 1830s, who by and large tended to live in smaller townships. This type of sociology also retains two aspects of Tocqueville's approach. First, it is primarily empirical in approach. Second, its findings as to the cultural state of Middle America are often ambiguous, stressing both the strengths and weaknesses of cultural life outside the big cities. A classic example of this sort of sociological investigation is Robert and Helen Lynd's study called *Middletown* (1957 [1929]). The title indicates that the small mid-Western city studied by the Lynds (in actual fact, Muncie, Indiana) was meant to be representative of other communities like it in Middle America. The Lynds carried out a systematic investigation of the city in the mid-1920s, utilizing an array of empirical research methods such as interviews, ethnographic observation and large-scale surveys. The idea was to look at almost every aspect of community life, from church-going to child-rearing, and to assess the impact that wider social and cultural trends occurring in America more generally were having on this particular community. Leisure pursuits were therefore treated as part of the overall network that made up social life in Middletown, rather than dealt with in isolation from other factors as the later cultural critics such as Greenberg and Macdonald had done.

The findings of the Lynds concerning leisure activities are an interesting set of assessments as to the effects of 'mass culture' on the inhabitants of Middletown. The Lynds compared the ways in which people of all classes entertained themselves in the 1890s with how they did so in the 1920s. The main change that had occurred in the intervening period was 'the coming of inventions, the automobile, the movies, the radio, that have swept through the community since 1890' (1957 [1929]: 226). The terminology 'swept through' gives an idea of the degree to which these products of 'mass culture' had transformed the social and cultural life of the town, according to the Lynds. When one inhabitant was questioned about the major changes he felt had occurred over the previous thirty years, he replied: 'I can tell you what's happening in just four letters: A-U-T-O!' (ibid. 251). Mass production of cars since before World War I had meant that automobile transport was increasingly an integral part of social life, even for those with quite low earnings. The Lynds discerned that the car altered cultural life in various ways. It had undermined Sunday church attendance, previously a fundamental part of what had been in the 1890s a very religious community. This change caused great consternation among the local preachers, who saw it as embodying a more general drop in ethical standards, especially amongst the young. Cars had loosened family relationships, with teenagers wanting to spend time riding in cars with their friends rather than stay at home with their families. In addition, the car had widened the possibilities of where to travel to. In the 1890s, a thirty-mile train trip to a nearby town had been regarded as a big event. But the car had made longer journeys possible and in its wake brought a wider set of experiences of other people and other places.

The widening of experience was also identified by the Lynds as one of the effects of the coming of radio and cinema to Middletown. One implication was that the coming of radio actually opened up a whole new series of artworks for people who had never been exposed to them before, for now 'great artists . . . are in the cabinet in the corner of one's living room' (ibid. 247). In other words, people in Middle America could now easily tune in to hear musicians who previously they would have had to travel hundreds of miles to the big cities to hear. It could indeed be argued that in some ways the advent of the mass media actually *strengthened* the position of 'high culture' rather than diminished or destroyed it. Cinema too was a way of broadening people's experience of the world. Romance movies were used by the young as models of how to behave when out on a date. While this was regarded as a great boon by young people verging on adulthood, who had often previously been left in the dark about such things by austere, strait-laced parents, the latter and the community's priests and teachers took a dimmer view. The effects of Hollywood movies on youth were seen to be making them 'grow up too fast', making young people worldly-wise, especially about sexual matters, at an age their elders thought was too young. Juvenile delinquency too was often blamed on over-exposure to the excitements that Hollywood had to offer. This kind of controversy continues today in most Western countries, over the alleged effects of television and cinema 'sex and violence' on young minds.

The job of the cultural critic is to attack what he or she sees as morally pernicious, and in so doing he or she brings to bear his or her own moral and political agenda on the issues under consideration. An important aspect of the Lynds' more distanced, sociological approach was that it attempted to represent moral dilemmas as they were felt by members of the community themselves. Whether the instruments of the mass media strengthened or weakened community ties was a question addressed from the point of view of people in that community. This is potentially a very valuable contribution to the understanding of cultural life, because it illustrates that moral responses to cultural issues are not the exclusive preserve of professional cultural critics, nor are their views unrelated to those of certain groups in society.

Despite this emphasis on showing how people in Middletown regarded the new mass culture age with which they were now faced, the Lynds also offered their own assessment of the effects this was having on the nature of communal life. From their point of view, the biggest difference between the 1890s and the 1920s was that in the earlier period many of the leisure time pursuits involved participation in clubs and other organizations of 'civil society', the very factors that Tocqueville had seen as preventing a retreat into selfish individualism on the part of most Americans. The coming of mass cultural activities such as cinema had made leisure much more passive. Instead of actively participating in a theatre group or a musical ensemble, more and more people of all classes were now likely to sit passively watching a screen or listening to the radio. The Lynds' conclusion was *not* that this necessarily leads to uncritical thinking and zombielike behaviour. In some ways, daily life continued just as before, despite these new forms of entertainment. But mass cultural pursuits were nevertheless having an effect on communal life, for, 'by breaking up leisure time into an individual, family or small group affair, [they] represent[ed] a counter-movement' against the forms of civic participation that many in America – after Tocqueville – had thought necessary to ensure the continuation of democratic social life (Lynd, 1957 [1929]: 265).

The Lynds' conclusion was not apocalyptic, unlike the style of both moralists in Middletown and the critics of mass culture. Nonetheless, they noted that what had once been a relatively isolated community in the mid-West was being brought into closer contact with the rest of America – and the rest of the world – by the car and by new communication media. While this opened up new possibilities, it also threatened the communal base on which American life outside the big cities had hitherto depended.

Taking America's pulse

A later study which is part of this vein of sociology is *Habits of the Heart* (1988), based on investigations carried out by a team led by Robert Bellah. In the early 1980s, this research group undertook, through interviews and other empirical methods, to investigate those 'ordinary practices of life' in communities beyond the big cities, which Tocqueville had called the 'habits of the heart' of ordinary Americans. Like the Lynds' study, Bellah and his group were interested both in the ways people in the communities they studied reacted to and thought about the social and cultural changes happening in America as a whole, and in sociologically diagnosing the effects of such processes on the nature of communal life. Of Tocqueville's original analysis that American life was torn between too much individualism and a tendency towards the individual being subsumed into the mass of people, cultural critics like Macdonald had emphasized the latter possibility as the outcome of the appearance of a mass society and a mass culture. By contrast, Bellah and his colleagues argue on the basis of their study that it is the former problem, that of too much individualism and a decline in community participation, that is the main dilemma in contemporary America. As Bellah et al. (1988: 285) phrase it, the 'American dream is often a very private dream of being the star, the uniquely successful and admirable one, the one who stands out from the crowd of ordinary folk who don't know how'. But if everyone is dreaming in their own personal way and acting in a self-centred manner, what happens to the bases of community life?

The Bellah team emphasize that the centrifugal forces of individualism are an important feature of American life today, especially among the suburban middle classes. In the suburbs, the main source of information and entertainment is the television, not the community hall. The people interviewed did experience a 'profound yearning for the idealized small town' that is part of American mythology, ironically enough partly as a result of Tocqueville's description of its civic life (Bellah et al., 1988: 282). But this recognition of the importance of civic participation often remained at the level of desire rather than of practice. Nonetheless Bellah and the other researchers found that the religious and political traditions of early America had not completely died out. Even in modern America, land of the automobile and twenty-four-hour television, 'somehow families, churches [and] a variety of cultural associations . . . do manage to communicate a form of life' that vaguely corresponds to the civic society described more than one hundred and fifty years ago by Tocqueville (ibid.). For example, organized religion continues to be an important focal point for many Americans. Although many of the more evangelical forms of Christianity are mediated through television, the local church retains its role as a centre of community life in many places. In addition, the ceremonies of American 'civil religion', such as Thanksgiving and the Fourth of July, provide a 'shared rhythm' to the lives of otherwise separated family groups.

On this rather optimistic view of the continuance of nineteenth-century America's habits into the twenty-first century, even 'the mass media, with their tendency to homogenize feelings and sensations, cannot entirely avoid transmitting' such ideals 'in however muted a form' (Bellah et al., 1988: 282). From this point of view, television – the mass medium par excellence – in its American form can be divided into two distinct thematic categories. On the one hand, there is the highly materialistic, self-interested vision of the American dream as a path towards fame and riches. This kind of ideal was portrayed very aggressively in 1980s soap operas such as *Dallas* and *Dynasty*, and arguably continues to be a theme of much television programming. On the other hand, there are shows which emphasize emotions, and caring and sharing values. The current popularity of 'relationship' shows like those hosted by Oprah Winfrey are a case in point. These reflect, in however indirect a way, the more community-based ideals that Tocqueville had identified as a bulwark against individual selfishness. As a result, Bellah et al. argue that the cultural products of a mass medium are not just wholly impersonal in nature. Rather, deep currents of American civil life continue to run through what seem like the shallows of American television. This argument can be criticized for what might be a certain naivety and a rather uncritical acceptance of American social conditions. Nonetheless, it opens up a perspective different from one which argues that in social terms Americans are wholly atomized individuals, and that culturally the United States is a hell of mass cultural malaise. This form of sociology agrees with the position of Shils and Gans on the nature of life in the metropolises that the terms 'mass society' and 'mass culture' do not do full justice to the complexity of cultural conditions across many different parts of the United States.

Towards multiculturalism

Since the 1960s, the two camps of cultural critics and sociologists have generally talked past each other. The former have seen the latter as relativists who are part of the cultural problems of modern America, encouraging an 'anything goes' attitude and, in so doing, contributing to further erosion of the standards of 'high culture'. Conversely, sociologists have often characterized cultural critics, especially those of a conservative political persuasion, as being wholly out of touch with the realities of social and cultural life. For example, the conservative cultural critic Daniel Bell (1996 [1976]: xxv) rails against what he sees as having developed exponentially since the 1960s – a mass consumer culture involving 'goods packaged in the glossy images of glamour and sex', and promoting a socially irresponsible, hedonistic lifestyle among the American middle classes. For a similar critic of American mores, Christopher Lasch (1991 [1979]: 4), the middle classes have become more and more self-obsessed and self-indulgent, taking up trivial and faddish activities such as 'getting in touch with their feelings, eating health food, taking lessons in ballet or belly-dancing, immersing themselves in the wisdom of the East, jogging, learning "how to relate" ' and so on. For those of a more liberal political persuasion, some of these activities might be taken to signify an opening up of previously rather rigid and prescribed middle-class tastes, in favour of a set of cultural dispositions more open to global influences. For sociologists such as Heelas (1996), the growth of New Age ideas in the United States and other Western countries is not to be condemned but, rather, is to be empirically examined, especially in terms of long-term processes of the decline of orthodox forms of Christianity. But from the point of view of Lasch, sounding a faint echo of Tocqueville's warnings about individualism diminishing the effectiveness of democratic institutions, such experimentation is indicative of a selfishness that prevents many Americans from taking an active part in the political process.

For the most part, debates on culture between left and right in America today no longer take the form of controversies around 'mass culture'. This has become so much an accepted part of American life that it has faded into the background of intellectual debates, occasionally resurfacing in the form of controversies over matters such as the alleged effects of cinematic and televisual violence on the young. In its place has arisen a whole series of disputes over the nature of political culture and the education of the young. As members of what some see as 'oppressed minorities' – blacks, gays, women – develop more assertive voices in intellectual and political life, debates have shifted towards the issue of whether the Constitution should recognize not just the rights of individuals but also those of these groups too, in order to compensate for the history of their oppression by the white, male, middle classes (Taylor, 1992). The educational corollary of this is the demand that the canon of works by dead, white European males, the backbone of white, upper-middle-class America's 'high culture' should be ditched in favour of teaching young people about the ideas and experiences of the oppressed.

For Afro-American thinkers like Cornel West (1990: 19), these twin processes would produce a more tolerant culture based on the recognition and celebration of 'diversity, multiplicity, and heterogeneity'. By contrast, for conservative cultural critics, the political effects of such proposals would be to shatter America's 'national culture' and encourage forms of warfare between different groups of Americans (Schlesinger, 1991). The cultural effects would be to relinquish judgements about what is good or bad in cultural terms in favour of a flaccid form of relativism (Lasch, 1996). It is now the issue of 'multiculturalism' rather than mass culture that convulses America's intellectuals of both left and right. This is also an issue that is increasingly at the forefront of arguments in Britain, Australia and other Western countries. What might the role of sociologists be in these disputes?

Conclusion

This chapter has considered the various ways in which cultural matters have been thought about and argued over in America. Tocqueville's original analysis stressed the fundamentally ambivalent nature of American life, showing it was subject to tendencies either in the direction of too much individualism or towards massification and the swamping of the individual by the group. Cultural critics throughout the twentieth century tended to argue that, as the United States was a mass society, it must have a mass culture. This culture was understood as being inferior to 'high culture' and the 'true' arts. Sociologists have challenged these views in various ways, pointing to the social diversity both of American cities and of the society in general, and arguing that mass culture is neither homogeneous in terms of its products nor passively consumed by its audiences. While the cultural critics have sought to explain society through the analysis of culture, sociologists have tended to work in a reverse direction, analysing a disparate social order and finding diverse cultural forms. These include a 'national' culture based on a belief in democracy, local cultures based around networks of friends, family and neighbourhoods, subcultural values based on a rejection of middle-class ideals, and ethnic and class-based sets of taste which are the basis of differentiations within an apparently monolithic mass culture. Sociologists have often emphasized the more positive sides of American culture – its openness and fluidity – as these were first indicated by Tocqueville.

We have set out the ways in which sociologists have challenged the views of the cultural critics, in which the ideas of the latter have been charged with being too narrow in focus, too speculative and empirically ungrounded, and blindly unaware of their basis in the tastes and dispositions of the (mainly) upper-middle-class groups from which the cultural critics derive. Yet it would be a mistake to think that sociology has all the answers and that cultural criticism is merely a product of class-based biases. What sociologists and cultural critics are engaged upon are two different enterprises. Sociology generally seeks to *explain* things, cultural criticism to *evaluate* them. There is surely space for both such approaches to cultural matters. There are of course many instances of sociologists seeking to evaluate things too, in light of certain strongly held – and sometimes not explicitly acknowledged – values and beliefs. But, on the whole, one of the main benefits of sociological understandings of culture is that they can involve standing back and evaluating why certain people have certain attitudes towards cultural matters, thus revealing the often tacit assumptions and interests that lie behind these views. This could be of great benefit in the current debates on multiculturalism – sociologists could point out to the combatants the often covert reasons why different groups argue as they do. Moreover, sociologists can turn their analysis upon themselves, revealing that their tendencies towards aesthetic relativism are also in part the products of the social groups from which sociologists derive and to which they belong. Sociology can foster a more sophisticated series of debates on cultural issues, in America and elsewhere, by encouraging those with different views to reflect upon the social reasons that lurk behind their most deeply cherished beliefs, and in so doing to turn the sociological gaze back upon their own 'habits of the heart'.

4

Reading from Right to Left: Culturalism in England

Introduction

In this chapter we will examine the distinctive ways of understanding culture that have developed in England. These bear some resemblance to ideas developed in Germany, France and the United States, but, nonetheless, English approaches to culture have their own particular emphases and tenor. The reason for this is that sociology as an academic discipline gained less of a sure foothold in England than it did in the other countries mentioned above. It was only as late as the 1960s that sociology really became a central part of the curriculum in English universities. As a result, most English thinking about culture was carried out by people who were not specifically sociologists. Literary critics especially have played an important role in the elaboration of the characteristically English ways of studying culture. As we will see in this chapter, this situation has produced a way of thinking about culture that can enrich more obviously 'sociological' views. But it has also meant that these English ideas often fail to look at the very things that French and German sociology has drawn attention to.

The main stream of thought that developed in England as to cultural matters is known as 'culturalism'. The development of this style of analysis will be the focus of this chapter. Culturalism has two key features that will be highlighted throughout this chapter. First, it has a strong *moral* component, which emphasizes how culture should be the basis for a healthy and contented social order. Second, culturalism puts a strong stress on *cultural creativity*, accentuating the creative capacities of 'ordinary people' to make their own forms of culture and to resist those manufactured for them by powerful groups. These characteristics of culturalism lead to both strengths and weaknesses in this position, as we will see. We begin by considering its antecedents in the nineteenth and early twentieth centuries. We then turn to look at its development after World War II, as outlined by the literary analyst Richard Hoggart. Then we will focus on two different styles of culturalism as they have developed in the recent past, setting out both the 'populist' version of culturalism to be found in the works of figures such as Paul Willis, and the more 'sociological' variant developed by Raymond Williams. We conclude with an assessment of what culturalism and sociological approaches developed outside of England can learn from each other.

Culture against society

In order to understand culturalism, we have to look at the historical context out of which it developed. The main background here is the industrial revolution, which transformed English life from the early nineteenth century onwards. From this time, a whole new society was being forged, one that left behind rural life in favour of city dwelling, saw the development of a new urban working class and witnessed the demise of older, aristocratic and religious forms of political power in favour of secular domination by a class of capitalist entrepreneurs. These huge changes in English social conditions were witnessed by many thinkers, especially those on the political right, with extreme dismay. For these conservative thinkers, such as the poets Coleridge and Wordsworth, the rise of modernity was a disaster. It was equated with anarchy, both in terms of ideas – the older religion was dying, leading to a spiritual vacuum – and in terms of politics (Williams, 1958). The great fear of conservatives was the dangerous new class of workers, concentrated in cities and often living in very awful conditions. The revolution in France in 1789 which had overthrown the aristocracy seemed to be a portent of the terrible power that potentially lay concentrated within an unruly and discontented working class. This class had, as the conservative historian Thomas Carlyle (1795–1881) put it, 'decreasing respect for what their temporal superiors command [and] decreasing faith for what their spiritual superiors teach' (Roe, 1936: 57).

Conservative thinkers reacted to this situation by turning to art, not just as a personal solace against what they saw as the ugliness of modern society, but as a way of remedying what they saw as the ills of modern life. Their ideas were part of the stream of thought known as Romanticism, which we examined in chapter 1. Romantic ideas were a reaction against industrial capitalist society in general, and its emphasis on rational, scientific ways of thinking in particular. Because they saw the society around them as being so degraded – so 'mechanical' because it lacked any spiritual values – Romanticists compensated for this by looking to 'culture', which they defined as being synonymous with Art (with a capital 'A'), while Art itself was indicative of human spiritual perfection. As Coleridge put it, culture was a process of 'cultivation', a 'harmonious development of those qualities and faculties that characterise our humanity' (Williams, 1958: 76). On this view, Culture (with a capital 'C') is 'above' society, in that it is morally and aesthetically superior to social conditions. Culture is not a component of society but is *out of* and *above* it. As a result, Culture is seen as the complete antithesis of Society, the one about beauty, the other about degradation.

This strongly moralistic view of culture was carried on by other English thinkers, both conservative and liberal, as the nineteenth century wore on. Most famous of these was the politically liberal Matthew Arnold (1822–88). The title of his major work, *Culture and Anarchy* (1995 [1869]), gives a good idea of his views. Echoing the ideas of German sociologists such as Tönnies, Arnold saw contemporary England as a 'mechanical' society bent more on making money than on developing individuals spiritually. There was, as a result, widespread spiritual anarchy, where the older religious standards of good and evil were being replaced by a nihilistic relativism. Only 'Culture' could save England from this woeful condition. When he spoke of culture, Arnold referred to its qualities of 'sweetness and light', that is, authentic culture was possessed of both great beauty and intellectual insight. Arnold's famous definition of culture emphasizes both its aesthetic and its cognitive capacities:

> [I] recommend culture as the great help out of our present difficulties; culture being a pursuit of our total perfection by means of getting to know, on all the matters which most concern us, the best which has been thought and said in the world, and through this knowledge, turning a stream of fresh and free thought upon our stock notions and habits, which we are now following staunchly but mechanically . . . the culture we recommend is, above all, an inward operation. (1995 [1869]: 199)

Arnold's view of culture is often represented as comprising the best works of art and philosophy that have been produced throughout the history of the West. While he does include those things ('the best that has been thought and said'), it would be wrong to think that Arnold sees culture as made up purely of material artefacts such as books or sculptures. For him, the pursuit of culture is the pursuit of spiritual perfection. Culture is thus not made up of objects, but is, rather, a *process*, whereby the best that the Western tradition has to provide is used to challenge the individual's most fundamental views and assumptions, to erase these if they are found to be stale or wanting, and to put in their place new ways of thinking and doing which are constantly cleansed by a 'stream of fresh and free thought'.

The benefit of this way of thinking is that culture can be used as an ideal against which contemporary society can be compared and found wanting. The idea of culture, therefore, can act as the basis for *social criticism*, interrogating current social conditions and suggesting ways of improving them if they are found not to be conducive to the development of individuals' intellectual, aesthetic and spiritual capacities. But despite this advantage, this particular way of viewing culture makes it impossible to relate 'culture' and 'society' to each other. The connections between culture, society, economy and politics are hidden from view. One cannot see how culture is made, nor how it affects people's everyday lives. This is because, on the Arnoldian definition, 'Culture' is an ideal rather than a part of actually existing societies. Thus, while this view of culture may be crucial for morally informed criticism of society, it is very unhelpful for answering more *sociological* questions about the nature of culture. Arnold (1995 [1869]: 107) himself may have been partially aware of the shortcomings of his own ideas in this way when he admitted that they fell 'very far short in precision of what might be required from a writer equipped with a complete and coherent philosophy'. Later English attempts to think about culture would try to rectify this.

Paradise lost

In the first half of the twentieth century, English thinkers developed the ideas concerning culture formulated by their predecessors in directions that preserved the moral – and often conservative – aspects, but which took these ideas in more explicitly 'sociological' directions. Two important figures here are T. S. Eliot (1888–1965), the American-born poet who was resident in England for most of his life, and the highly influential literary critic F. R. Leavis (1895–1978). In some ways, both of these figures were part of the general intellectual reaction to modern society, especially the rise of the mass media, of which the Frankfurt School thinkers and the American cultural critics were also part (see chapters 2 and 3). This led them both to make rather predictable denunciations of modern 'mass culture'. For Eliot (1939: 39–40), there is a 'steady influence which operates silently in any mass society organised for profit . . . [towards] the depression of standards of art and culture'. For Q. D. Leavis, F. R. Leavis's writing partner and wife (1990 [1932]: 67), mass culture's cheap thrills and tawdry shock-effects come not only to dominate the lives of those lower down the social scale, but it also inexorably begins to infect the cultural lives of the higher classes. This is particularly disastrous, as it is with cultural elites, drawn from the higher ranks of society, that lies the preservation of culture, the greatest works of art and forms of thought ever produced (F. R. Leavis, 1993 [1948]). Elites keep the flame of culture burning, maintaining the higher spiritual values. But that is now seriously under threat as the cultural elite (of whom both Eliot and Leavis see themselves as members) is increasingly marginalized, and as the wider society gets more and more 'dumbed down'. As with the members of the Frankfurt School, such attitudes are a product of the social backgrounds of those who espouse them: a rich, patrician upbringing in Eliot's case, and the imbibing of the views current in the University of Cambridge in the 1920s in Leavis's case, where he was an undergraduate student and then a lecturer.

Nonetheless, these highly critical views of contemporary social and cultural conditions were also informed by the strongly moral sense that had informed previous English thinking about culture. Moreover, these ideas were based on a conservative kind of sociology. For both Eliot and Leavis (as for Tönnies too), what was being destroyed was an older society based on community in favour of a new social order characterized by alienated, isolated individuals. The older community-based society was seen by both thinkers as 'organic', in that it was bound together by emotional ties between people, each person being an integral part of the whole group. Such a community had a 'common culture' which involved common thoughts and feelings, binding everyone together in a way that was now under threat. From Eliot's (1939: 16) point of view, the 'traditional social habits of the people' are destroyed, a sense of community atrophies, and this results in a society of atomized individuals, open to manipulation by advertisers and cultural commodity-producers.

For the Leavises, this 'organic' society was best exemplified by seventeenth-century England. In that context, both the lower and the upper classes had participated in the same culture, as witnessed by the fact that everyone from the lowest commoner to the highest aristocrat went to see Shakespeare's plays. By contrast, the twentieth century was characterized by an almost complete divide between the cultural activities of the 'uncultured' majority and the educated minority. The shift from a pre-modern 'organic' society to a modern 'mechanical' one is described by Q. D. Leavis (1990 [1932]: 57–8) as involving 'the substitution for village and small town communities of cities composed of units whose main contact with each other outside the home is in the dance-hall, the cinema, the theatre, social but not co-operative amusements'. Thus the non-communal nature of modernity produces a social situation of individual isolation and segregation rather akin to Durkheim's description of anomie (see chapter 1). The Leavises' reading of the Lynds' then-recent study of American small town life, *Middletown* (1957 [1929]), seemed to provide sociological evidence for this view of modern social life (see chapter 3). The Leavises read the book as showing how 'small town communities', previously characterized by common cultural activities, had been transformed such that individuals now carried out leisure pursuits alone rather than in groups. Where once there had been the active communal life of the town square or market, now isolated individuals gazed passively at a cinema screen or read trashy novels, both movies and books being nothing but low-grade, comforting cultural fodder.

It is obvious that the distinction between organic and mechanical societies owes a great deal more to a conservatively inclined political imagination than to an actual empirical investigation of social conditions. The idealized 'organic community' of the past may turn out on closer inspection to have involved quite as much misery and exploitation as the society of today. Nonetheless, the attitudes of Eliot and Leavis remain interesting because they draw upon sociological thought about the nature of community in order to make morally informed criticisms of present-day culture and society. They are therefore drawing upon sociology in a manner that fits with the English tradition of using culture as a way of interrogating the present and finding it lacking in terms of its capacities to provide spiritual sustenance for people. This *moral sociology* is a key element in the culturalist school of thought.

Towards a literary sociology

Eliot and Leavis developed this style of 'moral sociology' in two quite distinct ways. Eliot took up the definition of culture that was diametrically opposed to the Arnoldian one, namely the anthropological idea that culture is a 'whole way of life'. Eliot sees 'the best that has been thought and said' as characteristic of the culture of the elite in a given society. This 'high culture' is embedded within, and feeds off, the wider culture. This latter 'includes all the characteristic activities and interests of a people', the thoughts, religious beliefs, attitudes and habits of the general populace. Eliot (1954 [1948]: 31–2) defines the overall 'common culture' of England, which involves both its 'high' and 'low' aspects, as involving things like 'Derby Day, Henley Regatta, Cowes, the twelfth of August, a cup final, the dog races, the pin table, the dart board, Wensleydale cheese, boiled cabbage cut into sections, beetroot in vinegar, nineteenth-century Gothic churches, and the music of Elgar'. His selection of characteristic aspects of English culture ranges from works that might occupy a place in the high art canon, such as the music of Elgar, through 'typical' proletarian activities such as soccer matches, through to the most quotidian and everyday objects like pickled beetroot. This selection is indicative of his stress on the interrelated nature of the most 'high' and most 'low' aspects of a given culture. Eliot thus places the Arnoldian culture in a sociological context, in that he sees it as the culture of the elite. The role of the elite in any society is to preserve the high culture and to ensure that it guides the wider culture, thus maintaining the 'health' of the latter.

This raises a crucial question. According to the mainstream of sociological thought, such as is voiced by Karl Mannheim (see chapter 1), the 'social value of intellectual culture [read "high culture"] is a function of the social status of those who practice it' (cited in Hoggart, 1973a: 239). In other words, high culture is only socially valorized because it is the culture of the elite, and this group has the power to *define* its own culture as being superior to the culture of other groups. Therefore Eliot may have unintentionally destroyed the claims he otherwise wants to make about 'Culture' in the Arnoldian sense being superior to other forms of culture, by admitting that it is indeed the *product* of elites and part of their lifestyle. So-called 'high culture' is in fact just a form of class privilege. On the other hand, Eliot could claim that the *social genesis* of the products of high culture – classical music, artworks, etc. – is not synonymous with their *value*. This value is intrinsic to them because they are *inherently* 'better' – more sophisticated, more thoughtful – than the cultural forms produced by the 'ordinary people'. It is not that the elite have defined such things as 'good culture'. Rather, these things just *are* better than other cultural forms, the role of the elite being merely to preserve the cultural legacy bequeathed to them by their ancestors. Whether there really is a 'high culture', or whether it is just a way of elite groups maintaining power for themselves, is a central theme of chapter 7.

While Eliot was concerned to locate Arnoldian 'Culture' in a social context, F. R. Leavis was more oriented towards developing a sociologically informed way of interpreting the meanings of cultural forms.

As a literary critic, Leavis was of course primarily interested in the interpretation of books, but he was of the opinion that it is inevitable that 'serious literary interest develops towards . . . sociological [analysis]' (1962a: 188). But it is not standard sociological approaches to literature and culture that Leavis is here defending. Most standard sociology, when applied to literature, merely uses poems or novels as examples of general arguments, for example using the work of Charles Dickens to 'illustrate' mid-nineteenth-century middle-class concerns about the poor. But such 'illustrations' do not really engage with the particular work of literature itself. They remain 'external', bringing already-formed interpretations to the text. Leavis (1962b: 195) argues that the sociologist must have a 'more inward acquaintance' with literary works. The sociologist must read the text as would a literary critic, looking for the meaning on a 'close reading' of the entire work. The sociologist must in fact become a literary critic, scrutinizing the work closely so that it may reveal nuances and inflections of meaning that he or she had not already guessed at. For the sociologist to be able to do that requires that he or she be trained in literary critical skills – the abilities to attend to the subtleties of language. Accordingly, Leavis (ibid. 200) concludes that the sociologist 'will be a literary critic or nothing'. The literary sociologist must endeavour to read a text as much as possible *without preconceptions* and to let the text *itself* tell her what it has to teach about the society in which it was written. Only on a close acquaintanceship with the book's details and the patterns they form can the sociologist-reader come to know what the book 'means'.

The problem with this position, of course, is that nobody comes to interpret anything without preconceptions. Even when the interpreter thinks they are being 'neutral', they are not, because one form of bias or another will be underpinning their interpretation (Eagleton, 1976). There are always a huge number of tacit, unconscious assumptions being made about what aspects to highlight in the interpretation and how to make sense of them. Despite this, the idea of a 'literary sociology' might still be a useful one, because it suggests a close analysis of a particular phenomenon – a cultural text or a cultural context – and asks the analyst to attend to the fine-grained details that are embodied within it. Richard Hoggart gives a good example of this kind of method:

> You may find yourself intrigued by the charity shops which proliferate in British towns. Their different roles [in the life of the town] are quite hard to 'read'. Then one day, in a predominantly middle class town, yet another glance at the rack of discarded men's clothing holds your

attention. You notice for the first time that much of that clothing, all freshly cleaned and ready to go on display, is casual wear, sports jackets . . . grey flannels, short leather coats, Barbour jackets – all of very good quality and all, you suddenly see, in styles adopted by elderly professional men. Then you have a vision of middle class widows clearing out their husband's wardrobes as soon as they can bring themselves to do it and carrying it all down to Oxfam [a well-known charity shop] or one of its cousins. A little, whole world. (1996: 183)

This exercise in micro-sociology would perhaps not have yielded such a finely detailed analysis of the emotional currents running through cultural life if one had begun the interpretation of charity shops with a preconceived model (Leavis, 1986). Instead, the details of English provincial life, especially the moral and emotional aspects, are elucidated through a close reading of the situation, an interpretation that seeks to reconstruct what the charity shop might 'mean' to those in a small town who run it, donate to it, shop in it and so on. The insights that such a reading reveals could then be thought about in 'theoretical terms', for example how middle-class people might seek to retain their prestige and status by only donating the better quality items of clothing in their possession. Yet the initial insight would come from a close-up examination of a cultural context that is sympathetically reconstructed by the sociologist.

Richard Hoggart and mass culture

It was out of the diverse set of influences that we have examined above that 'culturalism' was born in the 1950s. It took on some of the ideas of previous English thinkers on culture, and rejected or modified others. It maintained the morally engaged aspect of earlier analyses of cultural life, seeking to ascertain how 'healthy' a particular culture was for the people who lived within it. But this critical assessment of cultural conditions was now carried out from a left-wing rather than a right-wing perspective (Johnson, 1979). Moreover, the older assumption that the products of 'mass culture' must be inferior to those of 'high culture' was rejected, in favour of an appreciation of how the former might have some value (Hall and Whannell, 1964). In addition, the 'common culture' (Williams, 1989 [1968]) of the everyday lives of 'ordinary people' was both analysed and celebrated, rather than being despised as it had been previously (though not by Eliot, as we have seen). These various themes were crystallized in the title of an early paper, 'Culture is Ordinary', by one of the main figures in culturalism, Raymond Williams (1921–88).

The Arnoldian definition of 'Culture' as somehow separate from and above society, was now comprehensively rejected in favour of the anthropological idea of culture as a 'whole way of life'. From this followed a new emphasis on the cultural creativity of people in the 'ordinary' contexts of living-room and shop-floor. Williams denied there was such an entity as 'the masses', but only real people living real lives. Recognition of this meant that one could say with confidence that 'the telly-glued masses do not exist; they are the bad fiction of our second-rate social analysis' (1980 [1961]: 361). 'The masses' was therefore merely a derogatory term coined by those wishing to defend an elite culture, that was itself a form of social privilege (ibid. 191; Carey, 1992).

Another central figure in the rise of culturalist ways of thinking was Richard Hoggart [b. 1918]. As the founder of the Centre for Contemporary Cultural Studies (CCCS) at the University of Birmingham in the mid-1960s, Hoggart was instrumental in creating the first designated institute of the new discipline of cultural studies in the world. Cultural studies was in its first phase primarily a child of culturalism. Hoggart's work illustrates the continuation as much as the transformation of the English tradition in cultural analysis. The central precept of all his writings is that cultural analysis must involve moral critique of culture and the social life that is bound up with it. The cultural 'health' of a society is what has to be diagnosed. As he puts it, 'the distinctive contribution of literary criticism to the discussion of cultural change is its attempt to define what is meant . . . by "changes in the quality of life" of a society' (Hoggart, 1973a: 126–7).

The desire to understand culture from a morally engaged stance was the driving force behind Hoggart's most important book, *The Uses of Literacy* (1962 [1957]), one of the founding texts of the culturalist approach. The book was in part an extension of the ideas of Eliot and Leavis, in that Hoggart (ibid. 24) claimed to identify a process whereby England was 'moving towards the creation of a mass culture; that the remnants of what was at least in parts an urban culture "of the people" are being destroyed; and that the new mass culture is in some important ways less healthy than the often crude culture it is replacing'. But Hoggart's way of criticizing such developments had a different basis from those of the older thinkers. Eliot and Leavis had set up a (mostly) imaginary 'organic community' of the past and used it as a point of comparison by which to criticize contemporary society for its *lack* of community. Hoggart sets up a much more immediate point of comparison, namely English urban working-class communities in the period before World War II.

Hoggart regarded the culture of such communities as having origi-
nally been created by working-class people as a means of accommo-
dating themselves to, and making more comfortable, the often very
harsh conditions of urban industrial areas. A distinctive working-
class culture had arisen as a result of the struggles of these people to
make their lives liveable. Hoggart describes in very positive terms the
'whole way of life' of the pre-war working class, emphasizing the
close ties people felt they had with each other, and how their leisure
pursuits, such as going to the pub and joining in with sing-alongs,
rose 'organically' from the community itself, rather than being imposed by outside forces. He then contrasts the virtuous qualities he
sees embodied in the cultures of these communities to what he sees
as the much less positive aspects of cultural life in his own period,
especially as it impinges on the life of working-class people.

The background to the destruction of the older (and, in Hoggart's
view, 'better') working-class culture was the increasing material wealth
of the working classes in the years after 1945. Hoggart (1962 [1957]:
244) feared that in place of older forms of naked economic subordination exercised by the powerful, new forms of bondage, this time
cultural in form, were being forged for the working classes. The rise
of mass media such as television, with their prepared and easy-to-
digest cultural commodities, were ousting more genuinely 'popular'
forms of entertainment such as community trips to the seaside. His
analysis of the ways in which a capitalist market in cultural goods
breaks down older and more 'organic' forms of leisure pursuit sometimes sounds very much like the earlier conservative authors such as
Eliot. The current cultural condition is seen to be moving danger-
ously close to a situation where 'the larger part of the population [is
reduced] to a condition of obediently receptive passivity, their eyes
glued to television sets, pin-ups and cinema screens' (ibid. 316). This
pessimistic strain in Hoggart's analysis, which goes against the more
positive appreciation of ordinary people voiced by Williams above, is
particularly well illustrated by his description of contemporary youth
culture. Writing of the then-popular 'milk bar', a café where teenagers
would meet to listen to the newest records on the juke-box, Hoggart
identifies the music being played as having been 'doctored' by the
music industry so that all the records had the same, popular rhythm.
The records are part of the overall mechanism of mass culture, which
(in a phrase strikingly similar to Adorno's on the same issues)
'premasticates' the content of the record (or book, or film) so that it
'shall neither bore nor tax anyone, shall not prompt any effort at
correlation or comparison' (ibid. 202). Here is the conservative theme
that critical thought and aesthetic judgement are being systematically

eroded through the consumption of the products of mass culture. This could be indexed in the low level of the quality of reading material that working-class people, especially younger ones, were increasingly attracted to (ibid. 234). In a now well-known passage, Hoggart compared the mass cultural 'milk bar' to the traditional pub, which yet retains some aspects of the organic working-class culture:

> Compared even with the pub around the corner, this is all a peculiarly thin and pallid form of dissipation, a sort of spiritual dry-rot amid the odour of boiled milk. Many of the customers – their clothes, their hair-styles, their facial expressions all indicate – are living to a large extent in a myth world compounded of a few simple elements which they take to be those of American life. (Ibid. 248)

Here we have both the despairing tone of earlier conservative critics and identification of an issue that had been spotted at least as far back as Arnold: that mass culture was an American import, seeping slowly but surely into the fabric of English cultural life. For Hoggart, the tawdry American cultural products increasingly enjoyed by working-class people – cheap thrillers and cowboy novels, detective shows on television – were subverting and destroying from within the 'whole way of life' of the working class. This had ramifications not just for the working classes but also for the whole of English society. Echoing Arnold quite explicitly, Hoggart (ibid. 194) argues that mass culture brings with it a destruction of cultural and artistic standards which involves 'a loss of sense of order, of value, and of limits . . . an endless flux of the undistinguished and the valueless'. Mass culture is seen to bring in its trail a form of spiritual bankruptcy.

This aspect of Hoggart's work can be criticized because it perhaps relies on an over-idealized picture of working-class life 'before' mass culture, just as Eliot and Leavis had constructed an unrealistic notion of the pre-modern 'organic community'. Hoggart has often been accused of sentimentalizing this 'traditional' working-class culture, overemphasizing its positive aspects – such as its strong sense of community and moral responsibility – and downplaying its more unpleasant aspects (drunkenness, wife-beating and so on). Certainly there is some reason for thinking that Hoggart (e.g. ibid. 40) is over-doing things somewhat when he tells us, for example, that the traditional working-class culture was 'a good and comely life, one founded on care [and] affection'. Drawing on his own childhood amongst the northern English working class, he is here rather guilty of looking at the past through a very nostalgic lens. But it is essential to realize that such a positive view of 'traditional' working-class culture is not just a result of naivety, but is an essential aspect of Hoggart's analytic method. By playing up the positive aspects of this culture, it can then be more effectively compared to contemporary cultural conditions, the nature of which is found wanting through the comparison.

Cultural creativity

The negative attitude towards mass culture and the present day found in Hoggart's views is balanced – or contradicted – by a much more positive set of attitudes which he also expressed. Mass culture may be pernicious but ordinary people are not necessarily its passive dupes. He thus raises what will become a key assumption in later culturalism: merely because people read a certain book or watch a certain film does not automatically guarantee that they will read or view it in the fashion intended by its makers. They could perhaps read or view such a product 'in their own way'. So even if mass cultural products are purchased and used, the reader (from the working class or another group) may be 'less affected than the extent of their purchases would seem to indicate' (1962 [1957]: 231). This idea became a central theme in Hoggart's later work. Aiming directly at Adorno's studies of popular music (see chapter 2), which assume a passive response to a song on behalf of the listener because the content of the song is identified as having been designed to induce passivity, Hoggart (1970c: 270) argues that such assumptions are invalid. One must empirically investigate what the listener (or reader or viewer) actually did in the process of listening, and what she actually takes from the song. Simplistic attitudes towards 'mass culture', including those of earlier English writers, had to be overcome in favour of an appreciation of the *complexity* (a favourite culturalist word) of the 'whole way of life' of different groups, especially the working class. According to this position, mass culture views assumed that

> mass art can be explained simply in commercial and economic terms; that it is wholly and deliberately a devised product, for an audience whose tastes are pretty exactly known . . . [V]iews like these . . . simplify the relationship between the producers and their audiences, the producers and their material, the audiences and the material, and the interactions between different forms and levels of taste. (Hoggart, 1970a: 32)

With this view, the focus shifts from assuming what the effects of 'mass art' *must be*, to investigating how people actually *use* it. The general culturalist position was that in order to understand the full complexity of such issues involved developing research methods that could get to grips with what 'really' happened in the cultural worlds of ordinary people. There is a move away from *assuming* what the working classes are like to investigating empirically what actually went on at the grass-roots level. Raymond Williams (1989 [1958]: 12) regarded this as a fundamental break with the previously unchallenged assumption that 'the observable badness of so much widely distributed popular culture is a true guide to the state of mind and feeling, the essential quality of living of its consumers'. In place of this, cultural analysis *must* involve detailed empirical research on how people actually make use of the cultural products they are offered.

Hoggart (1982: 130) argued that this outlook meant that the primarily literary-based English study of culture would have to become more 'sociological' in orientation, in the sense of sociology as an empirical investigation of human life. In his later writings, he advocated the adoption of what he called a 'cultural sociological' approach to the issues broached in *The Uses of Literacy*. He argued (1970b) that such an approach would investigate the social and cultural conditions of writers and artists, audiences, cultural opinion-formers who influenced how cultural products were viewed by other groups, the culture industries involved in the production of culture, and the relations between all of these groups. He therefore advocated a qualified shift towards sociological methods, away from some of the key conceptual tools of the earlier English tradition. 'Mass art' had to be examined in terms of its *reception* amongst groups of people, rather than by a comparison with 'high art', that is, through the usual analytic dichotomies of 'low' versus 'high', 'exploitative' versus 'non-exploitative', 'machine-like' versus 'creative' and so on (Hoggart, 1982: 126). We must examine in detail areas of cultural life we might have assumed to be dominated by mass culture, but which on closer inspection prove to be more alive and vibrant than might have been expected. Here we have a typically culturalist emphasis on how humans can change their conditions of existence. According to this view, humans always have the capacity to rework the cultural habits they operate with, such that they are not merely prisoners of the cultural system in which they live (Williams, 1980 [1961]: 137).

This emphasis on the creativity of ordinary people in how they dealt with the contexts in which they found themselves, and those involving mass cultural products in particular, became a key theme of later culturalist studies. Later scholars drew on the work of Hoggart, Williams and the historian E. P. Thompson (1924–93), whose most well-known work is *The Making of the English Working Class* (1976 [1963]). Thompson, a Marxist who had broken with the British Communist Party and its orthodox form of Marxist analysis, wished to set up a form of analysis of culture and society which emphasized Marx's original stress on how history is *made* by ordinary people in their everyday struggles. The emphasis was to be shifted away from seeing abstract 'social structures' as determining how people lived their lives, to examining how those people created and recreated social and cultural patterns. In terms of the sociological dualism of 'structure' and 'agency', Thompson definitely tended towards emphasizing the latter rather than the former. From this angle, later culturalists sought to examine how ordinary people were culturally creative. A particular area for study was the youth cultures emerging in England from the 1950s onwards. Partially recanting on his earlier views on the 'milk bars', Hoggart (1982: 128) indicated a theme that would become the dominant one in culturalist studies from the mid-1970s – that certain aspects of youth culture might betray 'an unsuspected energy, an implicit criticism of . . . mass society . . . a thrust back from the grass roots, and a kind of imaginative inventiveness that nothing in our assumptions gave us reason to expect'. Thus Hoggart pointed at what would become the main agenda of culturalist approaches: a shift from the 'elitist' assumptions of the previous English tradition of cultural analysis to the 'populist' view that people resist domination, and that the main aim of cultural analysis is to see how such resistance to power plays itself out at the grass-roots level.

Struggle and resistance

Much culturalist work in the late 1970s and early 1980s on such issues was informed by a combination of the ideas of Hoggart, Thompson and Williams, and the notion of hegemony forwarded by the Italian Marxist Antonio Gramsci (1891–1937). The central claim of Gramsci's (1971) reworked Marxism was that the power of the ruling class in a society is never guaranteed. Instead, all societies are riven with conflicts and struggles in which the ruling class *attempts* to impose its rule on other classes. Sometimes, compromise situations arise in which there is a *negotiation* between the interests of the powerful and the interests of the powerless. Whether a ruling class fully succeeds or not in gaining control over the other classes depends on the particular situation in a society at a given time, rather than being predetermined in advance. This empirically based model allows for the possibility that working-class people may resist and challenge the sources of power that confront them. Nevertheless, Gramsci acknowledges that in many cases the power of the ruling class is sufficiently strong to control and channel such forms of resistance, with the result that their power is contained. Quite clearly, Gramsci's focus on struggle and resistance fitted well with the culturalist idea that ordinary people creatively respond to the conditions they find themselves in (Bennett, 1986).

The editors of an influential mid-1970s collection of culturalist studies of youth culture expressed this point when they argued that '[n]egotiation, resistance, struggle: the relations between a subordinate and dominant culture . . . are always intensely active, always oppositional' (Clarke et al., 1976: 44). Studies of youth culture were carried out using ethnographic methods in order to find the fine-grained details of the cultural life of such groups, a search for particularities that had been enjoined, albeit for very different reasons, by Leavis and then Hoggart. Although there was at this time some consensus among culturalists that ethnographic studies allowed access to the nitty-gritty of everyday life, there was some dispute as to how to understand the findings of such studies. There were two main ways of understanding data gathered on youth cultures. The first possibility emphasized the ultimately determining factor of the power of the dominant class and the relative powerlessness of the working class. The other option was to argue that working-class people, especially youth, were highly culturally creative, and so were able effectively to resist attempts to control them.

The first way of examining the position of working-class youth examined youth subcultures in terms of their overall position within a capitalist society. Groups such as 'teddy boys' and 'mods' were seen as offering *imaginary solutions* to the problems experienced by working-class boys, such as being condemned to have to work in dull and unrewarding blue-collar jobs. Membership of a subculture was a way of making life both more bearable and more colourful. For example, the 1950s subculture of 'teddy boys' dressed in elaborate ways; one of their more distinctive forms of dress was a modified Edwardian gentleman's frock coat. Appearing like a 'dandy' and emphasizing one's own personal and idiosyncratic style provided an 'imaginary solution' to the greyness and boredom that such young men otherwise had to deal with (Cohen, 1980). Likewise, the strong group affiliations amongst members of a subculture like the 'mods' of the 1960s were interpreted as a semi- or unconscious attempt to recapture forms of working-class community that were being eroded by factors such as the demolition of older working-class housing areas (the very areas Hoggart had eulogized), and the relocation of their inhabitants to apparently more alienating locales such as tower blocks. But all such 'solutions' were merely 'imaginary', because the people who lived through them were in such a dominated position in society. From this point of view, resistance to the norms of middle-class life is possible but ultimately futile, because working-class youth lack any real power to change their situation. The whole society works against them, from the police who victimize them to the education system, which succeeds not in educating them but in turning them off formal education, and so confirms their future adult lives as workers in low-paid, unrewarding employment (Willis, 1977). Membership of a subculture is a form of *symbolic* resistance to power, but such forms of rebellion are 'fated to fail' because of the material, socio-economic power structures of capitalist society being so heavily weighted against young working-class males (Clarke et al., 1976: 47). This echoes Gramsci's point that, in most situations, the powerful groups in society will prevail.

The second way of understanding the cultural position of 'ordinary people' in general, and young working-class people in particular, reverses this analysis. This school of thought has been dubbed 'populist' because of its celebration of the apparently resistive capacities of ordinary people, especially those in the working class (McGuigan, 1992). Although it praises the popular culture of everyday people and is thus the antithesis to earlier English authors' defence of 'high culture', it nonetheless retains the highly morally engaged tone of earlier authors, in that it finds moral value in everyday contexts and situations. Instead of seeing symbolic forms of rebellion as doomed to impotence, this viewpoint sees such activities as being highly successful. This outlook stresses the other aspect of Gramsci's work, that subordinate groups are always engaged in struggles with dominant groups. Scholars in this camp likewise played up the earlier culturalist notion that people respond to the contexts they are in, even the most apparently unpromising ones, in active and creative ways. Taking Hoggart's initial ideas, these scholars emphasized that although mass cultural products are given to people by powerful interest groups, such as television and record companies, the meanings people in audiences take from these need not be those meanings intended by powerful groups. Cultural consumption is seen, rather, as an active process, whereby 'things are imprinted with new meanings, associations and values, which expropriate them from the world which provides them [i.e. of the culture industries] and relocate them within the culture of the working class' (Clarke et al., 1976: 55). The semiotic versions of these ideas developed by English scholars in the late 1970s are examined in chapter 5.

On the most extreme version of this view, which is associated with John Fiske (1989a, 1989b), in modern Western societies there are in fact two entirely separate realms. The first is the 'official cultural economy', where the culture industries such as record and publishing companies create mass-produced products. The second area, which is completely distinct from the first, is the 'popular cultural economy'. This is the aspect of life in which ordinary television viewers, record buyers and so on take the products that they buy and use them for their own purposes, conferring their own meanings on these manufactured goods. Although the forces of the official economy try to control the activities that go on in the popular economy, they rarely do so, because ordinary people are understood by Fiske to be *inherently* sceptical towards the overtures of advertising executives and other so-called opinion-formers. Fiske's attitude is the direct antithesis of that of Theodor Adorno (see chapter 2). While Adorno saw cultural consumption as being dominated by cultural production, and the products of the Culture Industry as determining the ways in which audiences respond to those products, Fiske's argument is that once a product such as a film or book is 'inside' the popular cultural economy, its meaning will be reinterpreted according to the needs and interests of the people who are viewing or reading it. For Fiske, cultural consumption is always about the creative *use* particular people make of the cultural goods they have purchased.

A similar position is put forward by Paul Willis, the other figure apart from Fiske who today is known for forwarding a 'populist' version of culturalism. Willis's shifts in attitude towards these issues are indicative of wider shifts in British cultural studies from the 1970s to the 1990s. In the late 1970s, Willis (1977) was advocating a Marxist analysis of the working class in the British school system, arguing that young working-class males were so alienated from the middle-class values upon which schools were based that they generally tended to rebel against the educational establishment, thus forfeiting the chance of gaining qualifications and so condemning themselves to an adult life in unrewarding types of work. In this way, capitalist society's need was met for people to do the jobs no one would want to do if they had the choice. But a decade later, Willis (1990) was arguing from a populist perspective that working-class youths are highly creative in their responses to difficult circumstances. On Willis's populist redefinition of 'common culture', everyday life is full of examples of people, especially young people, taking what is given to them and making creative uses of it in unexpected ways. In so doing, they 'humanize, decorate, and invest with meanings their common and immediate life spaces and social practices', through such means as spraying graffiti on the walls of their neighbourhood, or through choosing their own personalized styles of dressing (1990: 2). There exists a dialectical interplay between the Culture Industry and 'the streets': for example when clothing companies pick up on new styles emanating from youth groups and sell that 'look' on to a wider market, these clothes in turn become modified in terms of how they look and what they mean by young people. In terms of *meaning* and *symbolism*, therefore, there is not a homogeneous and monolithic 'dominant ideology'. Rather, the ideas of the powerful are always being undermined by the powerless, who, as a result, gain certain resources of power for themselves.

This is a very appealing picture, but from the point of view of a sociology that wishes to connect cultural life to sources of social, political and economic power, it seems like a very idealized view. Quite clearly, many of the activities highlighted by Fiske and Willis do occur – activities unrevealed by analysis that sees only 'mass culture' and utterly passive responses to it. But populist analysis fails to locate such activities in wider contexts of structured social inequalities. Both Willis and Fiske can be criticized for overstating their case, partly as a result of relying too heavily on limited forms of evidence. Moreover, Fiske's division of the world into 'official' and 'popular' realms seems arbitrary, a convenient analytic fiction that helps him make his argument, but it is a division that is far too simplistic to grasp the complexities of the actual cultural situation in modern societies, including how forms of power can indeed 'colonize' grass-roots contexts and come to control them (Habermas, 1984). In essence, both Willis and Fiske separate 'culture' from 'society', and give all their attention to the former without attempting to relate it to the latter, with the result that their interpretation of what occurs in cultural life is denuded of an adequate account of the dynamics of power which act upon and shape culture.

This problem can be traced back to the work of Hoggart. For example, he claimed that a focus on changes in the style and content of popular cultural forms such as magazines and newspapers could provide a useful index for assessing trends in social life in general (1962 [1957]: 170). He thus focused on one area – mass cultural products – without giving much attention to issues of social or economic structures, downplaying these in favour of an analysis of what was designated as a distinct 'cultural' realm. Thus, the serious failure to deal with the 'structural' components of social and cultural life, in favour of an overemphasis on 'agency' and 'resistance', is not merely due to the populist commitments that emerged in the work of later culturalists such as Willis and Fiske, but rather can be traced back to the literary criticism tradition out of which culturalism developed. This possessed many subtle ways of thinking about what it saw as an isolated realm of 'culture', but generally failed to relate 'culture' to conceptions of 'society' and 'social structure', the key issues dealt with by French and German sociology. Despite its left-leaning credentials, culturalism unintentionally reproduced some of the conceptual problems of the older conservative tradition, allowing 'culture' to remain a relatively free-floating realm unconnected to other areas of social life. As Hoggart himself admitted in his later work, 'sociological approaches allow more conceptual rigour to be brought to bear on literary cultural studies' (1982: 132).

The role of Raymond Williams

This gap in culturalist understanding might have been avoided if culturalist authors had paid more serious attention to the ideas of another founding figure of this way of thinking, Raymond Williams. All of Williams's work was addressed in one way or another towards relating the cultural and social aspects of human life. In his earliest work, Williams (1958) was concerned to escape from the chasm that the English thinkers of the nineteenth century had erected between Culture (in the Arnoldian sense) and Society. In place of this view, Williams argued that this division wholly misrepresented the actual situation, because 'cultural' and 'social' factors were always intimately bound up with each other. The link between them was to be found by recognizing that humans are fundamentally *creative* creatures. Echoing Marx (1981 [1844]), Williams develops the typically culturalist theme that humans have the capacity to make and remake the social and cultural conditions in which they live. Thinkers such as Arnold and Eliot had limited creativity to the production of Art, of 'Culture'. Williams, by contrast, argued that every aspect of the 'whole way of life' of a society was informed and produced by the creative acts of socially organized individuals. Thus the production of artworks is just one aspect of human creativity, along with making more apparently 'mundane' things like cars and other everyday tasks like shopping or raising a family (Williams, 1980 [1961]: 61).

This point of view has two important ramifications. First, the 'health' of a society can be measured in terms of how conducive it is to allowing individuals' creativity to be freely expressed. Societies that block up creative processes – for example, by being politically totalitarian – are seen from this morally engaged culturalist standpoint as being culturally inferior to societies which allow more freedom of expression. Second, culture and society are seen as always mutually interpenetrating rather than as separate entities. In his major work of the early 1960s, *The Long Revolution* (1980 [1961]), Williams argued that the apparently separate spheres of culture, politics and economics were not separate at all, but, rather, were inextricably linked elements of the whole *social process*, whereby societies were created and recreated by human beings. In his later work of the 1970s and 1980s, which united culturalist and Marxist ideas (1989 [1975]), Williams argued that the aim of a sociology of culture was to examine the total social process which constituted 'cultural', 'social', 'political' and 'economic' aspects of human activity. Each aspect is only ever relatively 'cultural', 'economic' or whatever, as they are never wholly inseparable from each other. Each of these elements, all of which are important, is understood not as a realm unto itself but as a factor constitutive of a 'complex unity' (Williams, 1977: 139). It is this focus on the interplay between 'cultural' and other aspects of human life, especially the ways in which powerful forces can shape the forms of creative action in which humans engage, that gets underplayed in less sociologically informed versions of culturalism.

Williams also contended that it was not enough to add Marxist ideas to culturalism to sort out the latter's various forms of myopia (1997a). Sociology too, especially its Marxist form, would have to be rethought. In this direction he argued that each society at a given period of time is made up of the ways in which the different cultural, economic, social and political forces exert pressure on each other. The pattern that pertains at a given time between 'cultural' factors and others will reveal the relationship between those cultural factors and modes of class power (Williams, 1977: 87). In other words, there is no constant relationship between all the factors. The relationship involves the particular balance of forces operative in a given society at a given time. There is no one universal relationship between 'culture', 'politics', 'economy' and 'society' (Williams, 1981: 33). There are only ever different, socially and historically specific constellations of relationships between all of the above factors. This was Williams's (1997b) riposte to the orthodox Marxist idea that in *every* society, the economic base directly determines the cultural superstructure. There are indeed some societies where 'cultural' factors, such as the production of films, are more closely connected to 'political' and 'economic' factors than in other societies (a case here would be a tightly controlled society like Nazi Germany, where cultural production was strictly controlled by the state). But there are other types of society (e.g. modern-day capitalist societies) where the links and relationships are much more diffuse (the state has very little *direct* control over cultural production). Here, Williams rejects the Frankfurt School idea that modern Western societies are run on the same propagandistic lines as totalitarian societies.

Williams recuperates Marx's notion that in modern societies the social and cultural situation might be riven with contradictions, because different powerful groups may have opposing interests. For example, government officials may wish to censor pornography, but certain capitalist entrepreneurs might want to make money from its sale. These two groups are therefore in conflict because they operate with two separate cultural ideals – in this case, 'morality' and the search for profits regardless of the moral consequences. Although in modern Western societies culture is not the direct off-shoot of economics and politics, nonetheless it is not the case that 'cultural' factors are wholly disconnected from the others. The aim of the sociology of culture is to make these connections, but in ways that are sensitive to the different historically specific ways in which particular societies are patterned (Williams, 1981: 213).

The final aspect of Williams's work we will draw attention to here involves his advocation of an approach to culture he dubbed *cultural materialism*. This is envisaged as a revamped form of Marxism that avoids some of the worst mistakes of a naive version of Marx's views. The base and superstructure model hid what should be seen: how culture is *made*, by particular people in particular circumstances (Williams, 1977: 97). It is a perspective that examines how forms of culture are produced in material ways. Cultural objects are viewed not as free-floating entities locked in the ethereal world of the superstructure, but instead are viewed in terms of how they are produced. Cultural activities such as writing a book or composing a symphony are as 'material' as the activities involved in the making of a ship or a tractor, and the latter practices have 'cultural' components too. Producing cultural goods involves a combination of 'material' factors (e.g. composing the book using pen and paper) and 'cultural' factors (the kinds of imaginative strategies used in generating the prose style). Such imaginative strategies themselves are regarded as intrinsically socially shaped. Both the thought that went into making a cultural artefact, and the product that is produced, be it a book or painting or whatever, should be seen as material, as part of the whole *material social process*, rather than as a secondary offshoot of it.

Cultural materialism has become an important strand in contemporary studies of literature (Milner, 1993), and it bears certain similarities to the 'production of culture' perspective explored in chapter 8. But this and other aspects of Williams's work have been relatively ignored by sociologists. In the discipline of cultural studies, too, contemporary scholars have tended to favour semiotic and postmodern models of culture (see chapters 5 and 6) at the expense of culturalist ideas in general, and Williams's mixing of such ideas with Marxist approaches in particular. Michel Foucault is perhaps now regarded as a more central figure in the history of cultural analysis than is Williams (Bennett, 1998). This is a pity, as Williams offered some valuable correctives to the sometimes myopic vision of culturalism, whilst drawing sociological attention to the central culturalist insight, namely that culture is the creative product of social actors. Together with his emphasis on the material aspects of cultural production, Williams's works comprise a resource that has yet fully to be tapped.

Conclusion

In this chapter we have outlined the main features of a specifically English way of studying culture. Culturalism's key features are (1) a stress on looking at the particulars of culture rather than theorizing in an empirically uninformed manner, (2) an emphasis on the creative capacities of human beings, and (3) morally informed analysis and critique of contemporary cultural and social conditions. Out of the conservative ideas of the nineteenth century which separated Culture and Society, and defended the former from the depredations of the latter, came an approach which sought to relate cultural to social factors, and which focused on and celebrated the ordinary, everyday struggles of people at the grass-roots level.

Both culturalism and its conservative forebears have their strengths and weaknesses. The particularly appealing aspect of culturalism is its orientation towards seeing how culture is actively made by people rather than just thrust upon them by external sources of power. On the other hand, culturalism can lapse into a relatively naive populism which overemphasizes the scope of ordinary people to resist such powers, and which betrays the original culturalist desire to connect cultural with social, political and economic factors (see Harris, 1992). Conservative cultural criticism, likewise, is fundamentally flawed in that it tends not to see culture as anything other than 'Culture', refuses to see this as a form of elite power, and cannot relate cultural factors to social factors. On the other hand, it challenges sociology to think about its tendency to write off the idea of 'high' culture altogether as purely a way for elites to gain power for themselves. Most importantly of all, conservative cultural critique bequeathed to culturalism the sense that, by analysing its culture, one can decide whether a particular society is to be praised or condemned. As Hoggart puts it:

> For all its looseness and lack of analytical rigour, the English tradition in literary-cultural criticism has always been concerned with making a deeply human critique. It has kept a firm focus on individuals, on what happens to people . . . [it] need not just stand at the side of the social sciences. It can challenge them and seek to modify their vision. (1982: 133)

5

The Empire of Signs: The Semiotics of Culture

Introduction

Semiotic approaches are amongst the most influential ways of studying culture that have appeared inside and outside sociology. This is because semiotic ideas have permeated into a whole series of methods of cultural analysis. Postmodernist thinking (see chapter 6) is to a very large degree a development of semiotic ideas. The sociology of culture advocated by Pierre Bourdieu (see chapter 7) is also greatly indebted to notions deriving from semiotics. In this chapter we will examine what semiotics is, and how it has been applied to the study of culture as a distinctive method of analysis in its own right.

What is semiotics? The word derives from the Greek term *semeion*, which means 'sign'. Semiotics (sometimes also called semiology) is, therefore, the study of signs. The semiotic approach to culture is distinctive in that it focuses upon sets or systems of signs, examining their relations to one another. From this point of view, culture is made up of patterns (systems) of signs, and it is these that make culture full of meaning. According to those who practice semiotics, namely semioticians, without patterns of signs *signifying* meanings, there would in fact be no such thing as 'culture' at all. Cultural phenomena can be regarded as *signifying forms*, and the ways in which these forms are created and interpreted can be regarded as *signifying practices*. Semiotics, therefore, is concerned with culture in terms of how meanings are made and how certain forms demonstrate and embody such meanings.

But the precise ways in which semiotics should operate is an issue that is open to controversy. In this chapter we will demonstrate the various ways in which semioticians have developed semiotic analyses of cultural matters. We will first turn to examine the ideas of the Swiss linguist Ferdinand Saussure, whose ideas on the study of signs have been the most influential in later semiotic studies of culture, both in France and elsewhere. We then turn to review how his legacy was taken up by later French scholars, most notably the literary scholar Roland Barthes. Next we look at how Saussure's ideas were put to use, and somewhat altered, by thinkers working in both France and England. In the final section, we consider the limitations of Saussure-inspired semiotics and how these might be addressed. Throughout the chapter we will be particularly concerned with the often difficult relationships that have pertained at different times between semiotic and sociological ways of thinking about culture and society.

Capturing signs: the ideas of Saussure

Semiotics is part of the broader intellectual movement called 'structuralism', which was particularly dominant in France throughout the mid-twentieth century. This approach seeks to identify the structured aspects of social and cultural life. One of the foundational figures of this trend was Durkheim. As we saw in chapter 1, in his later writings Durkheim (2001 [1912]) was concerned to see cultural forms, especially religions, as containing certain structured properties. The religious and moral outlook of a given society is characterized by a binary division between *sacred* matters on the one side and *profane* things on the other. Religions are essentially cultural structures which operate as a means of making sense of the world for the people in a certain society, by classifying it in certain ways. By understanding certain things as 'sacred' or 'good', and others as 'profane' or 'bad', religion functions as a cultural processing mechanism, allowing individuals within a society to have a sense of themselves, of their roles within society and of how the world works.

There are close affinities between these ideas and those of another founder of the general structuralist school, the Swiss linguist Ferdinand Saussure (1857–1913). Whereas Durkheim was a *social* structuralist, Saussure's *linguistic* structuralism subsequently became equally, if not more, influential in French intellectual culture. Saussure's essential contribution to the study of culture is his claim that culture is structured like a language. Moreover, Saussure also claimed that language itself is structured in certain ways. Thus he puts forward a particular model of language, and suggests cultural forms look like this model. Saussure's thoughts on these matters are collected together in his *Course in General Linguistics* (1959 [1906–11]), a compilation of his lecture notes collated by his students and published after his death. We will now examine the main aspects of his ideas as they impact on the study of culture.

Langue *and* parole

According to Saussure, language possesses certain structured properties. Saussure uses the French word *langue* to describe the idea of language as a structured system. Rather like Durkheim, he asserts that there are certain 'social facts', entities that are more than the sum of their parts. Pre-eminent among these is language, which is more than just the sum of all the linguistic capacities of all the people who speak a particular language. A language exists above and beyond each of these individual speakers. It is a structured entity in and of itself, and it is this aspect of language that Saussure labels *langue*. It is the 'social side of speech' (1959 [1906–11]: 14), a structured collection of words and rules for putting them together in meaningful ways. Individual speakers, in order to make their utterances meaningful to other people in the same linguistic community, must follow these rules in their verbal activities. Saussure refers to individual acts of speech as *parole*. This refers to specific utterances carried out by individuals. Saussure makes characteristically structuralist claims about the relation between these two aspects of language. Like Durkheim, he asserts that the overall social system is more important than its individual manifestations. This is because those individual forms of speech are predetermined by the rules of *langue*. Individual instances of *parole* are but specific implementations of *langue*. As a result, the latter is socially more important than the former. Moreover, if one truly wishes to understand how language works, one must avoid a focus on specific instances of *parole*. If analysis were to focus only on these, then the systematic properties of language, namely those referred to by the term *langue*, would remain invisible. Thus, just as Durkheim insists on relinquishing the study of individuals and their idiosyncrasies for the analysis of the structured properties of society and culture, Saussure urges a focus on the structures of the overall language of a community rather than the specific uses that individuals make of language.

Synchrony and diachrony

The next claim that Saussure makes follows on logically from the previous one. If the structures of *langue* are to be the centre of attention, then analysis must look at language as a system. This involves looking at how that system operates at a given point in time. The structures of that system can best be grasped if one takes a 'snapshot' of it, which freezes it in time. Only that way can the structures of a language be revealed. If one were to look at the historical evolution of a given language – as linguists before Saussure had tended to do – the picture would be muddied. Methodologically speaking, only a viewpoint which captures the system as it operates at a single point in time can reveal the systemic nature of *langue*. As a result, Saussure proposes that linguistic analysis be *synchronic* rather than *diachronic* in aspect, where the latter term means a focus on the historical evolution of a thing over time, and the former means a focus on that thing at one point in time. In essence, what Saussure is proposing is that the history of an object – in this case language – be bracketed off, so that its structural aspects can be clearly seen. History, time, movement and change are therefore downplayed in favour of analysing how an object – language – operates at a certain period of its existence.

Signs, signifiers and signifieds

Once this methodological move has been made, Saussure is in a position to set out precisely what he takes to be the structural aspects of *langue*. Obviously, language is primarily made up of words and the rules for using them. However, the exact nature of words has to be more precisely outlined. Saussure does this by replacing the term 'word' with that of 'sign'. The sign is the basic constituent component of the *langue* system. *Langue* is made up of a set of signs, which are ordered in systematic ways with each other. Signs are made up of two components, *signifiers* and *signifieds*. The signifier is the phonetic expression of a certain mental concept; that concept is the *signified*. Saussure's point here is not the obvious one that a particular word (a signifier) refers to a particular object (the signified). Instead, his claim is that a sign unites 'not a thing and a name, but a concept and a sound-image' (1959 [1906–11]: 66).

This is an important reformulation of the nature of language. It is *not* the case that language is a set of words that refer to things. Instead, language is made up of two related systems. The first is the system of signifiers, the particular sounds and written images involved in a particular language. The second is the system of concepts or ideas to which these signifiers refer. The relation between the two is mutually self-constituting. In each sign, Saussure argues, signifier and signified are 'intimately united, and each recalls the other' (ibid.). The meaning of a sign, the signified, is therefore inseparable from its representation, the signifier. The implication of this position is, Saussure argues, that there is no meaning possible outside of language. Moreover, different languages construct the world in different ways. The meaning of something (e.g. a sheep) does not rest in the thing itself. Instead, the meaning of a sheep for a person who exists within a particular community of language-users comes from the concept of a sheep created by that language. The concept of a sheep generated by that particular language is utterly bound up with the word used by that language to designate something called a 'sheep'. For example, users of the French and English languages linguistically regard a sheep in different ways. The French word 'mouton' refers both to the living animal and also to the meat of the dead animal. But English uses two separate words, 'sheep' and 'mutton', to refer to these ideas. Thus the French signifier 'mouton' refers to a different signified (which covers both the living and the dead animal) than does the English signifier 'sheep' (which covers only one of those meanings).

Just as Durkheim argued that the cosmology of a given society generated the meanings which people in that society attribute to the world around them, Saussure argues that it is the language of a given group of people that dictates how they make sense of their environment. Meaning does not rest in physical objects, but in the system of *langue* drawn upon by those people. It is through language that meanings are created and understood. It is the language of the group that structures how people in that group view reality. 'Without language, thought is a vague, uncharted nebula. There are no pre-existing ideas, and nothing is distinct before the appearance of language' (Saussure, (1959 [1906–11]: 112).

The arbitrary nature of the sign

It follows from the previous point that there is no *natural* relationship between the object being referred to, such as a sheep, and the representation of that thing in language, the concept of that thing (the signified). There is nothing in sheep themselves that dictates that they be understood in a particular way. The understanding of them is purely the result of how a particular language makes sense of them. There is also no natural relationship between a given signified and signifier. The concept (signified) of 'sheep's meat' in English does not *have* to be represented by the signifier 'mutton'. After all, the word is just a sound, and it has no natural or necessary connection to the idea of sheep's meat. According to Saussure, this is the case with all signifiers and signifieds. The relationship between each of these in a particular sign is *arbitrary*. Any signifier could be used to denote any signified. It is purely a matter of convention which signifier refers to which signified. It is only because the language has laid down a rule for its speakers to follow, such that, for example, 'mutton' refers to the signified 'sheep's meat', that a given signifier is understood to refer to a certain signified. One of the main characteristics of *langue* therefore is the *arbitrary nature of the signifier*.

However, although it is purely a matter of social-linguistic convention which signifiers refer to which signifieds, it is not the case that chaos results, and that any signifier can be taken to mean anything whatsoever. This is for two reasons. First, the system of *langue* imposes certain habits and customs upon the people who use it. It enforces a kind of conservatively oriented rule upon them, such that particular signifiers are habitually accepted as referring to particular signifieds. As 'mutton' has since time immemorial referred to sheep's meat, then English speakers accept the word as referring to that signified. It is custom and habitual use of particular signifiers which ensure that meanings of signifiers remain relatively stable and fixed over time. Second, the structure of *langue* itself operates to ensure that meaning remains relatively stable. We saw above that *langue* consists of two interpenetrating systems, that of signifiers and that of signifieds. Saussure understands each as being characterized by a *system of differences*. This means that each element in each system only has a meaning because it is *different from* each of the other elements in the system. In the system of signifiers, each signifier has the particular meaning (signified) it has precisely because it is a different sound-image from all the other signifiers. In English, therefore, 'mutton' has a distinctive meaning precisely because in terms of sound and the written word it is different from 'sheep'. 'Mutton' as a signifier has no value in and of itself. But it takes on value and meaning when it is contrasted against other words such as 'sheep', just as 'sheep' takes on meaning when contrasted with 'mutton'. In fact, each particular word in a given language possesses meaning only because it is unlike *all* the other words in that language. 'Mutton' has a value not just because it contrasts with 'sheep', but also because it is different from every other word in English. A language, therefore, is not chaotic because each signifier in it has its separate meaning guaranteed by the fact that it does not sound or look like any other signifier in the system. The system is orderly, with each signifier's meaning being generated and guaranteed by all the others being different from it.

Syntagmatic and paradigmatic relations

The basic structure of each *langue* is that it comprises a series of differences, with each signifier located in a system of differences from all the other signifiers. Saussure specifies in more detail the structural aspects of *langue*. There are two main axes which analysis can focus upon. The first is the *syntagmatic* relation. This involves the ways in which particular words are joined together in sequences to form phrases or sentences. The sentence 'the cat sat on the mat' is a syntagmatic relation of words. It follows the placement rule of basic English grammar: noun (cat) followed by verb (sat). Each of the signifiers in the sentence 'acquires its value only because it stands in opposition to everything that precedes or follows it' (Saussure, 1959 [1906–11]: 123). Thus 'cat' here has a meaning (the signified of a feline) because it is not the same sound or written image as the other signifiers 'sat' and 'mat'.

The other way in which signifiers gain their meaning by being contrasted with other signifiers is through the *associative* axis of language. Linguists after Saussure have come to call this the *paradigmatic* relation. Here signifiers take on their specific meanings through being contrasted with other signifiers that have quite similar yet nonetheless somewhat different meanings. For example, the English words 'tuition' and 'apprenticeship' refer to similar kinds of activity. But English nonetheless makes a distinction between these two activities, and this difference at the level of signifieds is expressed at the level of signifiers in the fact that the words 'tuition' and 'apprenticeship' are different. Saussure regards the associative or paradigmatic axis of language as something implicit within a person's knowledge of a given *langue*. Generally, we do not consciously contrast different words in this way, but implicitly we are doing so all the time. It is only in this way that the words we use make any sense to us.

The idea of semiology

Saussure's ideas on language have subsequently become the basis for French developments in semiotics. Saussure himself pointed the way towards how his doctrine of linguistic signs could be used in this regard. In the *Course*, he notes that a 'science that studies the life of signs within society is conceivable ... I shall call it semiology ...

Semiology would show what constitutes signs, what laws govern them'
(1959 [1906–11]: 16). Saussure argued that language was but one
system of signs, amongst myriad others to be found in human life.
Nonetheless, he added that language was the most important of all
these sign systems, partly because it is involved in every aspect of
human life, and partly because it constitutes the reality as perceived
by members of a particular linguistic community. Although Saussure
indicates that he thinks semiology will be a science carried out
primarily by psychologists, he does suggest certain 'sociological' and
'anthropological' dimensions to this new form of analysis. Semiology
could concern itself with such systems of signs as 'symbolic rites
[and] polite formulas' (ibid.). These can be understood in terms of
the doctrine of the arbitrary nature of the sign. As Saussure puts it:

> every means of expression used in society is based, in principle, upon
> collective behaviour or – what amounts to the same thing – on conven-
> tion. Polite formulas, for instance, though often imbued with a certain
> natural expressiveness (as in the case of a Chinese who greets his
> emperor by bowing down to the ground nine times), are nonetheless
> fixed by rule; it is this rule and not the intrinsic value of the gestures
> that obliges one to use them. (Ibid. 68)

Each gesture used by people in a given society can be treated as a
signifier. It only has the meaning it does because it is contrasted with
all the other signifiers/gestures in a given society's semiological system. It follows that the same gesture (e.g. blowing one's nose) can
have very different meanings in different societies (something that is
considered acceptable in one society might be very rude in another).
The main point here is that particular signs only ever make sense in
relation to all the other signs in the system of which the particular
sign is a part.

Saussure's legacy

Saussure's analysis of language is the bedrock for later French
semiotic analyses of culture. Before we move on to them, it is worthwhile considering the assumptions to which a Saussurean approach
has committed later semioticians (see Merrell, 1986). In general terms,
semiotic systems are said to operate not just in the same way as
language, but also in the same way as *Saussure* says language operates. Such systems are to be analysed in terms of their overall structure (*langue*), and treated synchronically (i.e. as they operate at a

single moment in time) rather than diachronically (i.e. over time). One does not concern oneself with the historical *production* of semiological systems, but with their functioning at a given point in time. As a result, the particular uses that individuals might make of semiological systems (*parole*) are to be downgraded in favour of analysis of the system 'itself', which is treated as a self-sufficient, self-maintaining entity. This commits analysts to assuming that 'structures' are generally not present in the consciousness of actors. Just as the speakers of *parole* are generally unaware of the systematic properties of the *langue* they are dependent upon, so too are the 'users' of semiological systems generally unconscious of the systematic nature of these latter. The methodological implication of this is that analysis must focus not on what such users think they are doing, but on data that reveal the nature of the underlying – perhaps almost completely hidden – signifying system or 'code' itself. An assumption has to be made that such a code in fact exists, and that the semiological analyst can reconstruct it.

A further crucial Saussurean assumption is that the signifiers of each system are wholly arbitrary: they only derive their meaning from being contrasted with all the other signifiers in the system. Thus one of the key assumptions of later semiotics, but one that is already nearly fully explicit in Saussure's ideas, is that in the human world there is nothing 'natural'. All meanings result from the semiotic 'code' that operates in different societies: there are therefore no 'natural' meanings, only semiologically constructed ones. Thus, meanings are never natural or inevitable, but derive solely from the systems of arbitrary signifiers that constitute the cultures of each society. On this view, culture is a wholly human product, completely unconnected to the natural world.[1] Each person is caught within the webs of meanings spun by the semiological codes of the culture in which they are constrained to operate. As a result, humans are seen as being fundamentally alienated from extra-human nature, and compelled to think, see and feel in ways entirely dictated by the cultural context in which they live. As a result of this way of thinking, there is a certain strain of pessimism in French semiotics as to whether humans are capable of altering the cultural and social contexts in which they are

---

[1]   It is interesting to note that in the passage cited above on p. 119, Saussure seems not to follow through fully his own line of argument. The meaning of the Chinese man bowing to the emperor presumably derives solely from the semiological system of Chinese culture in the imperial period. There is, following Saussure's general reasoning, presumably no 'natural expressiveness' about such bows of submission, because different societies might have different signifiers for submission before a superior.

compelled to live. This is partly a result of Saussure's methodological bracketing off of questions about the active creation and production of culture by human beings, an elision that he argued was methodologically driven, but which some of his later followers hardened into a denial of the need to look at such matters at all.

Roland Barthes and the semiotics of popular culture

The first major figure to develop the ideas of Saussure towards the study of culture was the French anthropologist Claude Lévi-Strauss (b. 1908). Combining Saussure's ideas with those of Durkheimian sociology, Lévi-Strauss argued that anthropology (and, by implication, sociology too) should be semiotic in nature, studying particular systems of significations. In addition to the types of signifying system mentioned by Saussure, Lévi-Strauss (1987 [1973]: 9) added that anthropology should be concerned with many others, including 'mythical language, the oral and gestural signs of which ritual is composed, marriage rules, kinship systems, customary laws, and certain forms of economic exchange'. Although he himself focused on such systems in non-Western, generally pre-literate societies, scattered throughout his writings are tantalizing hints on how such analyses might be carried out in the modern West. For example, fashion in clothes was susceptible to semiotic elucidation:

> we rarely take note of why a particular style pleases us or falls into disuse . . . [but] this seemingly arbitrary evolution follows definite laws. These laws cannot be reached by purely empirical observation, or by intuitive consideration of phenomena, but result from measuring some basic relationships between the various elements of costume. (Lévi-Strauss, 1986 [1963]: 59)

Although Lévi-Strauss did not carry out such analysis himself, the implications of how a modern phenomenon such as fashion could be studied semiologically were taken up by other French scholars in the 1960s.

Foremost among these was Roland Barthes (1915–80), perhaps the most important figure in the development of French semiotics after Lévi-Strauss. His writings in the late 1950s and throughout the 1960s were concerned with utilizing semiotics as a form of analysing contemporary French culture, especially its more 'popular' forms. Barthes summed up his approach to such matters in an article written in 1964:

A garment, an automobile, a dish of cooked food, a gesture, a film, a piece of music, an advertising image, a piece of furniture, a newspaper headline . . . all are signs. When I walk through the streets – or through life – and encounter these objects, I apply to all of them, if need be without realizing it, one and the same activity, which is that of a certain reading: modern man, urban man, spends his time reading. He reads, first of all and above all, images, gestures, behaviours: this car tells me the social status of its owner, this garment tells me quite precisely the degree of its wearer's conformism or eccentricity, this aperitif (whiskey, Pernod, or white wine and cassis) reveals my host's lifestyle. (1988 [1964]: 157)

Signs, according to Barthes, are everywhere. 'In a single day, how many really non-signifying fields do we cross?' he asks. The answer, he says, is very few. He gives the example of someone going to the seaside: 'Here I am, before the sea; it is true that it bears no message. But on the beach, what material for semiology! Flags, slogans, sig- nals, sign-boards, clothes, suntan even, which are so many messages to me' (1993 [1957]: 112n.). Just as Saussure had denied that there were any 'natural' meanings arising from physical objects, so Barthes indicates in this example that the terrain of semiology is the sets of signs that humans are hemmed in by. To capture this idea more fully than he thinks is evident in Saussure, Barthes replaces the notion of 'sign' with 'sign-function'. This is the notion that no physical object only has a utilitarian function. It also carries meanings, because each object is itself a sign. For example, telephones obviously have the mundane function of allowing people to talk to each other. But there are different *types* of telephone, each of which has different meanings attached to it: in modern Western culture 'a white telephone always transmits a certain notion of luxury or of femininity; there are bureaucratic telephones, there are old-fashioned telephones which transmit the notion of a certain period', and so on. In other words, 'there is no object which escapes meaning' (Barthes, 1988: 182). Not only physical objects, but also everything that falls within human purview has some kind of semiotic value (meaning) attached to it.

The task of semiology is to identify these systems of signification, and to show how they work. In the mid-1960s, it seemed to Barthes and many others that the science of signs first mentioned by Saussure promised to become a new general way of carrying out social and cultural analysis. In addition to the 'economic, historical, [and] psy- chological' factors previously analysed by social scientists, 'a new quality of phenomena', namely cultural meanings, would now become an object of analysis (Barthes, 1988: 158). This new approach would focus on processes of *signification* as its primary unit of analysis, replacing positivist science's focus on 'facts' (ibid. 159). Semiology analyses not the *content* of signs, but, rather, their *form*. The analysis is therefore interested not so much with *what* a particular set of signs signifies, but with *how* it signifies the meanings it possesses (Barthes, 1993 [1957]: 111). Moreover, semiology does not look at particular signs and things in isolation, but looks at sets of signs and sets of things, seeing each element as part of a system, and the meaning of that element deriving solely from its position within the system (Barthes, 1988: 163).

Barthes at this period understands the realm of signification as one which is connected to, but analytically independent of, the 'psychological, sociological or physical' aspects of things. When studying a particular subject matter, these aspects of the things under study 'must themselves be treated in semiological terms, that is to say that their place and their function in the system of meaning [signification] must be determined' (Barthes, 1977 [1964]: 95–6). In other words, semiological analysis is separate from sociological analysis, if the latter studies the aspects of a subject deemed to be outside the level of signification. Semiology nonetheless is supposed to analyse the ways in which 'sociological' factors impinge upon systems of signification, as we will see below.

The meaning of myth

So far, Barthes has not done more than restate certain themes identified by Saussure. His innovation – and this is perhaps his most lasting legacy to semiotics – was to yoke such ideas to a kind of quasi-Marxist notion of social power. It is not just that sign systems signify; they signify in particular ways that work in the interests of powerful groups within a society. Barthes here translates the Marxist account of ideology into structuralist and semiotic terms. Systems of signs contain within them, either on the surface or buried deeper within them, a certain 'social charge', an ideological significance which shapes meanings in ways conducive to the continuing rule of powerful groups in society (Barthes, 1988: 155). Thus, Barthes' version of semiotics is an explicitly *political* exercise, carried out with the intention of exposing to view the forms of power contained within systems of signification. Semiology on this view is essentially an exercise in stripping away common-sense views of the world, because the latter are products of ideologies which are not recognized as such. 'We all understand our language [and other sign systems] so "naturally" that it never occurs to us that it is [actually] anything but "natural" in its signs and rules' (ibid. 158). To get beyond the ways of thinking stimulated by sign systems that hide power rather than reveal it requires an 'incessant shock of observation' on behalf of the analyst, so that one can escape, at least to some degree, from the webs of meaning in which everyone is caught (ibid.).

The semiotic analyst must therefore try to stand outside the sign systems in which everyone else is trapped, and to disabuse people of the myths they live under. This is the project developed by Barthes in one of his most famous works, *Mythologies* (1993 [1957]). He proposes that the semiotic analyst must assume the role of 'mythologist', someone who deciphers the meanings not of pre-modern myths, as did Lévi-Strauss, but the myths of the present day, the ideologically loaded ways of thinking and perceiving under which present-day people in Western societies live. The context of Barthes' analyses of such myths is the booming consumer-driven society of early post-war France, where older ways of life were being left behind in favour of a new social order based upon consumerism and advertising. It is the signifying systems of this new socio-economic condition that Barthes is primarily interested in interrogating. From the viewpoint he adopted in the later 1950s and early 1960s, contemporary society seems to Barthes increasingly like a cage of signifying systems out of which any kind of authentic feelings or moralities have disappeared. In their place are the signs of mass media, advertising and consumer culture, wrapping people up within nets of falsity and inauthenticity.

From adverts for soap powder to recipes in fashionable magazines, Barthes is concerned to set out not just what signifying systems present as their meanings, but the ways in which they address their recipients, the consumers and members of audiences that make up the French public as a whole. A signifying system is identifiable as mythical in character by the means through which it addresses people (Barthes, 1993 [1957]: 109). 'Mythical' meanings and messages are those which simultaneously operate at two different but interrelated levels. At the first level, which Barthes describes as the level of *denotation*, is the apparently basic meaning of the advert, or photograph, or film or whatever object is being analysed. For example, an advert for soap powder tells you that the particular product washes clothes whiter than its competitors. At this level, the signifier (the advert) refers to a signified, the basic meaning of the object (the soap powder). But this is not the only meaning of the object. The signifier and signified of this denotative level together make up a further sign. In mythical signification, this sign leads on to a second order of meaning, that is, the denotative sign is transformed into a signifier of another level of meaning. This second level is what Barthes terms the *connotative* level. This is the mythical or ideological level of the object. It is a secondary language that *infiltrates* the primary language of the denotative level. For example, in the case of the soap powder advert, the connotative – mythical – meaning is that happiness resides in the purchasing of clothes and other consumer goods, and that warmth, comfort and joy can be obtained through the means of the capitalist economy.

Advertising therefore works in such a way that the mythical connotative language of a consumer capitalist ideology pervades the banal denotative language that instructs consumers to buy things. The hidden underpinning of advertising is a signifying system that encourages people to assume it is *natural* to buy not only soap powder but every other type of commodity that capitalism makes available (Barthes, 1988: 176). In this way, a particular set of historical circumstances, in this case consumer capitalism, is signified as something both *natural* and *inevitable*. Thoughts about other possible ways of living are foreclosed in favour of making current social conditions seem *eternal*. The way Barthes puts this point is that capitalist society is *naturalized*, being made to seem as if it is the only possible form of social organization. Mythological thought thus aids in the reproduction of capitalist society (Barthes, 1993 [1957]: 139–40).

There are various problems with the position Barthes sets out in *Mythologies*. In the first place, mythological analysis is said to be the sole preserve of an elite, disengaged from the myths under which 'ordinary' people labour. The mass of consumers are seen as dupes of systems of signification that they swallow without thought or reflection. This kind of position runs into some of the difficulties associated with that of the Frankfurt School (see chapter 2). Not only is the (left-wing) intellectual assumed to be 'outside' of ideologies and possessed of a superior knowledge of reality than that held by 'ordinary' people; it is also the case that the deciphering of myth operates wholly at the level of the analyst interpreting signifying systems. It is *assumed* that people passively accept mythological thought, but this is not proven empirically in any way. As a result, the claimed effects of such thought – making the mass of the population more passive and accepting – is *asserted* rather than demonstrated.

There are also problems with how Barthes deals with the non-signifying, 'sociological' factors mentioned above. He admits that semiological analysis on its own is not sufficient for a full understanding of the cultural dynamics of contemporary societies. Its synchronic analysis of signifying systems needs to be supplemented with a diachronic account of how these systems were generated and formed historically (Barthes, 1993 [1957]: 112). But Barthes does not tell us how to connect either the diachronic and synchronic analyses, or the 'sociological' and 'semiotic' factors. In addition, it is not clear in his other writings of this period what these 'extra-semiotic' factors look like, or of what they are composed. In fact, since the thrust of Barthes' argument vis-à-vis sign-functions is that *everything* has semiotic significance, it is not at all clear if there do in fact even exist 'sociological' factors that are non-semiotic in character (i.e. they are 'pure' objects that lack any meaning). The upshot of this confusion is that there is a tendency in his work to view signifying systems as wholly autonomous processes, which have generated themselves rather than having been created by people, and which operate in completely automatic – and unchallenged – ways (see e.g. Barthes, 1993 [1957]: 131).

Thinking fashion

Some of these problems are dealt with in Barthes' slightly later writings on semiotics, dating from the early 1960s, where he deals with further aspects of contemporary popular culture such as the nature of cuisine and styles of consumer goods such as cars and furniture (1977 [1964]). It is worth noting that this focus on *popular* culture is not a mere idiosyncrasy of Barthes, but is in fact an outcome of the Saussurean semiotic position as a whole. If all meanings and values are social fabrications, and are purely the results of systems of arbitrary signifiers, it follows that all assertions of cultural value are based not in the 'natural' value of things, but are merely the products of signifying systems which operate in the service of particular social groups. For example, the distinction between 'high' and 'low' culture does not rest in the intrinsic properties of cultural objects themselves. Rather, it is wholly the result of an arbitrary signifying system which asserts that there is a difference between 'high' and 'low' cultural products. Such a system operates in the service of certain groups, such as artists and the 'cultured' bourgeoisie, those who claim cultural superiority on the basis of their consumption of such goods (Barthes, 1988: 164). As there is nothing intrinsic to a particular object that makes it *naturally* part of something signified as 'high culture', then it follows that the very idea of 'high culture' is a fabrication, part of a signifying system that attempts to pass off as *naturally* superior things that are not in fact possessed of any natural qualities at all. From this point of view, a work by Shakespeare is, in essence, just as 'good' (or 'bad') as a television soap opera, because the values ascribed to these products are not intrinsic to them but are merely ascribed to them by tendentious systems of signs. This notion of a *cultural arbitrary* has been particularly developed by Pierre Bourdieu (see chapter 7).

The main aspects of Barthes' 1960s semiotic writings can be discerned in his analysis of clothing fashions. In *The Fashion System* (1985 [1967]), he attempts to dissect the ways in which the French system of *haute couture* operates. Fashion, he believes, is a particularly good subject for semiological analysis in that it is a system wholly based on convention. Fashion is in fact like a language as Saussure describes the latter. There is nothing inherently 'stylish' about a particular garment. Its stylishness (or lack thereof) derives entirely from the labels it has been given by the fashion industry. The system of signification of the fashion industry arbitrarily dictates what is 'in' and what is 'out', what is *à la mode* and what is *passé*. The ways in which this is done can be analysed in terms of Saussure's use of *syntagmatic* and *paradigmatic* relations. Barthes analyses statements as to what is fashionable found in fashion magazines such as *Elle* in terms of the ways in which the words deployed both fit with each other (syntagmatic relations) and are in contrast to each other (paradigmatic relations). The syntagmatic relationship involves three terms: object, support and variant. For example, in the statement that fashionable this season is a 'sweater with a closed collar', the object is the sweater, the support is the collar and the description 'closed' is the variant. The paradigmatic relation involves the various mutually exclusive possibilities of the variant. Thus collars can be either 'closed' or 'open'. The signifying system of fashion arbitrarily decides what is fashionable or not by playing with the various permutations possible syntagmatically and paradigmatically. For example, during one season sweaters with closed collars are fashionable, while in another they are not (paradigmatic variation) – or dresses with closed collars are 'in' (syntagmatic variation: sweaters are replaced by dresses).

Fashion is a system that makes very excessive demands on the people who follow it. Even a tiny slip in what is acceptable at a given time (e.g. wearing the *wrong type* of blue) might mean social humiliation. Barthes argues that it is precisely because the language of fashion is so arbitrary that it demands so much of its adherents, the 'dedicated followers of fashion' who read magazines like *Cosmopolitan* and *Marie-Claire* and who shop in 'exclusive' boutiques. Fashion, as it were, compensates for its arbitrary nature by passing itself off as being 'natural' and 'inevitable'. One must not question the judgements of fashion, for to question them is to reveal how lacking in style or chic one is: quite simply, a certain type of blue is 'in' this year, and there is nothing more to be said. The language found in fashion magazines reinforces this kind of belief. Statements of 'fact', such as 'coats will be long this autumn', imply that this situation is both natural and inevitable. It is as if what is fashionable is an unfathomable but natural process. Although it is entirely arbitrary what types of garment are selected as being fashionable, the language used to describe them makes it seem as if their fashion value were an intrinsic part of them: 'skirts are becoming shorter', as if skirts had minds of their own. Thus, what is arbitrary is disguised as being inevitable. In *Mythologies*, Barthes had generally ignored the ways in which such mythical thought was actually produced. In the analysis of fashion, he focuses on the fact that the language of fashion does not generate itself (although it appears to). Instead, it is created by particular groups of people who have an interest in creating it, primarily fashion journalists and people in the clothing trade. Such groups of people make 'the decisions and deliberately elaborate . . . the code' of fashion language (Barthes, 1977 [1964]: 26). Such a focus on the particular groups of people who create signifying systems means that Barthes' later semiotic writings have more of a sociological specificity about them than the arguments contained in *Mythologies*.

There nonetheless remain several problems with this type of analysis. In the first place, we are still left with the assumption that the consumers of fashion accept without question the significations peddled by the fashion industry. There is no acknowledgement of how they might resist or modify the judgements handed out from on high by the fashion industry (Rylance, 1994: 41). This is not just a result of Barthes' particular position, but comes from the key Saussurean assumption that one must look at *langue* (here, the language of the fashion industry) rather than *parole*, the uses made by people of *langue*, in this case the ways in which fashion consumers might adopt and adapt clothing items to their own ends. Consumers are *assumed* to be doing certain conformist things, but again, this is not demonstrated empirically.

In terms of the analysis of the fashion *langue* itself, there are further problems. Barthes analyses only the system of Parisian *haute couture*. But contemporary fashion might be said to be made up of multiple languages, each of which exist in relations of implicit or explicit tension and antagonism. For example, there is a big difference between the statements of fashionability produced by the fashion houses of Paris and Milan on the one hand, and those generated by designers and other interested parties targeting their wares at groups such as goths or punks. There is potentially not just one 'language' of fashion but a whole series of them, each trying to downgrade and discredit the others.

There are also problems with the data selected for analysis. Barthes analysed the photograph captions from a year's issues of the style magazines *Elle* and *Jardin des Modes*. The criteria for such a selection were that the data collected for semiotic analysis must be (a) varied enough to provide a sufficient selection of paradigmatic and syntagmatic permutations; (b) similar enough to each other to be able to make meaningful comparisons between them (e.g. all the data should come from fashion magazines, rather than from a wide mixture of different sources such as newspaper articles and TV programmes); and (c) from a similar time period so that a synchronic analysis of the *langue* can be given as it operates at a particular point in time (Barthes, 1977 [1964]: 97–8). These criteria are all in fact designed to collect data which allows one to discern the *langue* of fashion (or indeed any other system of signification). The obvious problems here are twofold. First, is data being collected that provides 'evidence' of a structure that might not in fact exist? The semiologist *assumes* there is a *langue* to be found, but how can we know if it really exists in actuality when the data have been collected in a way that assumes that such a thing really exists? The danger is that the means of data collection might be biased in such a way that it merely confirms original assumptions in a very misleading way. Second, the criteria of selection might be said to be unnecessarily tightly defined. Surely it would be useful to collect data from various years of magazines, so that we might be able to see how the language of fashion changes over time? The structuralist demand for synchrony over diachrony might efface the possibility of finding *contradictions* in the world of fashion, such as the conflicts between rival sets of fashion languages described above. Overall, the conception of data collection deployed by Barthes seems overly controlled by a too narrow focus on *langue* rather than *parole*, and on synchronic rather than diachronic factors.

Finally, there are also problems with how social and economic factors are to be dealt with in relation to the semiotic analysis. Barthes' position in his mid-1960s writings is that '[f]ashion . . . has economic and sociological implications; but the semiologist will treat neither the economics nor the sociology of fashion: he [*sic*] will only say at which level of the semantic [signification] system of fashion economics and sociology acquire semiological relevance' (Barthes, 1977 [1964]: 96). Not only is this statement very vague, it also reproduces one of the crucial problems deriving from Saussure: it brackets off issues of how linguistic and/or semiotic processes are to be related both to economic factors and to social structures comprised of patterned interactions. This is a methodological decision on Saussure's part – he wants to forget about other factors so he can get at the *langue* system without hindrance. But in the case of his later follow-ers, including Barthes, the methodological decision to keep such factors out of the equation hardens into a tendency to see semiotic systems as actually truly *separate* from social and economic phenom-ena. This failure to account for the ways in which these various realms might affect each other haunts a great deal of semiotic writ-ings, and essentially involves a failure to think through adequately the relations between 'culture' (as signification) on the one side, and 'society' on the other.

Semiotics of resistance and everyday life

Of the various problems identified by critics as to the type of semiotics that Barthes was carrying out in the 1960s, the main one was that it overemphasized the study of *langue* rather than adequately examining particular cases of *parole*. As a result, it focused too much on the 'official' languages and other semiotic systems produced and used by powerful social groups, and did not look at the 'unofficial' languages and signifying practices of less powerful groups. One of the major trends in semiotic analysis since the 1960s has been in this latter direction.

In Italy, Umberto Eco drew on another type of semiotics, rather different to that of Saussure. This brand of semiotics was put for-ward by the American philosopher Charles Sanders Peirce (1839–1914). His version of semiotics insists that particular systems of signs do not signify 'automatically' as if they had a complete life of their own. Instead, signs only mean anything if they are interpreted by particular people. Therefore, what the semiotician has to look at is how particular groups of people *interpret* and *use* the signs that con-front them in their daily lives (Greenlee, 1973). Eco took this Peircean theme of active interpretations of signs being generated by people in particular social contexts and applied it to the study of the mass media. He stressed that one cannot only look at the codes of the signifying systems of television and other forms of broadcasting. One must also analyse the various ways in which different groups of people located in particular contexts *decode* (i.e. interpret) those messages. Analysis must be open to the possibility of empirically find-ing cases of 'aberrant' readings, where particular groups of people actively interpret the messages they are given, and make sense of them in ways not intended by those who produced the messages (Caesar, 1999; Eco, 1987 [1967]).

With this focus, Eco's position in the 1960s was far ahead of his contemporaries in France and other countries. It was not until the late 1970s that the British scholars associated with the 'culturalist' strain of cultural studies, particularly those associated with the University of Birmingham's Centre for Contemporary Cultural Studies (CCCS), took up some of the semiotic ideas put forward by Barthes (see chapter 4). Given culturalism's stress on the creative capacities of ordinary people, these scholars tended to emphasize *parole* over *langue*. They did so on the basis of a reworking of Saussure's ideas, rather than after reading Peirce. They particularly worked out a focus on *parole* in terms of the study of television news broadcasts. Rather like Barthes' view of myth-making, they argued that television news stories are presented ('coded') in such a way that they mesh with the semiotic systems that operate in the interests of the socially powerful. Perhaps the most dominant of such systems operates around the assertion that capitalist society is both 'natural' and inevitable. So ingrained is this mentality in the minds of a large part of the population of Western countries that it is not seen as one possible way of conceiving things, but as an incontestable fact, and 'just the way things are'. Television news stories are coded by journalists – who are unaware that they are doing it, so much has this way of thinking entered common sense – such that they fit this dominant *langue* (Hall, 1993 [1980]). For example, stories concerning how badly the economy is faring are presented as being partly the result of trade union activism, rather than the result of the crisis-ridden tendencies of the capitalist economy itself. In such a mode of presentation, unionists are blamed for economic troubles, and management generally escapes blame. Moreover, the word 'capitalist' is never used to describe 'the economy', making it look as if a capitalist economy is a natural state of affairs rather than being just one possible way of organizing economic relations. In this way, the interests of the powerful classes are constantly being re-secured by television news, as it demonizes deviant groups such as trade unionists, and it 'naturalizes' capitalism by presenting it as the inevitable state of affairs.

So far, the argument has been very like that of Barthes in *Mythologies*. However, in the late 1970s, the Birmingham scholars and others like them turned towards the analysis of how particular acts of interpretation (*parole*) affect how dominant systems of meaning (*langue*) are understood. In this way they reached the same conclusion as Eco had done earlier. Powerful groups produce certain types of semiotic code, but the code can be 'decoded' in unexpected ways by other groups. There is therefore no guarantee that the semiotic systems of the powerful will succeed in imposing themselves as the only ways of thinking about things or seeing the world. They may come up against the worldviews of groups such as the working classes or blacks, who already in certain senses have their own particular ways of interpreting things, techniques of decoding that are sceptical towards or which challenge the dominant semiotic systems in society (Hall, 1993 [1980]). Empirical studies of viewers of television in general, and television news in particular, such as that carried out by Morley (1980) seemed to back up this theoretical position. Some groups, such as businessmen, tended to accept completely the assumptions built into television news broadcasts (trade unionists are trouble-makers, all blacks are criminals, etc.). But, and perhaps unsurprisingly, other groups – especially those labelled negatively by news broadcasts, like blacks and students – tended not fully to agree with such assumptions, sometimes accepting in part the presentation of certain news stories, and sometimes rejecting them outright. This emphasis both on empirical study of what mass media audiences think and on the capacities of certain groups to resist dominant meanings is very far from the Frankfurt School assumption that such audiences inevitably accept the messages they are given. For this particular version of semiotics, it is not just the sociological analyst who is a semiotician – everyone uses signs all the time, sometimes accepting the systems of signs they are faced with, and sometimes rejecting them in favour of others.

It was not only television audiences who were reinterpreted by CCCS scholars as having the capacity to resist the meanings imposed upon them by dominant semiotic systems. Young people, especially those in particular style-based subcultures such as punks, were seen to possess the power not only to resist the meanings of a society dominated by parents, police and other sources of authority, but also to forge their own distinctive and resistive 'languages'. These were not just ways of speaking but also ways of *looking*. According to Dick Hebdige (1998 [1979]), subcultural style is a form of *parole* that seeks to reject the dominant ways of thinking and acting in 'mainstream' society. It does so by developing a visual code of dressing and acting that goes against the codes of 'ordinary', middle-class decorum. The way the punks dressed, for example, with their outrageous hairstyles and ripped clothes, 'interrupt[ed] the process of normalization', whereby mainstream society enforces cultural norms of appearance and behaviour on its members, such as dressing soberly and having a 'normal' haircut. In its place, the punk 'look' comprised 'gestures, movements . . . which offend the "silent majority" [and] . . . which contradict the myth of consensus' (ibid. 18). The punks were a 'spectacular' subculture, part of whose very existence was to be involved in often violent clashes with mainstream society and the organs of social control such as the police. More peaceable, but still apparently highly semiotically 'resistive', were the groups of young women studied by McRobbie (1994 [1989]), who challenged the codes of fashion laid down by style magazines and couture houses by purchasing second-hand clothes and remaking them in such a way that their own distinctive styles were created. Here we have a focus on active meaning-generating forms of *parole* in the world of fashion, which looks at what happens at the grass-roots level of everyday life, and which is the diametric opposite of Barthes' original emphasis on the official *langue* of fashionability as this was created by journalists and style gurus.

These themes also came to influence French semiotic writings in the 1980s. Foremost among such authors was Michel de Certeau (1984), who presented a picture of modern urban life in which ordinary people resist the powers exercised over them by governmental agencies, and so on, through a creative manipulation of sign-systems that have been imposed upon them. For example, a tenant in a drab housing block can decorate her home in her own idiosyncratic form of significatory 'style' in such a way as to make the place 'liveable', and in so doing rejects the dreary and bureaucratic nature of the housing that the authorities have provided her with. On the basis of de Certeau's writings, one Anglo-American writer, John Fiske (1989a, 1989b), who has also drawn on certain culturalist themes in his work, went so far as to claim that the cultures of modern societies are characterized by a 'semiotic democracy'. This is a situation where people in less powerful groups *always* negotiate and reject the meanings proffered to them by the mass media, government and other social institutions (see chapter 4).

But this emphasis on the creative power of significatory *parole*, which dominated much British cultural thought in the 1980s and after, comes at an analytic cost (McGuigan, 1992). It downgrades the efficacy of the various *langues* of governmental agencies and suchlike to constrain, label and control the activities of the people that de Certeau and Fiske celebrate. Thus an extreme emphasis on one end of the *langue/parole* dichotomy is arguably replaced by an opposite but equally excessive focus on the other side of the equation.

Semiotics beyond Saussure

There are, however, resources at hand that can be drawn upon to avoid this oscillation between extreme emphases on the semiotic power of either powerful groups or apparently subordinate ones. Some contemporary semiotic analysts (e.g. Hodge and Kress, 1988) have based their approach upon the reformulation of Saussure's position carried out by the Russian linguist V. N. Voloshinov.[2] The remarkable aspect of Voloshinov's book *Marxism and the Philosophy of Language* (1973 [1929]) is that, despite being written in the late 1920s, it sets out a far more nuanced and sociologically sensitive version of language and other semiotic systems than was generally developed by semioticians before the 1970s. Voloshinov's critique of Saussure centres around the claim that Saussure is too interested in seeing language as an abstract, isolated system set apart from the social contexts in which language is used. In essence, Saussure overstresses the systematic nature of *langue* and underplays the active role played by individual speakers in the elaboration of instances of *parole*. Writing from a Marxist position, Voloshinov argues that it is social – especially class-based – contexts which shape the nature of language, not the self-enclosed system of signifiers postulated by Saussure. It is forms of organized social activity which shape the uses that people, both individually and collectively, make of language. Actors do not just enact *parole* through the unthinking application of rules. Instead, language is *used* in the various different contexts of social life in which it is needed, such as 'unofficial discussions, exchanges of opinion at the theatre or a concert or at various types of social gatherings, purely chance exchanges of words, one's manner of verbal reactions to happenings in one's life' and so on (Voloshinov, 1973 [1929]: 19–20). It is in these exchanges that the meanings of signs can be altered, and new connotations created.

Voloshinov's position obviously puts much more emphasis on the *activity* of language speakers and other sign-users than do Saussure and most of his followers. In this regard, it is akin to the views of de Certeau, Fiske and the British thinkers mentioned above, which stress the ability of ordinary people to challenge and rework dominant semiotic codes. Yet Voloshinov's account of the creativity of *parole*-users is arguably more satisfactory than the positions of all of these scholars. This is because it attempts to strike an analytic balance between looking at the power of officially sanctioned *langue*, and at unofficial, localized instances of *parole*. Voloshinov insists that signs are *multi-vocal* (Dentith, 1995: 26, 29). They have coded into them *both* the meanings of ruling groups, *and* the connotations derived from the activities of the powerless. Semiotic life is therefore part and

---

[2]   There is some controversy over whether Voloshinov was a real person or, in fact, the pen-name of the literary scholar M. M. Bakhtin. See Clark and Holquist, 1984.

parcel of social life, and both are sites of struggle, struggles between different groups (especially classes) being expressed through conflicts over meaning, there being a constant oscillation between signs connoting official or unofficial meanings.

There are certainly problems with Voloshinov's account. When reading his book, one is struck by a sense of indecision as to whether he wishes to see the social production of semiotic systems in light of an orthodox Marxist account of economic base and cultural superstructure, or whether the production of meanings is to be regarded as due to localized struggles in the kinds of particular social contexts described above. Nonetheless, his account is perhaps a more satisfactory yoking together of semiotic and (one version of) Marxist analysis than was Barthes' attempt in *Mythologies*, because the latter was focused solely both on *langue* at the expense of *parole*, and on the wholly 'official' nature of the former. Voloshinov attempts a more 'middle way' approach to these issues (similar to that of Gramsci – see chapter 4), which also avoids the perhaps rather naive populism of figures such as de Certeau and Fiske.

As a result of a rethinking of some of the more questionable assumptions of Saussurean semiotics, the present-day research agenda in semiotics has involved not only a ditching of the idea that the Saussurean linguistic sign *must* be the model for all signs, but also has developed a focus on 'context, the specific and the concrete' (Winner, 1986: 183). The contemporary approach known as 'social semiotics' or 'socio-semiotics' has various axiomatic principles, deriving from the ideas of both Voloshinov and Peirce. First, and unlike some post-structuralist and postmodernist accounts of signs (see chapter 6), such approaches insist upon the need for the social contexts of the production, transmission, reception and reinterpretation of sign systems to be taken into consideration, and the relations between these analysed. Second, sign systems must be related to other factors such as power relations and the material conditions of social life (Hodge and Kress, 1988: 23). Third, semiotic analysis should be based on empirical analysis rather than simply on abstract theorizing. This involves an open-minded approach as to whether the significatory systems produced by powerful groups actually have the effects intended by those groups upon subordinate populations. Issues of control and resistance are to be researched empirically, rather than being decided beforehand. Moreover, the role of the privileged analyst, who is assumed to know more about significatory systems than the actors who make or are confronted by them, must be reflected upon and not abused or misused. To this end, analysis must seek out various forms of data that can be used to back up its claims, not only analysing texts that embody particular significatory systems, but also perhaps deploying interview-based methods with both the producers and the consumers of such codes (Gottdiener, 1995: 29). Although the full implications of such imperatives for research are yet to be ascertained, this new agenda in semiotic studies nonetheless itself signifies a break with some of the more restrictive assumptions and practices associated with semiotics in the past.

Conclusion

Semiotics as a means of studying culture has been used both as a method in itself and as a resource drawn upon by cultural analysts who wish to yoke its insights to other forms of study. The benefits and drawbacks of semiotics per se also figure as some of the strengths and weaknesses of these more hybrid approaches. The two main streams of theory of culture covered in this book that have involved a use of semiotic perspectives are postmodernism and the sociology of Pierre Bourdieu. In the next two chapters we will see how these two types of cultural analysis have been affected by their acceptance of certain assumptions made, in particular, by Saussure and Barthes.

On the plus side, semiotics provides us with a way of understanding some of the detailed characteristics of cultural forms. It allows us to see the specific signs of which a cultural form is composed, and how people might react to, understand and use that form. Barthes coupled semiotics to a Marxist understanding of ideology, allowing an exploration of how sign systems are interwoven with sources of social power, and providing an account of how certain ideologically loaded sign systems attempt to present particular views of the world as natural and therefore unchangeable. Semiotic-inspired viewpoints have also enabled us to think about the ways in which ordinary people can reject or resist such dominant sign systems.

On the negative side, semiotics has often lacked a sociological component. It has had difficulty in relating sign systems to sources of social, political and economic power. It can show how these impact on sign systems, but because it is designed only to look at sign systems, it has lacked adequate understandings of factors that are irreducible to signification alone, especially the *material* power of particular elite groups. In other words, semiotics is good at understanding 'culture' but not so well adapted to comprehending 'society', especially the material aspects of the latter. This focus on culture and meaning at the expense of more material elements of social life is the main reason why so many semiotic-inspired studies of the resistive capacities of subordinate groups could be said to be quite naive. The *cultural* capacities of such people are celebrated, but this type of analysis fails adequately to locate such people within the material contexts of social, economic and political power. As a result of this overemphasis on culture alone, the resistive capacities of ordinary people are arguably overstressed, because 'sociological' issues are not factored into the equation. Semiotics therefore may be seen as inadequate in itself for the purposes of the sociological analysis of culture. But when it is attached to frameworks that can grasp the things that it cannot, it yields indispensable insights into the workings of culture and society.

6

Phantasmagoria: Postmodernism and Culture

Introduction

Over the last twenty years or so, the word 'postmodernism' has been on many people's lips, both inside and outside universities. For the more philosophically inclined, the term refers to new ways of thinking about a multitude of things, from how the social sciences should operate to the nature of social and political struggles. For those interested in the dynamics of contemporary society and culture, 'postmodernism' signifies the appearance of new attitudes, cultural products and styles, which, taken together, may have changed fundamentally the lives of people in Western societies. Postmodernism, therefore, seems to indicate a novel situation, where things are not as they were before. In terms both of what is happening socially and culturally, and of how we are to think about these developments, postmodernism is taken to mean a break with the past and moves towards a future situation the like of which we have not seen before.

In this chapter we will look at the two main aspects of ideas associated with postmodernism. First, the notion that new modes of thinking are required truly to grasp the nature of life in contemporary Western societies. We will refer to these novel forms of conceptualization as *postmodernist* in character. Second, we will look at the view that the social and cultural orders of Western societies have now entered into a qualitatively different phase from the previous one, namely the period of *modernity*. We will refer to the new type of *society* that is alleged to have been born as *postmodernity*. The new type of *culture* that is said to go with it we will designate as *postmodern culture*. Many authors of a postmodern persuasion argue that only if we think in postmodernist ways will we be able really to understand the nature of both postmodernity and postmodern culture. This has profound ramifications for how sociology is to operate, postmodernist authors often calling for a complete rejection of the ways of doing sociology set up by the classical sociologists. By contrast, the critics of these authors argue either that modernist ideas are the best way to grasp postmodernity and postmodern culture, or that the latter two phenomena do not in fact exist at all, being merely the imaginative fantasies of postmodernist thinkers. For these critics we are still in modernity and nothing really has changed very much, either in culture and society or in the ways we should think about them.

The conflicts between modernists and postmodernists have been both complicated and often very bitter. This is to a large degree due to the highly politicized nature of these debates. Postmodernists argue that modernist ideas of politics are now defunct and that a new postmodernist form of politics has to be forged. Conversely, modernist authors argue that postmodernists have given up on struggles towards political change in favour of an uncritical acceptance of current social and cultural conditions. At stake in these often very rancorous arguments is the role of the person who wishes to analyse society and culture: from what angle should he or she come at social and cultural situations, and on what basis should he or she assess them? These fundamental questions about social and cultural analysis and critique are what are being addressed in the debates on postmodernism. We begin by looking at the various ways in which postmodernism and ideas associated with it have been defined, both by academic writers and by others. We then turn to examine the ideas on postmodern culture of one of the main postmodernist thinkers, Jean Baudrillard. His central concept is that of 'hyperreality', which we set out and evaluate. We will then consider how his views on cultural consumers have been adopted and adapted by other postmodernist authors. Baudrillard has challenged sociologists to rethink the ways in which they understand society and culture. The final section deals with the various responses to Baudrillard made by those who wish to defend modernist ways of thinking. We conclude with an assessment of the contribution of postmodernist ideas to the sociology of culture in particular, and sociology more generally.

What is postmodernism?

Postmodernist thought emphasizes transgression and rejection of established parameters and boundaries, and a scepticism towards any attempts to identify the nature of something once and for all. As a result, it is rather paradoxical to try to give a single, fixed definition of what postmodernism, postmodernist thought, postmodernity and postmodern culture are. This would defeat the purpose of postmodernist thought, which is to escape from such essentialist ways of thinking. There are, in addition, many different types of postmodernist author, working in different academic disciplines, each with his or her own view of what postmodernism is or could be. A crucial feature of the intellectual terrain that constitutes postmodernism is its profusion – if not confusion – of different ideas and attitudes. However, it is precisely the confusion and the ambiguity that most postmodernist authors champion, in contrast to what they see as the overly restrictive notions that underpin their great enemy, modernist thought. For most postmodernists, modernist thought is characterized by a scientific desire to create fixed categories which claim to be utterly true and objective. A central tenet of postmodernist thought, by contrast, is that claims to know something comprehensively and objectively are a fiction. On this view, both things and their meanings are anarchic, refusing to be captured in the overly simplistic terms that modernist thought operates with, especially in its so-called 'scientific' form.

This situation shows us some important things about postmodernism. Despite the multiplicity of different authors and views, there are nonetheless common emphases and ideas among the apparent chaos. These shared themes are centred on a rejection of what are taken to be the typically modernist ideas of scientific knowledge, certainty and order. The opposite principles of subjective understandings, uncertainty and disorder are stressed and championed. Although postmodernist thought is suspicious of dualisms, which it takes to be overly simplistic and constraining, the differences between modernism and postmodernism can nonetheless be represented as involving oppositions between these sorts of value: stasis/movement, design/chance, determinacy/indeterminacy, and certainty/uncertainty (Hassan, 1985). This places postmodernists in opposition not only to modernist thought but also the society they take to be its embodiment, namely modernity. This is usually seen (distantly following Max Weber – see chapter 1) as a social order based around a bureaucratic and repressive form of rationality. A more anarchic and irrational – therefore more fluid and open – society informs the political desires of many postmodernist thinkers.

We noted above that the two main ways in which postmodernism has been developed by its proponents are in terms of, first, *postmodernist thought* and, second, ideas of *postmodernity* and *postmodern culture*. In terms of the first aspect, probably the most influential advocate was the French philosopher Jean-François Lyotard (1924–98). Like his compatriot Jean Baudrillard (see below), Lyotard was one of the generation of French intellectuals who, by the 1970s, had grown very disillusioned with the Marxist promise that revolution would sweep away existing injustices in favour of a better world. With the failure of the 1968 anti-government student protests to make any lasting difference to social life in France or elsewhere, Lyotard and other intellectuals, such as Michel Foucault, moved towards a 'post-Marxist' outlook, one which often retained the rebelliousness and anarchism of Marxist thought, but which rejected what they saw as its more authoritarian aspects, especially the claim that Marxism was a true science of society and as a result was the only way of having 'objective' knowledge about social conditions.

As one of the leading proponents of post-Marxist ideas, Lyotard's postmodernism embodies a fundamental rejection of Marxism's claims to be the only objective knowledge of society. Indeed, Lyotard goes further than this, drawing upon the ideas of the philosophers Friedrich Nietzsche and Ludwig Wittgenstein, to argue that the idea of pure objective knowledge is itself a myth. His account of postmodernist thought, *The Postmodern Condition*, defines it as 'incredulity towards metanarratives' (1984: xxiv). 'Metanarratives' are grand stories about human life, especially those concerning freedom and emancipation, that have been current in Western social and political life for the last several centuries. Among these are the liberal belief in increasing democracy and progress, and the Marxist idea of total revolution and the complete emancipation of the working class in a future communist society. These were the ideas that have, according to Lyotard, underpinned the development of Western modernity. From a postmodernist perspective they are fictions, the ideas of particular interested groups who pass them off as being of universal interest and applicability. This view strikes a dim echo of Marx's account of ideology as a particular set of interests being represented as if they were for the good of everyone. However, unlike Marx who thought communism was the solution to all problems, Lyotard holds that there are no universal solutions. The best that can be done is to recognize that knowledge is always particular and subjective rather than universal and objective. Different groups each have their own 'narratives' – their own particular ways of understanding the world and themselves. What must be recognized is that each of these 'mininarratives' is in and of itself valid, and that one cannot be evaluated or criticized from the point of view of another, because no narrative is more 'objective' or better than another. What Lyotard is arguing for is a view of knowledge that sees it not as involving a natural scientific monopoly on truth, but as disparate, fragmented and involving multiple different viewpoints. The ideas of multiple truths rather than one truth, and fragmentation and chaos rather than unity and order, are key motifs, not only in Lyotard's work but also in that of most other postmodernist authors.

Lyotard's argument is that knowledge has always been made up of different and incompatible viewpoints, but that modernist knowledge – of which natural scientific positivism and Marxism are the two greatest exemplars – hid this from view. In this sense, 'postmodern' conditions of uncertainty and subjectivity have always been part of human life, and therefore part of modernity too, even if such a society was based on covering up this condition (Readings, 1991). But in the present day, 'most people have lost the nostalgia' (Lyotard, 1984: 40) for the absolute truth and certainty that modernist knowledge peddled. The implication of this view is that contemporary Western society could in that sense be characterized as 'postmodernity'. This is because it is a social order based around a postmodern culture, a culture involving a form of consciousness which has relinquished the illusions of modernist knowledge and has embraced the principles of doubt and a lack of certitude about anything.

There are two main problems with this view. First, in revealing something – the postmodern condition – that was not yet fully apparent, Lyotard has in fact acted like the sort of modernist, especially Marxist, intellectual that his theory is criticizing: he has shown us the 'truth' of the situation. This contradiction is at the heart of most postmodernist thought. Is not such thought itself a 'metanarrative' which claims to know everything and be a privileged perspective on all things? Faced with this paradox, many postmodernist authors have adopted an ironic stance, claiming that such paradoxes should not be sources of embarrassment, but should, rather, be embraced, because inconsistencies are what postmodernism is all about, rejecting a modernist compulsion towards order and consistency. Thus while modernist authors see such a paradox as a problem with postmodernism, postmodernist authors see it as a positive virtue. The second issue that arises from Lyotard's views is that he is claiming that now 'most people' have embraced the postmodern condition of uncertainty and scepticism. But what evidence does he have to back up this claim? How could it be proved? Are people in all different parts of society equally of this mindset? For many postmodernists, such questions are the products of an outdated 'scientific' mentality which seeks 'facts' when actually there are no facts (except, apparently, the fact that there are no facts). According to this kind of view, the search for empirical evidence is based on a fantasy of finding out the single and unalterable 'truth' about society (Game, 1991). For those who reject postmodernist ideas, one of the main flaws in this way of thinking is that it is based more on philosophical speculation and assertion than on empirically based investigation and proof. This issue is one of the main dividing lines between postmodernist and modernist versions of sociology, as we will see below.

Postmodern style

At the same time as Lyotard and other French thinkers were moving away from Marxism, certain people in the United States were also developing their ideas as to what might constitute postmodernism. The earliest developments in this direction actually occurred in the field of architecture. For certain younger American architects of the 1970s, modernist architecture was now on its last legs. In this field, 'modernism' was associated with styles that had been developed since the 1920s, which emphasized geometrical shapes, straight lines and plainness of design. Such architecture was primarily ascetic in temperament, eschewing bright colours and any forms that were not rigorously and mathematically 'pure'. The iconic figure in this kind of style was the Swiss architect Charles-Edouard Jeanneret, known as Le Corbusier (1887–1965), who had pioneered the modernist movement in architecture, which he saw as being based around a 'spirit of order' (Le Corbusier, 1986). Such modernists had thought that the world could be rebuilt in such a way as to eliminate disorder and to foster perfected forms of living. What had seemed revolutionary and hopeful in the 1920s had by the 1970s come to seem hopelessly utopian, overly authoritarian and politically corrupted. Many modernist designs for housing estates in America and Europe had become alienating slums rather than the utopian communities their designers had imagined (Jencks, 1984). This raised the question of what type of architecture would arise *after* modernism had expired? For a member of the younger generation of architects, such as Robert Venturi, architecture that was literally *post*-modernist would turn the values of modernism upside down. There would be a rejection of 'a view of life as essentially simple and orderly' in place of an outlook that saw things as 'complex and ironic' (Venturi, 1966: 23). There would be 'richness of meaning rather than clarity of meaning' (ibid. 17). This would be achieved by mixing and matching different styles that had hitherto been kept apart, in a collage effect marked more by disorder than by unity. Such architecture comprised 'a hybrid language' (Jencks, 1986) which took different styles and 'quoted' from them in an ironic and playful way. This knowing and worldly attitude is very often semi-serious, in ways that postmodernists see as contrasting strongly with the unsmiling seriousness of modernist art. Conversely, those of a more modernist bent see this kind of outlook as rather cynical and shallow, lacking a critical perspective on the world and the powerful groups that control it.

Postmodernist architects found a particular model of an ironical style in the architecture of the casinos of Las Vegas (Venturi et al., 1977 [1972]). This involved mixing together all sorts of apparently incompatible forms of design, from medieval castles to Roman amphitheatres. Each style is a pastiche of the original; that is, a deliberately phoney and plastic variant of that original (e.g. the blatantly unreal nature of the copies of castles to be found in theme parks like Disneyland). The commingling of all these faked styles, as occurs in Las Vegas, breaks all the rules of modernist aesthetics as to artistic 'purity' and keeping the 'high' ('serious' architecture) separate from the 'low' (kitsch reconstructions of Roman palaces, etc.). Postmodernist architects revelled in creating a look that destroyed all the modernist rules. This outlook perhaps signifies the most fundamental break between modernist and postmodernist ideas, not just in architecture but also in the aesthetic and artistic realm more generally. Whereas modernist aesthetics generally operated around the view that Art was separate from and superior to 'mass culture', postmodernist thought embraces the latter, seeing in it quite as much interest and value as the Art of modernism, if not more so (Huyssen, 1984). In fact, the idea of the artistic 'genius' as an innovative creator of completely 'original' and novel works is regarded as a modernist fiction. Postmodern art involves mixing together previously existing styles rather than forging wholly new ones. This view often goes together with a rather pessimistic view that all true originality is now dead and that all one can do is play around with the pieces that are left, reassembling them in various different permutations. Artists who make this kind of art, and who attempt to break down the Art/ mass culture distinction, are particularly enthusiastically assessed by postmodernists – for example, Andy Warhol's 'pop art', which drew upon such 'mass culture' imagery as comic books. Opening up cultural creation to everyone, rather than relinquishing it to a coterie of avant-garde artists and modernist critics, is one of the main themes of postmodernist cultural politics. For modernists sceptical of such claims (e.g. Jameson, 1992 – see below), such a viewpoint actually makes artistic creation even more subordinate to commercial impulses, making it more of a commodity in the capitalist marketplace than ever, and reducing artistic achievement to the level of developing new images for advertising purposes. The politics of whether postmodernist art is politically progressive or retrogressive is one of the central disputes between modernists and postmodernists.

Las Vegas appealed to the postmodernist architects not only because of its chaotic interpenetration of different styles, but also because they saw its architecture as challenging modernist assumptions about meaning. The bright, gaudy façades of the casinos hid utterly bland modern buildings that actually housed the hotel and gaming spaces. Everything was therefore on the surface – there were no hidden meanings to be discovered and decoded. One recurrent theme of postmodernist thought, not just in architecture, is that since every cultural artefact has shallow rather than profound meanings, there is actually no meaning at all. This is the more pessimistic strain in postmodernist thought. It is countered by a more optimistic viewpoint, a part of postmodernist thinking also emphasized by the American architects writing in the 1970s. Rather than having no meaning, postmodern culture is alive with multiple meanings, and manifold interpretations of them are possible. Postmodernist architecture was meant to be more 'democratic' than its modernist predecessor. In the latter, the meaning of the design had been the prerogative of the architect. But given the multiple combinations of style and effect in postmodernist architecture, the meaning was now supposed to be less fixed, more open to the interpretative imaginations of members of the public who could look at a postmodernist building and find their own meanings within it. The same is often held to apply to other phenomena that are held to be part of postmodern culture: there is a vast array of meanings, and no fixed or 'correct' way to interpret them. No one group has the monopoly on what to do or how to do it. Everything, from ways of thinking to cultural styles, is in flux and constantly subject to change, and all certainties are thus redundant in a new age characterized by an abundance – if not an *over*-abundance – of information. This is one of the key themes developed by Jean Baudrillard, as we will now see.

Semiosis unlimited

In chapter 5 we examined the development of the semiotic and structuralist ideas of Saussure by, in particular, Roland Barthes (1983 [1970]). Much postmodernist thought is inspired by post-structuralist philosophy, which has been developed by certain French philosophers since the 1960s. As its name suggests, post-structuralism is a more radical version of the original structuralist notions of Saussure (Jameson, 1972; Harland, 1987). If one wishes to understand postmodernism, one *must* have a good grasp of semiotic ideas, otherwise matters will remain very unclear indeed (and we would therefore recommend the reader unfamiliar with semiotic ideas to peruse chapter 5 before continuing with this chapter).

Post-structuralist thought has been particularly developed by another French philosopher, Jacques Derrida (1978). Although rejecting the label 'postmodernist' to describe his own position, it has been Derrida's aim to take to the extreme some of Saussure's original contentions. Saussure had suggested that the signifier was arbitrary in that it got its meaning from its difference from all the other signifiers in the linguistic system of which it was a part. Nonetheless, Saussure argues that each signifier refers to a certain signified, the concept of a thing in the 'real' world. By contrast, there is a movement in post-structuralism in the direction of a stress upon the *completely* arbitrary nature of the signifier. Post-structuralist thought cuts off the signifier's relationship with the signified, and thus with the 'real' world. The *only* source of the signifier's meaning is seen to be its place in the system of signifiers, for now the signifier is no longer seen to have any attachment at all to 'real things'. Indeed, 'real things' are in fact not 'real' at all – they are the products of the images produced by signifiers. We can never have direct access to 'reality', but always see it through a particular cultural lens, that lens being systems of signifiers. To claim otherwise is to indulge in a false 'metaphysics of presence', as Derrida calls it, the spurious idea that we can have direct and unmediated access to a pure 'reality'.

Immanuel Kant argued much the same thing – without the terminology of signifiers – two hundred years ago. The more radical possibility that Derrida points to is that there is no 'real world' at all, just our images of it. And those images are arbitrary because they are not rooted in anything that would guarantee their reality. On this view, language and other significatory systems are not means of representing the world, for they only ever signify themselves. That is to say, signs never point to the 'real' – because there is no such thing – but to other signs, signs referring to signs that refer to other signs, in a never-ending chain. As Derrida (1978: 281) puts it, 'the play of signification . . . has no limit'. There is therefore no escape from systems of signs into 'reality', because the latter is the product of signs.

Having eliminated the 'real world' by seeing it as purely the product of different systems of signifiers, Derrida highlights what he sees as the wholly arbitrary nature of these systems. Each system – each 'language' – is unstable, subject to shifts and changes, such that the meaning of each signifier is constantly open to alteration and disruption. The result of this situation is that each signifier does not relate to one signified, but potentially to a multiplicity of them. In other words, signifiers are *polysemic* – they possess multiple meanings – rather than *monosemic* – having only one, stable meaning. There is only ever *difference*, that is, meaning is generated through the differences between different signifiers, rather than on the basis of mirroring 'reality'. In order to press this point home, Derrida argues that the true nature of language rests not in *speech*, which seems to be connected to 'reality', but in *writing*, which is a wholly arbitrary series of semiotic conventions. Writing does not represent the 'outside world'. Instead, and this is the most radical implication of Derrida's position, writing creates its own multiple, plural, transient realities. The world is made up of different 'texts', each of which has constantly shifting and multiple meanings. From this point of view, meaning is never stable and the significance of anything is never fixed. This is because all meaning is conventional and arbitrary, a situation which means nothing is guaranteed or inevitable. Here we have a semiotic version of Lyotard's ideas about uncertainty and multiplicity being characteristic of a postmodern situation.

Baudrillard beyond Marx

One of the major theorists of postmodernism, Derrida's countryman Jean Baudrillard (b.1929), takes up these post-structuralist ideas and applies them to the sorts of phenomenon that Roland Barthes had pioneered the semiotic study of – fashion, advertising, the mass media and so on. Baudrillard could be described as a post-structuralist, postmodernist semiotician. His contribution has perhaps been the most provocative analysis of the contemporary cultural condition from the postmodernist camp. His early works (1996b [1968]; 1998 [1970]) analysing interior design and consumerism bear strong similarities to Barthes' work on related issues. These see contemporary life as one where Nature has disappeared altogether, being replaced by systems of signs, 'a world no longer given but instead produced' by endless series of signifiers (1996b [1968]: 29). In such a world all objects are manufactured commodities, deprived of any 'natural' meanings they may once have possessed. There is also a Marxist component in these arguments, which holds that while semiotic analysis is best for understanding the meanings embodied in phenomena such as the consumption of consumer goods, there also has to be a more Marxist dimension which looks at how and why these goods are made. But by the early 1970s, Baudrillard had relinquished this balance between semiotic and Marxist approaches in favour of a wholly semiotic analysis of culture, and one which bore more and more resemblance to the version of semiotics suggested by Derrida.

The reason for this shift was Baudrillard's rejection of what he saw as the unacceptable assumptions built into Marx's views. Like other 'post-Marxist' thinkers at this time, Baudrillard was keen to bury Marxism and move on to new styles of thinking, the most productive of which seemed to be the type of post-structuralism associated with Derrida. Baudrillard (1975) rejects Marxist analysis for two main reasons. First, it is out of date. This is because Marx analysed the production of *commodities* but did not account for what would occur in a later phase of capitalism, namely the production of *signs*. Signs are now the most important part of capitalism's functioning, rather than the material objects the signs connote. What Baudrillard has in mind here is that in contemporary consumerism, it is not the object itself that has any value but the sign attached to the object. For example, it is not the pair of jeans that are important but the designer label on them, for it is the label 'Versace' or 'Gucci' in which resides their value. The second reason why Baudrillard rejects Marx's views is that he sees them as being founded on a myth. This myth is that ultimately the value of any product can be explained by the amount of labour that went into making it. But for Baudrillard, as we have just seen, the value rests in the sign of the object, not the object itself.

The implication of this position is that there is no such thing as a 'true' human need for things, which Marx had designated as the *use-value* of particular objects. Instead, according to Baudrillard, there is only ever what Marx had called *exchange-value*, the arbitrary value of objects dictated by fluctuations in price on the capitalist market. Baudrillard goes further and sees exchange-value not as involving economic prices but as signs, the value of the object residing in its sign, such as its designer label. Given this, contemporary capitalism is seen by Baudrillard to be much more irrational, uncontrollable and beyond human intervention than Marx had ever dreamed of (1975: 122). Baudrillard sees this system as operating according to its own inscrutable logics rather than due to the manipulations of a ruling class. The idea of class-based domination is dropped in favour of seeing systems of signs as wholly autonomous of other factors and running away from human control, towards ever more frenzied forms of directionless change. This is Derrida's doctrine of signs, applied to the modern economy, with systems of signification being seen to have, as it were, a life of their own. Here we have the postmodernist version of the modernist idea of alienation, formulated by many authors, including Marx himself (see chapter 1), where what were once human products are viewed as taking on their own independent existences and coming to threaten and dominate the people who made them.

A further ramification of Baudrillard's critique of Marx is that there is now no distinction between truth and falsity, as Marx had thought. There is no 'reality' based in use-values to compare to the falsity of exchange-values. Instead, the whole value of a thing rests in its sign, which is completely on display. In this way, Baudrillard attempts to argue that the Marxist critique of ideologies is now dead, because it relied on making a distinction between the surface appearance of a situation (its ideological representation) and the actual truth of it (the power of a ruling class to control the production of things). But in the age of the sign, everything is apparent, and every meaning is on the surface and entirely open to view. There are no hidden depths to be penetrated. If this situation cannot be grasped in a Marxist fashion, then a new way of thinking is required to grasp it. This involves 'surfing' along the surfaces of systems of signs, watching how they mutate and transform themselves, without seeking to find a more profound truth behind or below them, because there is literally nothing beneath them. Analysis must accept that all that exists are surfaces with no substance whatsoever.

Baudrillard beyond the real

In his work in the 1970s and after, Baudrillard took these ideas about how the contemporary capitalist economy works and applied them to the analysis of culture in general, especially that produced by the mass media, which he sees as the dominant form of culture in the contemporary West. It is the utterly unpredictable, irrational and unbridled nature of systems of signs in contemporary media culture that Baudrillard (1983b) emphasizes. He is concerned to 'surf' the waves of the systems of signs, taking in the undulating transfigurations of meaning that the media produce. He refers to the media's production of meaning as 'simulation'. This does not involve the creation of false systems of images, because 'truth, reference [to "real" objects] and objective causes [of events] have ceased to exist' (ibid. 6). Particular signs do not now stand for the objects they apparently refer to. Rather, because real objects no longer exist, the sign creates the object. As Baudrillard's mentor Derrida (1978: 280) put it, the 'substitute [the sign] does not substitute itself for anything which has somehow existed before it'. Such signs Baudrillard dubs *simulacra* (singular: *simulacrum*). These are images that fabricate a reality that has no existence except for their fabrication of it. In other words, instead of reality generating images of itself, images now create reality. Baudrillard refers to this situation as the *hyperreal*. Contemporary culture is characterized by hyperreality, a reality created solely by shifting and unstable systems of signs. There is nothing 'real' being hidden by this hyperreality. The only reality is the fabricated reality produced by systems of signs. The contemporary world is characterized by a 'death of the real'. But this situation was not intended or brought about by any particular social group. It was the result of the uncontrollable proliferation of signs in a media-dominated world (Baudrillard, 1996a).

Just as the postmodernist architects were drawn to Las Vegas as an emblem of their aesthetics of depthlessness, so too is Baudrillard attracted by sites that seem best to demonstrate his ideas. Disneyland is an obvious exemplar of the notion of the hyperreal, with its faked European palaces and the proffering of a make-believe world of cartoon characters. However, Baudrillard regards Disneyland as having a distinct social function (despite the fact that the idea of a particular entity having a social function is part of a modernist style of sociology that he otherwise rejects). Disneyland is not simply an ideological hymn in praise of the American way of life. Instead, it exists in order 'to conceal the fact that it is the "real" country, all of "real" America, which *is* Disneyland . . . Disneyland is presented as imaginary in order to make us believe that the rest is real' when in fact they have now entered the condition of hyperreality (Baudrillard, 1983b: 25). Thus the sign that is Disneyland does not hide social reality as Marxist analysis would claim – that it covers up the exploitative nature of American capitalism – but, rather, what it hides is the fact that there is nothing to hide, because America is now in a hyperreal condition where all meaning lies on the surface.

American dreams – and nightmares

It is this aspect of the United States that Baudrillard goes in search of in his book *America* (1994 [1986]), which is a travelogue of a tour he took around the country. The book is in one way a pastiche of a certain genre of travel writing, whereby Europeans journey around the United States offering their impressions as they go, the most famous author in this genre being Alexis de Tocqueville (see chapter 3). Baudrillard offers up some explicitly Eurocentric views, which may or may not be intended as self-parody, such as '[w]e in Europe possess the art of thinking, of . . . subtlety and conceptual imagination' whereas Americans apparently do not (Baudrillard, 1994 [1986]: 23). If this is intended ironically, then it can be seen as part of the overall style of the book, which is made up of disconnected observations and fragments, rather than of a sustained and rigorous argument. In writing this way, Baudrillard intends to escape from modernist definitions of what an 'argument' involves – that it should be rigorously logical – in favour of a style that itself grasps the fragmented nature of postmodern culture. As he puts it, it 'is not enough for theory to describe and analyse, it must itself be an event in the universe it describes' (1987: 99). He thus attempts to put himself in the position of the tourist, who skims over the surfaces of American culture, just as the television viewer skims over systems of depthless images. Touring in a car across the desert, Baudrillard goes in search not of 'social and cultural America, but the America of the empty, absolute freedom of the freeways, not the deep America of mores and mentalities, but the America of desert speed, of . . . the marvellously affectless succession of signs, images, faces, and ritual acts' to be found whilst travelling at speed on the open road (Baudrillard, 1994 [1986]: 5). For Baudrillard, America is a series of empty signs and surfaces that signify nothing except themselves. It is a country where hyperreality reigns supreme.

According to Baudrillard, America indicates the way the rest of the world is going under conditions of hyperreality. In a hyperreal situation, information and meaning are paradoxically both utterly clear and totally incoherent. Baudrillard refers to the former situation as the 'obscenity' of communication. Because there are no hidden depths to images, and all their informational content is on the surface, their meaning is utterly apparent. They are 'obscene' in the same sense as pornography is obscene: everything is totally clear, nothing is hidden, there are no disguised subtleties or nuances. In this sense, hyperreality is a condition where 'things are clear' because everything is on the surface (Baudrillard, 1990b: 181). But in another way, hyperreality is a situation in which things become ever more unclear. This is because there is so much information being produced by the media that it all starts to make no sense. Baudrillard is here thinking of the masses of different TV channels available in America, all pumping out vast amounts of information, in many cases twenty-four hours a day. These different messages combine into an informational jumble that makes no sense at all. Baudrillard (1987) describes how the viewer deals with this informational overload using the terms 'vertigo' and 'ecstasy'. Confronted by so much meaning, the individual feels a sense of dizziness, as if peering into an endless abyss from a great height. That abyss is the televisual world from which all meaning has leaked. The senses are stimulated so much that nothing makes sense any more. The 'ecstasy of communication' lies in the 'dizzying over-multiplication' of messages, where 'all sense is lost' (Baudrillard, 1990a: 9). Contemporary societies pay witness to a total 'collapse of meaning' where processes of signification point to nothing at all except a desert of information where nothing lives.

In such a situation, the mass media no longer operate as propaganda tools. The identification of certain messages as propagandistic requires finding a 'true' situation that they disguise. But that distinction is precisely what is obliterated by a condition of hyperreality. This is the background to Baudrillard's suggestion that the Gulf War of 1991 *did not happen* (Brooker and Brooker, 1997). Such a media spectacle played on the world's television screens like a film or video game, rather than as coverage – biased or otherwise – of a real event. The series of signifiers that purported to describe what was really happening actually signified only themselves – images referring to other images that refer to other images. In addition, argues Baudrillard, propagandistic messages no longer have any effects on the audience. The 'masses' no longer respond to any sorts of message, being wholly disinterested and impassive. They are no longer duped because they believe nothing at all. Information provided by the mass media 'flows through them . . . but diffuses throughout them without leaving a trace' (Baudrillard, 1983a: 2). They are neither alienated – because there is no 'reality' to be alienated from – nor are they deceived – because deception is impossible in a world where all meanings are both immediately understandable and yet beyond comprehension. On this view, life is an empty plane where nothing means anything any more. The realm of 'social life' has been erased in favour of the phantasmagoric play of signs that is the condition of hyperreality. The image that catches this best is a room full of chattering television screens, sending out vast amounts of meaningless information, and playing only to themselves.

The limits of hyperreality

Baudrillard's ideas are difficult to assess sociologically because what he is doing involves a deliberate rejection of 'mainstream' sociological accounts of society and culture. Just to criticize his views from the standpoint of such a sociology could be dismissed by Baudrillard and one of his followers as betraying an out-of-date modernist standpoint (Owen, 1997). His highly poetic and allusive style of writing is set up in opposition to what he sees as modernist attempts to describe social and cultural conditions 'scientifically'. What seem like outrageous claims – for example, that the Gulf War did not happen – are meant as ironic and playful provocations. So denouncing them as irresponsible – for example, by asking why he ignores the fact that tens of thousands of people *died* in a war he sees as having played out like a movie – seems like the product of an old-fashioned, over-serious moralism. To a great degree, one either buys into Baudrillard's project completely or one does not. Either you accept that signs are completely arbitrary in a condition of hyperreality and that postmodern theory's fragmented style is the best way of describing this condition, or you do not. If you do not, then Baudrillard's claims can be assessed in light of the criteria held by more 'modernist' forms of sociology as to what makes a convincing or unconvincing argument (Lash, 1990).

If looked at in a more sceptical light, it might be said that some of Baudrillard's ideas are useful, if decoupled from his overall hyperbolic position. For example, the condition of hyperreality, where signs endlessly refer to other signs in such a way as to fabricate a new form of 'reality', has obvious utility for thinking about the internet and cyberspace. In fact, Baudrillard was pointing to a realm of wholly semiotically constructed realities long before use of the World Wide Web really took off in Western countries. In that sense he can be said to have been highly innovative in anticipating important new cultural phenomena, both the unreal spaces of the cyberworld, and also perhaps the mental dispositions of those who spend a great deal of their time navigating it. If hyperreality is applied not to *every* aspect of contemporary culture but to a specific phenomenon like the internet, then from the viewpoint of a modernist sociology it has a certain use in helping us to understand an area that hitherto had not been explored thoroughly.

However, a modernist viewpoint also has a good many more critical things to say about Baudrillard's ideas. A glaringly obvious issue from this point of view is the almost complete lack of empirical evidence behind most of his assertions. Baudrillard of course would dismiss this criticism as a residue of modernist delusions about how 'scientific' ways of thinking should operate. But if no evidence is to be furnished, then we are left only with the possibility of believing his assertions because they are *his* views. This arrogates to Baudrillard himself the authority to say what he likes without being challenged, because to challenge him on the basis of a lack of evidence is to be seen to be in the grip of modernist delusions about 'proof'. This potentially means that Baudrillard is arrogantly saying that he is beyond criticism, the kind of high-handed attitude towards having a monopoly on the truth that he and other postmodernists criticize in sociology, Marxism and other modernist ways of thinking. In fact it could be argued that Baudrillard is actually a modernist himself. His emphasis on developing a particular style in order to grasp things better betrays a typically modernist obsession both with finding an 'appropriate' writing style (see the case of Adorno in chapter 2) and using it to represent the true 'reality' of the phenomena being written about. John Docker (1994) argues that Baudrillard's study of America is actually highly modernist in tone, because it seeks to reveal to (European) readers the 'truth' of the United States, and is based on a metanarrative that claims to explain everything we need to know about that country.

The problem of proof applies to all of Baudrillard's claims. In particular, how does he know that people experience the output of the mass media in the ways he asserts? In what way can he actually *demonstrate* – rather than merely *claim* – that the 'masses' are as he says, utterly passive and completely unfeeling? This begins to sound like a version of the empirically uninformed tirades against both the mass media and their audiences formulated by the mass culture critics of the mid-twentieth century, and they were modernists *par excellence* (see chapter 3). They too argued that audiences were wholly passive and that mass media output was completely trivial if not wholly meaningless, arguments that sociologists were not slow to challenge on empirical grounds. Baudrillard (1983a: 5) argues that the 'masses' are beyond sociological investigation, beyond division into categories of class, race, gender and so on. But why should we take his word for that? There is much compelling evidence (e.g. Morley, 1992) to suggest that mass media audiences are in fact divided on these sorts of lines. From the viewpoint of an empirically based sociology, Baudrillard's work seems more like a speculative *philosophy* of culture rather than a grounded *sociological* approach. If the latter is regarded as being more informative than the former, then Baudrillard's ideas would seem to have to be taken with extreme caution.

This is particularly so if one wishes to stick with a more modernist view of the relationship between cultural analysis and politics. Critics of Baudrillard sympathetic to Marxism argue that his work is marked by the same profound pessimism to be found in the writings of other post-Marxists. He has relinquished the intellectual's critical edge in place of, at best, a passive contemplation of the systems of signs he gazes at, and, at worst, he is in effect an uncritical apologist for capitalist society. By denying there is any 'real' underneath the surface, he denies the truly exploitative, cruel and harsh realities of contemporary capitalism that are, for Marxists, at the root of all forms of culture today (Kellner, 1989).

Towards the 'real'?

Whether this critique is accepted or not depends on one's own attitudes towards the utility or otherwise of Marxist theory. Nonetheless, the Marxist response to Baudrillard does highlight what many, including non-Marxists, would take as the limitations of his approach, which focuses on systems of signs to the exclusion of most other factors. In the previous chapter we examined some of the problems associated with semiotic approaches to the study of culture, especially that developed by Roland Barthes. Baudrillard's version of these ideas arguably has all the same flaws. By concentrating on systems of signs that apparently generate themselves, semiotic analysis downplays both how these systems are made *by people* and how they are responded to *by people*. In his earlier, more Marxist work, Baudrillard acknowledged that all the systems of signs in consumer society were the 'product[s] of . . . human activity' (1998 [1970]: 26). But this awareness of how human beings make signs, and how potentially they can change them and make their own uses of them, was dropped when the Marxist emphasis on the production of goods was rejected in favour of seeing sign systems as fully possessed of a life of their own. A perspective which focuses on how cultural goods are really produced challenges this inattention to how signs are actually made (see chapter 8). The ways in which signs are received by people in particular social contexts is likewise downgraded in much semiotic thought, and especially in Baudrillard's version of it. For example, he deliberately searches for the systems of empty signs he sees at the heart of American life, rather than for the 'deep' America that involves looking at actual communities and observing what people actually do and think. Baudrillard arguably has to suppress these aspects of everyday life because, being ordinary and prosaic, they do not fit with his theory's emphasis on the extraordinary and hyperreal. Again, in his earlier work, he was aware of the need to examine the ways in which signs are dealt with in particular locales and by particular people. At that point he claimed that each social environment is a 'directly experienced mode of existence, and it is very abstract indeed to apply to it' ideas that do not take account of how people actually *live* their lives (1996b [1968]: 27). This was a theme he in fact explored briefly in the mid-1970s, when he argued that contemporary people have learned how to 'play' with signs in ironic and knowing ways. This is a different, more active account of people's practices than what can be seen as the highly pessimistic account offered in the analysis of the passive, unmoving 'masses'.

This kind of more positive approach to everyday life has been taken up by authors who also see themselves as postmodernist in orientation. Such authors are implicitly critical of Baudrillard's general emphasis on systems of signs over what happens at the everyday level. In this kind of postmodernism, what is identified and celebrated is postmodernity's capacities to free up the lives of ordinary people. Under the conditions of a postmodern society, people are less constrained to act in the ways that are demanded by modernity's rules and regulations. A common theme here is the claim that the barriers between 'high' and 'low' culture have now been abolished, opening up a new, more fluid arena of cultural activities that mix elements of what were once considered completely opposed forms of culture. The mass culture theorists in the mid-twentieth century had also identified such a process (see chapter 3), but whereas they condemned it, postmodernist authors celebrate it. This situation is argued to have effects at various levels. At the level of cultural goods, postmodern mass media – television being the most cited example – are said to mix up and mingle cultural forms of all varieties, from 'high culture' goods such as recordings of classical music concerts, to the 'lowest' forms of tabloid programming. In so doing, a typically postmodern collage of cultures is presented to the audience (Twitchell, 1992). That audience itself, contrary to the opinions of both mass culture theorists and Baudrillard, is, it is argued, fragmented into a plurality of different groups and is therefore postmodern in character (Fiske, 1989a, 1989b). At the social level, class boundaries, and the taste cultures that went with them (see the argument of Gans in chapter 3), have broken down, engendering a more actively participatory cultural realm where those previously excluded from 'high culture' can now join in (McRobbie, 1994 [1989]). Less respect is accorded to 'high culture', popular culture now being embraced by 'ordinary people' as a wholly valid form of experience that no one need feel ashamed of (Chambers, 1986). Finally, at the level of identities – which much postmodern thought focuses on rather than on the Marxist notion of ideologies – subjectivity in the contemporary period is argued to be fragmented, fluid and open. Such a postmodern identity is never fixed, static or based on one key element – e.g. seeing oneself only as 'working class' – as these identities are not tied to social structures but are more free-floating, and open to change and alteration. They involve multiple affiliations and orientations, even when these are logically contradictory according to modernist criteria of logic – e.g. seeing oneself as Indian *and* British, or as black *and* lesbian (Minh-Ha, 1989; Hall and du Gay, 1996).

Some of these views have been put forward by scholars in the field of cultural studies, a discipline where semiotic and postmodernist ideas have come to be particularly influential. From a more orthodox sociological perspective, such claims can be challenged as being more indicative of how these theorists would *like* contemporary society to be, rather than as reflecting what it is *really* like. In the next chapter, we will see how the French sociologist Pierre Bourdieu has argued that all the empirical data available point to a situation whereby class remains central in European countries as *the* central source of social inequality. As a result, divisions between class-based taste cultures, between 'high' and 'low' cultures, generally remain in place, as do class-based identities to some extent. Even in the United States, historically less class-bound than European countries, inequalities in wealth and status are still major aspects of the social scene (Lamont and Fournier, 1992). From this kind of sociological perspective, the claims of the postmodern theorists above owe more to their political dispositions – the desire for a more open social order, and sympathy for the practices of 'ordinary people' – than to the actuality of capitalist societies today. In their defence, it might be argued that the social structural sociology of Bourdieu and others like him is not well equipped to grasp the kinds of change going on in culture to which postmodern approaches are sensitive, especially the fluid nature of contemporary identities. Whatever side is right, both of them have focused attention on the realms of sign production, social structure and everyday life, three areas that Baudrillard's position, which focuses on sign systems alone, is arguably ill-equipped to deal with.

Marxist ripostes

The response of Bourdieu to the more optimistic claims above is part of the sociological backlash against postmodernist thought, which perhaps reached its highest levels of influence in the late 1980s and early 1990s. Both Marxist and non-Marxist writers have attempted to deal with what postmodernism has to say, especially as to whether contemporary society is best characterized as 'postmodernity'. This has involved rejecting the postmodernist critique of sociology which sees it both as hopelessly ill-equipped for dealing with the new cultural conditions of postmodernity, and as having no authority to proclaim the 'truth' about such matters, being merely one more 'narrative' that is no better than other types of knowledge. For sociologists who have refused to accept this critique, a *postmodernist sociology* in the style of Baudrillard and others is not required. Rather, what is needed is a *sociology of postmodernism*, which interrogates phenomena often described as 'postmodernist' using the conceptual tools of (modernist) sociology (Featherstone, 1991; Bauman, 1992).

For a red-blooded Marxist like Callinicos (1989), postmodern theory is a socially uncritical form of thought that hides the realities of capitalist society by passing the latter off under the much nicer label of postmodernity. This kind of view assumes that postmodernism has nothing to teach Marxism, which is already fully equipped for the job of telling us what contemporary society is 'really' like. For those of a less enthusiastically Marxist persuasion, this might seem like a maintenance of a dogma rather than a genuine openness to new conditions heralded by what has been described as postmodernity.

For other Marxists, postmodern ideas do in fact have some truth about them. For David Harvey (1989), 'postmodern' is an accurate description of the kind of cultural 'superstructure' now produced by the capitalist economy. On this view, Baudrillard's emphasis on constantly and rapidly changing systems of signs as characteristic of contemporary culture is correct, except that Baudrillard fails to account for how and why these phenomena are produced. For Harvey, they are the products of a culture which is itself a creation of a socio-economic 'base' centred on 'flexible accumulation'. By this, he means a new mode of capitalist production based on novel ways for companies to make profits. At the level of production of goods, this type of capitalism responds very quickly to opportunities in new markets, laying off workers in one country when production has to be moved to another to exploit emerging opportunities. In addition, other ways of generating profits are engineered through instantaneous electronic flows of communication across the globe, such as through playing currency markets, corporate raiding and asset-stripping (Harvey, 1989: 163). The result of this economic situation, characterized by dizzyingly rapid movements of both information and people 'in ways that seem almost oblivious of the constraints of time and space' (ibid. 164), is the kind of culture often described as postmodern, one which is in permanent flux and transition.

The criticisms of the original 'base' and 'superstructure' model of Marx can also be put to Harvey's theory (see chapter 1). It reads cultural phenomena purely as the outcome of economic factors. In so doing it denies that 'postmodern' culture could have come about for any other reason than that of new forms of capitalist activity. It therefore seems to exclude the possibility that postmodern culture is anything other than an ideological smokescreen of capitalist society, the very idea that much postmodern thought has been trying to move beyond. Nonetheless, it does highlight a fact ignored by many postmodernist thinkers. An account of capitalist *modernity* as involving rapid change and constant chaos was emphasized by Marx a century and a half ago (Berman, 1983). Such a focus on novelty and uncertainty is not itself new or unique to postmodernist theory. Postmodernists have arguably taken up Max Weber's more pessimistic assessment of modernity as a bureaucratic 'iron cage' in order then to differentiate it from postmodernity and show it as a more open form of social organization. The 'unique' nature of postmodernity would perhaps not have seemed so compelling if Marx's emphasis on the creative, open and changeable aspect of modernity had also been accounted for (Rojek, 1995).

We saw in chapter 2 how Adorno and Horkheimer had attempted to overcome the problems of Marx's base and superstructure model with the idea of 'totality', which viewed cultural, social, political and economic factors as being combined with each other to form a complex unity. The contemporary American analyst, Fredric Jameson, accepts that there is indeed something called 'postmodern culture', and uses the ideas of the early Frankfurt School in order to explain why such a culture has the characteristics it does. Adorno and Horkheimer (1992 [1944]: 126) had, arguably, anticipated postmodernist themes of hyperreality back in the 1940s, when they had warned of how the Culture Industry creates a situation whereby '[r]eal life is becoming indistinguishable from the movies'. Jameson (1992: x) holds that his own theory has the 'same relationship to Horkheimer and Adorno's old "Culture Industry" concept as MTV . . . bear[s] to fifties television series' – that is, it is an upgraded and updated version fitted to analyse postmodern conditions. For Jameson, postmodern culture is both the expression of and part of the totality that makes up 'late capitalism'. This is the new, faster and more devastating form of global capitalism in which transnational companies, tied to no particular home country, are involved in economic transactions characterized by a 'vertiginous new dynamic' (ibid. xix) of production for consumer markets round the world. Postmodernism describes a situation first pointed to by Adorno and Horkheimer, where every single aspect of culture has come under the sway of capitalist commodification processes.

At the level of stylistics, this situation is embodied in particular types of cultural good which are primarily pastiches of previous cultural styles. Jameson singles out for special attention films made in the mid-1980s, such as David Lynch's *Blue Velvet*, which involved deliberately 'fake', hyperreal representations of small-town America in the 1950s. In such movies the 'real' 1950s – of puritanical sexual morals, Cold War repression of communists, rampant racism – are ignored, replaced by the flat surfaces of images taken from such 1950s television series as *I love Lucy*. The past is reduced to being a mere succession of stereotypical images – houses with white picket fences, cars with fin-tails – and sounds – rock and roll hits from the period. As a result, a real history of oppression and exploitation is conjured away in favour of Disneyland-type hyperreal surfaces. The problem with this kind of culture, argues Jameson, is that it encourages audiences to forget how things really were and are. Thus postmodern culture is a form of 'opiate of the people', encouraging a passive acceptance of the status quo. In line with the usual problems of this kind of Frankfurt analysis of audiences (see chapter 2), Jameson can be accused of having very little evidence to back up claims about the effects of such films, ironically enough placing his empirically inadequate position rather close to that of Baudrillard. Moreover, the kinds of film he focuses on can hardly be said to be representative of all cultural goods produced today, therefore calling into question how good an index they are of contemporary cultural production. Postmodernists point to the vast diversity of different forms of culture being produced under what they see as postmodern conditions, so one type of film (nostalgia pictures) in only one medium (cinema) could hardly be said to be indicative of all cultural production in contemporary society. In addition, the reasons why they were made at all may have only a tenuous connection to issues of postmodernism (see chapter 8).

Postmodernity or late modernity?

Outside Marxism, sociologists have attempted to reassert sociological concepts as the way of understanding contemporary social and cultural dynamics. Foremost among this group is Anthony Giddens (1990), who argues that sociological tools remain crucial for analysing the current situation. These methods of analysis remain relevant because Western societies today are in a condition of 'late' or 'radicalized' modernity, rather than postmodernity. Late modernity involves an extension and deepening of the tendencies of modernity first identified by the classical sociologists, including both cultural fragmentation and economic integration at a global level. Late modernity in particular involves further transformations of time and space, such that individuals' experiences are reshaped in novel ways. The sense of time becomes less rooted in local contexts when, for example, one can travel to the other side of the world in half a day. Local spaces become modified by global forces, such as the mass media bringing flows of information from distant parts of the world into a person's living room. These are the structural and institutional bases which create the sense of fragmentation and dispersal that postmodernists describe as postmodern culture, but which is in actual fact the experiential corollary of late modernity.

Although such conditions can increase feelings of unease and dislocation, they are also potentially empowering, because they can contribute towards a heightening of the *reflexive* capacities of individuals, that is, their ability to reflect on and question the cultural forces that have shaped their ways of thinking. A good example of this kind of scepticism towards accepted habits and modes of conduct is given by John Urry (1990) in his account of a certain type of contemporary tourist, the *post-tourist*, who seeks neither the mass culture pleasures of traditional holiday 'resorts' nor the supposed cultural 'authenticity' that self-described 'travellers' desire. Instead, the post-tourist sees tourism as a game, aware that no tourist site is genuinely authentic but has been packaged and commodified. Far from being horrified by this, the post-tourist revels in the fact that what he or she is presented with is so fake. While this disposition could be seen as the result of a fluid postmodernist identity centred around an ironic and playful view of the world, an analysis deriving from Giddens would see it as ultimately deriving from late modernity's opening up of individuals' capacities to reflect critically on their own tastes and preferences. From this point of view, mentalities such as that of the post-tourist are mislabelled if characterized as postmodern. They are modern through and through, legacies of modernity's capacities to encourage self-awareness and to escape from the dead weight of cultural traditions.

Conclusion

It is difficult to come to any firm conclusions about the strengths and weaknesses of postmodernist ideas as to society and culture, mainly because there are so many different emphases within postmodernist thought. Quite simply, postmodernism and postmodernity mean different things to different people. Some of the different strands directly contradict each other, most notably Baudrillard's view on the 'masses' and the more positive responses by other postmodernists as to the cultural capacities of 'ordinary people' under postmodern conditions. Condemning or praising one form of postmodernism or one particular postmodernist theme does not necessarily mean supporting or denying the usefulness of another form of post-modernism or another theme. In addition, one has to enter into the complex debates as to whether postmodernist thought is superior to more mainstream forms of sociology. If we are living in a wholly new social and cultural environment that is substantially different from that which is describable as 'modernity', then postmodern theory would seem to be a plausible form of thought. But if we are not living within a period that involves a radical break with modernity, then the tools of sociology first forged by the classical sociologists would seem to be of continuing relevance. Which way this dilemma is answered in turn depends on what we take 'modernity' to mean – the repressive social order first characterized by Max Weber, or the more ambiguous society, open to constant change and characterized by uncertainty, as emphasized by Marx.

Despite these difficulties, we can say that, if one accepts the con-tinuing utility of sociology as it has been historically constituted, postmodernist ways of thinking about culture run up against various problems. In particular, the often highly speculative accounts of con-temporary conditions proffered by postmodernists such as Baudrillard often seem untroubled by the need for empirical proof of the claims that are made. A tendency also to downgrade social and economic factors in favour of focusing almost exclusively on cultural phenom-ena is, furthermore, a flaw that runs through much postmodernist writing, a problem inherited from the indebtedness to the style of semiotic analysis outlined in the previous chapter. Conversely, post-modernism has perhaps done mainstream sociology a great service by challenging it to avoid complacency and to rethink itself in light of emerging, often novel, social and cultural conditions. The identifi-cation of things that might be happening to us in a highly mediated, information-saturated world, issues that had not yet been fully dwelt upon by more orthodox means of study, is perhaps the most useful legacy postmodernism has had to offer the sociology of culture.

7

In the French Style: The Sociology of Pierre Bourdieu

Introduction

Pierre Bourdieu (1930–2002) was undoubtedly one of the foremost sociologists of the late twentieth century. Professor of Sociology at the Collège de France, his highly influential ideas become a force to be reckoned with not just in his native country, but also on the global sociological scene. Bourdieu's ideas on society, culture and the nature of sociology itself stand at the present time as one of the major trends in how sociologists seek to understand the world around them. His voluminous writings range in scope from ethnographic studies of French and Algerian peasants, through theoretical excurses on the nature of social action, to detailed analyses of contemporary cultural habits and attitudes. Bourdieu's notion of 'habitus' has become one of the most central – and controversial – terms within contemporary sociological discourse. No study of the sociology of culture written today would be complete without reference to his analysis of cultural matters.

Bourdieu's position is a blend of a diverse set of influences, drawing on, among other things, Marxian, Weberian, Durkheimian and semiotic ideas in order to produce a distinctive form of sociology (Lane, 2000). In this chapter, we will set out the key components of Bourdieu's claims both as to how the sociology of culture should operate, and his substantive findings about the nature of modern cultural life. We begin by examining the key concepts Bourdieu utilizes in his rethinking of sociology as a whole. This is followed by an outline of Bourdieu's analysis of the nature of class-based forms of cultural taste. We look in turn at each of the main forms of taste that Bourdieu has delineated. His ideas are not without their critics, and it is to challenges of his position, and his defence of it, that we turn our attention in the closing section.

Rethinking sociology

Understanding what Bourdieu says about cultural matters involves examining the ideas and concepts his brand of sociology involves overall. Bourdieu took up the ideas of previous sociological analysts and reworked them with the aim of overcoming what he saw as the dualistic assumptions that had hitherto crippled sociological thinking. Throughout its history, he argued, sociology had been split into rival groups of thinkers, who tend to champion one side of the divide between more 'objectivist' approaches to the study of culture and society, and more 'subjectivist' approaches. The former include Marxists and Durkheimians, the latter include action theorists and ethnomethodologists. Bourdieu's sociology is an attempt to overcome this objective/subjective divide, and the other binary oppositions that derive from it, such as social structure versus social action, and materialism versus idealism. Bourdieu's aim (1988b; 1990a: 34–5; see also Wacquant, 2000) was to draw upon the more productive ideas of previous thinkers in both main camps, and in so doing to get beyond the either/or logic that says one must have *either* an objectivist *or* a subjectivist approach to the study of social life.

Bourdieu's approach imposes certain demands on the sociologist. First, in terms of methodology, he or she must not sever the fundamentally important relationship between empirical data, research methods and sociological theory. Each is a crucial element of the research process (Bourdieu et al., 1991). Diverse methods of research, from large-scale surveys to detailed ethnographic studies, must all be used in order to investigate a particular situation (Inglis et al., 2000). This emphasis on having to justify one's theories with empirical evidence distances Bourdieu's approach from more speculative positions like that of the early Frankfurt School, which mainly rest content with pure theorizing rather than insisting on empirical proof. Bourdieu claimed he was not interested in making grand theoretical claims. Instead, he wished to examine particular areas ('fields') of social life in particular contexts at specific times, for example the field of education in France in the period 1960–90. From these particular studies he would venture to make more general claims, such as accounts of how education systems in modern Western countries in general might work. But he remained insistent that his approach was contextually sensitive and was not a form of arrogant grand theorizing.

Second, in terms of the focus of sociology, analysis must relate different factors to each other. For too long, argues Bourdieu, sociology has been made up of separate areas of study, like the sociology of religion, sociology of education, sociology of the family and so on. The problem with this academic division of labour is that it neatly parcels up into distinct areas ('religion', 'family') aspects of life that are in reality all connected with each other (Bourdieu and Passeron, 1979: vii; 1990 [1970]). In place of this, sociology must seek to relate all these various factors, showing how each affects the others. As we will see below, Bourdieu argues that the sociological study of culture cannot be adequately carried out without examining how culture is instilled in the young by systems of education. So the sociology of culture must simultaneously be a sociology of education too. Drawing inspiration from both Marx and Weber, Bourdieu argues that all aspects of social and cultural life must be examined in terms of the power relations they embody. On this view, the sociology of culture is always an exercise in the sociology of power (Honneth et al., 1986: 46). Bourdieu sees the main aim of sociology in Enlightenment terms (see chapter 1) – as the exposing of the power of elite groups in society, power that would not be fully open to view without the sociological exposure of it. Lurking under all cultural forms, therefore, are the forms of power held by elites, a situation sociology seeks to reveal.

But unlike the traditional Marxist approach to culture, which sees it as a mere offshoot of allegedly more 'fundamental' socio-economic factors, Bourdieu wants to view culture in a way that synthesizes 'materialist' and 'idealist' approaches (see chapter 1). He has given particular attention to cultural matters, but not because he sees them as 'privileged explanatory factor[s] for understanding the social world' as postmodernism does (Bourdieu, 1993b: 36). Instead, the aim must be to show how culture is intertwined with relations of material power, whilst demonstrating that cultural factors have their own logic of operation. The sociology of culture must recognize that cultural factors are irreducible to other (material) factors, whilst nonetheless being thoroughly permeated with relations of power (see Garnham and Williams, 1980).

Thinking the habitus

In a similar way, Bourdieu saw his version of sociology as over-coming the dualism between 'objectivist' approaches that stressed the importance of 'social structure' in shaping what people do, and 'subjectivist' approaches which emphasize the ideas and values of social actors in motivating their actions. He claims these approaches are reconciled within the key concept of 'habitus'. This is a term that is supposed to capture how social conditions act upon and shape individuals' actions, as well as demonstrating that people are – within certain limits – capable of creative responses to the situations they find themselves in. Habitus (plural: habitus) refers essentially to the characteristic ways of thinking, feeling, acting and experiencing shared by all members of a certain group of people. The term is defined by Bourdieu (1992a: 172) as a 'system of practice-generating schemes which expresses systematically the necessity and freedom inherent in' the collective conditions of life of a certain group of people. The point to grasp here is that 'habitus' concerns both the socially shaped dispositions *and* creatively generated activities of a particular group. It describes the conjunction between how social structures act on individuals in that group, *and* how they respond to the social situations they find themselves in.

A habitus of a given group of people therefore involves both objective and subjective, passive and active, and material and ideal elements. The more 'objective' and 'material' aspects of a habitus are the life conditions of the group (whether they are wealthy or not, whether they possess power or not, and so on) and the socialization processes that make people part of that particular group. Socialization involves the inculcation of the habitus into the individual. From birth, individuals are instilled with the values, ideas and attitudes of the group. But such socialization is not just a *mental* process. It is much deeper than that, because the individual's *body* gets shaped by socialization too, such that it takes on the characteristics of that group's habitus. Such tacit forms of inculcation embed in the very physical constitution of an individual 'the most automatic gestures or the most apparently insignificant techniques of the body [such as] ways of walking or blowing one's nose, ways of eating or talking' (Bourdieu, 1992a: 466). Overall then, early socialization in child-hood, which is reinforced as the child grows up within the group, means that both the mind and body of the individual are shaped in ways typical of the group's characteristic ways of thinking and act-ing. Even the tiniest details of an individual's behaviour, such as the way they stand, will be reflective of the ways in which other members of the group do these things. In essence, the habitus generates the particular ways of thinking and acting that members of the group live their lives by.

It is not just the case that everyone in the group tends to think and act in similar ways. It is also the case that each individual person's various activities will tend to 'fit' with each other in terms of style (Bourdieu, 1977: 143). By this, Bourdieu means that there are *homologies* (similarities) between each of the activities a particular person carries out. For example, if a person is a member of group X, he or she will have been socialized into the habitus of group X. Each of the activities he or she engages in will be done in the style of the habitus of group X. He or she will play sports in ways that are like the fashions in which other group X individuals play sport, and will have tastes in food generally like everyone else in group X. The connection between apparently different activities such as playing sport and eating food is that the group X person will have a *group X-style* way of doing these seemingly unconnected things. Quite literally, then, a habitus involves a person living a particular *lifestyle*, where everything they do, no matter how apparently unconnected, is expressive of that lifestyle.

For the most part, individuals are not fully aware that everything they do is expressive of the habitus they have been socialized into. Instead, the habitus disguises itself by making people see the world in common-sense ways, and these ways do not allow actors to turn their critical reflection upon the habitus. People just experience things 'as they are', generally without realizing that what they experience as 'common sense' is actually the result of their habitus. This common-sensical view of the world is what Bourdieu (1977: 80, 164) calls *doxa*, the unexamined ways of acting that are at the root of each group's mode of being in the social world. This situation has important ramifications for how cultural *tastes* operate. The particular tastes and dispositions seem to the individuals who possess them as 'natural' and 'inevitable'. This is because such tastes are part of the socialization into a particular group's habitus. This socialization profoundly roots tastes and preferences not just in the individual's mind but in their *body* too. Hence tastes are experienced as if given by 'nature' (e.g. a person thinks she just naturally hates the taste of meat) but are actually products of society (the group to which she belongs is vegetarian). Thus according to Bourdieu (1977: 78), who is here extending the ideas of Roland Barthes, there is nothing either natural or inevitable about a particular set of tastes and dispositions. They are *arbitrary* in the sense that they are the product not of 'natural' dispositions but of socialization into the group's style of life (habitus). What Bourdieu means by the term *cultural arbitrary* is a situation in which a particular group's tastes and preferences are *misrecognized* by people in that group or in other groups as natural and inevitable, rather than as the products of (mostly unconscious) social training. As a result of being so influenced by their habitus, people forget that their tastes could have been different, a situation that would have occurred if they had been socialized into the habitus of another group.

On the other hand, there are certain ways and circumstances in which individuals *are* aware, albeit dimly, of their habitus. In the first place, they realize, mostly in a vague way, that their personal preferences and ways of acting are not completely unique to them, but are in fact in some ways similar to the tastes and activities of other people who are felt to be 'like them'. For example, there is a sense that this is what 'people like us' eat, or drink, or enjoy. Second, individuals are aware that their own tastes and activities, both in purely personal terms and in terms of the vague sense of group membership just mentioned, are *unlike* the habits of other groups. In fact, the distinctiveness of 'our' tastes only really becomes apparent when we compare them to the practices and tastes of other people, 'them'.

The games that people play

Although the tastes and preferences of particular individuals are produced by their habitus, and so are rooted in the unconscious aspects of a person's existence, nonetheless the person subjectively experiences those tastes and acts on the basis of them. Bourdieu therefore emphasizes that the habitus has for a particular individual both unconscious and conscious aspects. This is the basis for Bourdieu's understanding of people's actions. These are generally neither the result of fully conscious decisions on behalf of the individual, or of wholly unconscious dispositions compelled by social structures. Instead, actions are produced at a *semi-conscious* level. Bourdieu replaces the word 'actions' with the term 'practices' to describe this situation. In their practices, individuals are partly aware and partly unaware of the implications of what they are doing. They are both living out the dispositions that their habitus demands, whilst fitting the habitus's demands to the social situations they find themselves in. Individuals are therefore always simultaneously *both* relatively passively expressing the demands of society *and* active shapers of their own activities.

Bourdieu describes how this paradoxical situation operates in terms of seeing the generation of practices as being like *playing games*. Each social context a person finds themselves in involves playing the game associated with that context. That person is a *player* in that particular game. For example, within the university context an academic 'plays' at being an academic, enacting all the things that are expected of academics. In playing a particular game, individuals are in some ways not aware of what they are doing, but are aware of what they are doing in other ways. To be able to play the game at all requires the person to feel the game is worth playing. The feeling held by actors that the game is worth playing is referred to by Bourdieu (1998c: 77) as the *illusio* of the game. This is the sense both that the game is worthwhile participating in, and that the stakes involved in playing it are worth pursuing. On the whole, this feeling is embedded in the unconsciousness of the actor, within the habitus, with the importance of the game never fully being reflected on. Mostly, people just accept that the things they do are what they do, as they live within the common-sense terms (*doxa*) of their everyday lives. To that extent, practices are generated at an unconscious level. On the other hand, individuals *are* aware of what they are doing to the extent that they are capable of engaging in particular forms of interaction with others, that is, of being able to 'play' the particular game in question (for example, the academic taking part in a seminar, and knowing what are the appropriate things to say, and the acceptable ways of saying them). The practices – the forms of playing – that the game involves are to that degree consciously engaged in.

So practices – the playing of different types of social game – have both unconscious and conscious elements, and thus are *semiconscious* in character. Bourdieu (1992b; 1993b; 1998c; 2000) refers to this situation as being characterized by *practical reason*. It describes how, without fully reflecting on it, actors have a *feel for the game*. If a particular 'move' *feels* right, it will be carried out, but if it *feels* wrong, it will not be. These feelings derive from the socially instilled criteria of rightness and wrongness embedded in the habitus. In their playing of games, actors are constantly deploying *strategies*: these are actions oriented towards achieving something without the actor being fully aware (or fully unaware) of what he or she is trying to achieve (Bourdieu, 1976). The basic point here is this: practices (ways of playing games) are generated in ways beyond the full conscious awareness of actors, as they are produced by the habitus of the group a particular person is part of. But the actor has a 'practical' (semi-conscious) sense of how to play the games they are involved in. In that sense, they have some, but not full, control over what 'moves' to make in the playing of the games. They have a *practical* rather than fully reflective sense for the game being played.

The idea of playing games lies at the heart of Bourdieu's sociology. The games metaphor describes not only how Bourdieu sees the way people act, but also is the way that he describes social structures. The *shape* of modern societies can be described as involving the main types of different games that people play. In chapter 1, we saw how the classical sociologists such as Spencer and Durkheim described modernity as involving a high level of *structural differentiation*. Modernity was split into different, relatively autonomous and separate spheres: the areas of politics, religion, education, art and so on. Bourdieu describes these different areas as *fields*. Sociology examines two things. First, the relations *between* different fields, e.g. the effects that religion and politics have on each other (Bourdieu, 1998b; Bourdieu and Haacke, 1995). Second, what goes on *inside* each field. This involves looking at the particular game being played by the people who operate within that field (Bourdieu, 1987). If a field is separated from other fields, the game will have its own particular *rules* (legitimate ways of playing the game), *resources* (the assets on which players can draw to try to win the game) and *stakes* (the benefits that come from being successful in the game).

The idea of game playing is also the way Bourdieu describes social – and cultural – hierarchies. In each game, there are players who are more or less successful. Their success or failure as *individuals* depends to a great extent on how powerful in the game is the group (the 'team') they are part of. Each group has a certain amount of resources at its disposal, upon which individual members can draw. Resources in each game are unevenly distributed, and this affects the success or otherwise of particular players. Some groups have a lot of resources useful for playing the particular game, whereas other groups are at a disadvantage because they lack those resources. Some groups have a lot of resources that make them successful in some games, but which cripple their performance in other games, because those resources are not appropriate in those games (metaphorically, knowing how to play tennis well won't help you in a golf match).

Within each game, the conscious aim for each player, of course, is to be as successful as possible. But at a less conscious level, the aim is for one's own team – the group you are part of – to be successful too. The team's continuing success helps your own performance in the game. This point is generally never fully consciously thought about by each player, but it underpins their playing at a deep level nonetheless. Each game, then, can be seen as a constant competition between different teams. The aim of each team is to be dominant over the other teams in the game. As the game never stops, the objective of each successful team is to retain its dominance in the game over time, while the purpose of less successful teams is to try to improve their position, and overthrow the domination of those teams that have up until then been successful.

Bourdieu (1991b) took this idea from Max Weber's analysis of the game being played in the field of religion. In that game, there is usually a dominant team, the Established Church, that tries to monopolize control over all religious activities in a particular country. It does so by defining its own practices as legitimate – as the 'true' religion. It also defines the activities of other religious groups (teams) as illegitimate, as sacrilegious or as superstition. But these other teams, sects or cults, negatively labelled by the Established Church, try to topple the power of the latter by resisting these definitions and in turn labelling the Church's practices in a very negative way. Sometimes these attempts to usurp the authority of the powerful team can be successful. But mostly the dominant team retains its power, because it has more resources at its disposal in the competition. In particular, the Established Church's damning judgements on the other teams are often regarded by most of the players in the game as carrying more authority than its rivals' negative descriptions of it. If the dominant team says that the play of the other teams is either unacceptable or of a low level of skill, then that judgement will generally be accepted, thus degrading the position of those teams in the game, and keeping them in a subordinate position over time. The authority that a powerful team has to make such judgements in turn derives from the power it has accrued for itself. From this derives one of Bourdieu's key claims. Although it is not *inevitable*, it is *probable* that a team that has a lot of power (i.e. many of the relevant resources) in a particular game will retain its power. Conversely, teams that have low levels of power (i.e. small amounts of the appropriate resources for the game) will continue to be subordinate.

The main principle of social power is that, although there can sometimes be upsets for the powerful and unexpected triumphs for the weak, *the winners keep winning and the losers keep losing*. A particular social group that fields teams that are winners in most of the games played in a society is likely to be the dominant group overall in that society. It retains its dominance because each of its teams in the various games has resources at its disposal that are appropriate for the particular games being played. Each of these teams are *more skilled* (or can *define* their play as being more skilled) in the playing of these games than the other teams involved, these latter deriving from other, less powerful, social groups.

Rethinking class

For Bourdieu, class is the main type of social group in modern societies. But he views classes in ways that are significant reworkings of the understandings of previous sociologists.[1]

The dominant class in society retains its power because its members are equipped with resources that allow them, individually and collectively, to keep triumphing in the various different social games. By contrast, the dominated classes are kept subordinated because their members keep losing the games they are involved in. Bourdieu refers to the resources that dictate why particular classes keep winning social games and others continue losing as *capital*. Capital involves both *resources* – the ways in which actors can play the game – and *stakes* – what players are playing the game to get more of, i.e. the advantages that can be won or lost by playing the game.

There are two main types of capital (Bourdieu, 1993b: 32–3).[2] The first is *economic capital*, the level of monetary resources a person has at their disposal. The second is *cultural capital*, the cultural resources that a person possesses in the playing of different games. This is the amount of socially recognized prestige attached to a person's various practices. It is also the amount of knowledge and know-how a person has about 'high' cultural matters ('art', 'literature', etc.). It is partly embodied in a material form, in the educational qualifications a person possesses. The higher the diploma a person has, the richer he or she is in cultural capital. There are also particular types of cultural capital.

[1]   Bourdieu's understanding of the nature of social class owes less to Marx's definition of class in terms of a group's relationship to the relations of economic production, and more to Max Weber's definition, which sees a class as a group of people with shared sets of opportunities in a labour market. In some senses, then, Bourdieu is as much indebted to Weber as he is to Marx.

[2]   There is also *social capital*, the amount of resources a person has in terms of networks of relations with other people (how many people they have relationships with, and the *type* of people that they are involved with in one way or another). However, this form of capital is less crucial in the writings of Bourdieu that we are here assessing, and thus we will leave it out of the discussion.

Particularly important here is linguistic capital (Bourdieu, 1991a), which involves the varying levels of social validation given to different ways of speaking, these forms of speech being class-based. For example, in modern European countries, working-class speech is less socially valorized than middle-class speech, hence a middle-class person possesses more linguistic capital than a working-class person. The general point here is that the habitus is the lifestyle of a particular social class. Being possessed of a particular habitus (e.g. a working-class habitus) equips one with a certain amount of cultural capital, with certain habitus providing more cultural capital than others.

The *amount* of capital of each type that a person possesses, mostly on the basis of their class habitus, is the basis for how successful they might be in the game in each particular field they are part of (Bourdieu, 1990a: 117).[3] It is not just a question of *how much* capital of each type one has at one's disposal. Relative success or failure in a field depends also on whether the *type* of capital one has is appropriate to the particular game being played within it (Bourdieu, 1993b: 34). Thus a large amount of economic capital might be very useful in a direct way within the field of *big business*, where the reputation of a businessperson rests on how much economic capital he or she possesses (or how much other players in the game *think* he or she possesses). But in another field, where cultural capital is the most important factor, economic capital might only have an indirect benefit for its holder. For example, in the field of art production and consumption, cultural capital (for example, being seen to know a lot about different types of art) is much more useful than a direct utilization of economic capital. This is because the other players in the field might find it 'vulgar' if someone is seen to be throwing lots of money about buying paintings without apparently knowing very much about art. It should be emphasized that Bourdieu argues that individual players feel these things mostly in semi-conscious, *practical* ways, rather than as a result of explicit awareness and reflection.

Generally speaking, those with high levels of cultural capital will succeed in games where cultural capital is the main factor, whereas

---

[3] For Bourdieu, a person's habitus very directly determines the level of that individual's cultural capital, at least in childhood and adolescence. The relationship is more indirect between habitus and a person's level of economic capital. For example, on this view, a working-class person could have a large income relative to other working-class people. But this person was brought up within the terms of the same habitus as these others, and so retains, despite his or her higher income, a similar (i.e. small) amount of cultural capital.

those with low levels of cultural capital will tend, naturally enough, to perform poorly in such games. The person with high levels of cultural capital will have an advantage over the less well equipped player because he or she will both feel more 'comfortable' playing that type of game and will know how to enact more effective techniques of play than the less advantaged player. This is because his or her habitus (based on high levels of cultural capital) will be attuned to the cultural capital-based type of game. Conversely, the player without much cultural capital will feel 'awkward' in a game he or she feels unfamiliar and uncomfortable with. This feeling derives from the player's habitus being badly attuned to the nature of the game, the game requiring familiarity with cultural matters that person has had little or no exposure to. He or she has not been 'trained' appropriately for this type of game, whereas someone raised within the habitus of a class with high levels of cultural capital will feel very comfortable with it indeed. The players with high cultural capital can always 'trump' other players in the game because they have the confidence not only to try out more 'daring' forms of play, but also because they have the power to define their own forms of play as being intrinsically better than the play of less advantaged players. Again, this facilitates a situation where the winners keep on winning. This process tends to get repeated over time. The people in winning teams (dominant classes) pass their economic and cultural capital to their children, who are nurtured within a habitus that teaches them how to make effective use of this inheritance in the games they will play in their lives. Conversely, those without much initial advantage in social games tend to lose constantly, and so pass on this disadvantage to their children. This is how the class structure of modern societies gets constantly reproduced.

From the basis of the two main types of capital that are important in modern societies, and the amount of cultural and economic capital possessed by particular groups, Bourdieu constructs a typology of the different classes that compete with each other for power in such societies. The result is that, very generally speaking, there are three major class groupings, each possessed of different levels of economic and cultural capital:

1   *Upper-midddle class*. This contains two subgroups:
    • economic bourgeoisie: intermediate cultural capital, high economic capital;
    • cultural bourgeoisie: high cultural capital, intermediate economic capital.

2   *Lower-middle class (petite bourgeoisie)*: intermediate to low cultural capital, intermediate to low economic capital.
3   *Working class*: low cultural capital, low economic capital.[4]

The upper-middle class, made up of two subgroups, tends to be the group to which belong the individual winning players in the various games played in modern societies. People from the lower-middle and working classes are almost always the losers. We will now look at each of these groups in turn.

The field of cultural consumption

Bourdieu's major work *Distinction* (1992a) is concerned with the system of cultural tastes and preferences that existed in France in the 1960s and 1970s (see Garnham, 1986). A series of research methods were employed to study this field, including large-scale surveys on cultural practices which yielded statistical data, interviews with people from different social backgrounds, and ethnographic observation of the lifestyles of different class groupings. In this way, Bourdieu hoped to achieve a comprehensive picture of French cultural life of the period.

However, more general conclusions about the nature of this type of field in other countries can perhaps be drawn from the study. The implications of this French study for cultural life in other modern, Western societies are twofold. First, Bourdieu's analysis of the role of culture in a modern society hinges on his identification of the cultural

---

[4]   The outlines of these groups should be seen only as very approximate representations of social reality. Bourdieu was quite aware that the complex nature of modern societies can hardly be represented by such a simple model. However, he believed complexity could be modelled by looking at the different groups *inside* each of the classes outlined above. He breaks down each of these classes into subgroups, each of which is defined on the basis of shared job types. For example, differences *within* the lower-middle class can be mapped by looking at varying levels of economic and cultural capital between, say, primary (elementary) school teachers and nurses. Both groups are part of the lower-middle class, and may have similar levels of income (hence roughly equal levels of economic capital), but there may be variations in the types and levels of cultural capital each group has (e.g. teachers may have a slightly greater preference for 'art' movies than nurses, because their profession is slightly more 'arty' and 'intellectual' than that of the nurses). But these variations will only be relatively slight in comparison with the very large variation between all lower-middle-class subgroups and the subgroups in the other main classes, such as the upper-middle class.

tastes of each of the classes described above. Each class's habitus produces a particular set of tastes that are distinctive of that class. These socially generated tastes, the product of socialization into the habitus, make individuals oriented to certain things that 'fit' with the habitus, and dislike other things that do not fit with it. This is Bourdieu's version of Max Weber's notion of an 'elective affinity' between a certain group of people and particular *types* of things (see chapter 1). Weber applied this idea to the appeal particular types of religion had for particular types of social group. Bourdieu broadens this to include *all* cultural goods, from food products to movies.

Second, each class-based set of tastes exists in a hierarchy, with the dominant groups having the most socially legitimate tastes and the subordinate groups having the least legitimate. This situation helps to reproduce the overall power of the dominant groups in society. The area in which this hierarchy operates is the *field of cultural consumption*. It is within this field that individual players from the different classes compete in the 'game' of attempting to define their own tastes and preferences as the most 'distinguished' and socially legitimate (hence the title of Bourdieu's book). Once again, it has to be emphasized that this form of *cultural class conflict* is generally carried out by individuals in more or less implicit, semi-conscious, 'practical' ways, rather than wholly consciously or deliberately. This distances Bourdieu's version of these issues from the classic account of Thorstein Veblen (1994 [1899]), which stressed the more conscious aspects of class-based snobbery. But although actors are not fully aware that when they disparage a particular taste or another individual's preferences, they are negatively defining the overall class from which that person comes, that is nonetheless the implicit effect of their actions. Taken together, all of the individual judgements made by dominant groups about the tastes of subordinate groups have the unintended effect of reproducing the cultural power of the dominant groups.

Bourgeois culture

One of Bourdieu's main criticisms of more traditional forms of Marxist analysis is that they tend to identify the dominant class in modern capitalist societies as unified and homogeneous, a class identified as the *bourgeoisie* (upper-middle class). Bourdieu argues that there are in fact two distinct groups that together make up this class. They were identified above as the *economic bourgeoisie* and the *cultural bourgeoisie*. These are two distinct groups because the members of each possess different types of capital. People in the economic bourgeoisie

– those working in the higher levels of big business – tend to have more economic than cultural capital. Conversely, those in the cultural bourgeoisie – such as authors, literary critics, people involved in the arts, top-level academics and so on – tend to have more cultural than economic capital. Between these two groups lie an intermediate selection of people who have high levels of both types of capital, those working in well-paid professions that nonetheless require quite large amounts of cultural capital to operate effectively, such as top-level lawyers and government officials (Bourdieu, 1998d). The relations between the economic and cultural bourgeoisie are characterized by both conflict and cooperation. On the one hand, each group is in competition with the other, seeing its own form of capital as the more prestigious. The typical judgements made by each group are that, for the cultural bourgeois, the economic bourgeois is 'vulgar' because all he or she thinks about is money rather than the 'finer things in life', while for the economic bourgeois, the cultural bourgeois often seems like an arty and pretentious idiot who has got very little grasp on 'reality'. Nonetheless, there exists, according to Bourdieu, a kind of truce between these warring camps when it comes to dominating the lower social classes. The power of both the economic and cultural bourgeoisie depends on them working together, intentionally and unintentionally, to keep the other classes in their place, and so both economic and cultural power are waged by *the bourgeoisie as a whole* against the lower classes. This situation creates what Bourdieu (1998c) calls a 'division of labour of domination' – the two parts of the bourgeoisie work together to retain their power, one keeping the lower classes down economically, the other culturally.

The field of cultural production is based around the ways in which lower groups are kept culturally subordinated, primarily by the cultural bourgeoisie. In *Distinction* (1992a), Bourdieu attempts to show how this is achieved. For him, the successful reproduction over time of the power of the cultural bourgeoisie rests in the very lifestyle of that group itself. That lifestyle is a product of the cultural bourgeoisie's habitus, which is socialized into children of this class from birth. The habitus itself is based on the material situation of this group, which Bourdieu characterizes as *a life of ease*. This class's existence is supported by relatively very large amounts of material wealth, and, as a result of 'the suspension and removal of economic necessity', the habitus is based upon a sense of 'distance from practical urgencies' (ibid. 54). The results of this in terms of the typical styles of acting (practices) of this group are that individuals generally feel very *at ease* with themselves and their surroundings, demonstrating an apparently effortless confidence in most situations. This is because these individuals are semi-consciously ('practically') aware of being highly refined, knowing how to act 'well' and not embarrass themselves, and aware that they will not encounter anyone with significantly more cultural capital than themselves. As a result, the cultural bourgeoisie exhibits a relaxed and 'easy' manner in the company of members of its own and other classes, a style of acting which is a fundamental source of its cultural power, due to the very nature of its habitus.

An 'elective affinity' exists between this habitus-based style of acting and certain types of cultural goods. Bourdieu's argument is that the habitus of the cultural bourgeoisie orients its members towards liking things that are characterized by their *superfluity* rather than by their *necessity*. For example, there is no pressing urgency that requires a cabinet to be made of a more expensive wood like teak rather than of a cheaper and less prestigious wood like pine. But upper-middle-class taste is oriented away from objects that express a direct function (a pine cabinet to keep cutlery in) and towards objects that express a certain sense of refinement and 'taste' (the teak cabinet is more than just a cabinet, for it is also felt to be a 'tasteful' object that blends well in the kitchen with other equally 'refined' objects). In other words, upper-middle-class taste is centred on a privileging in each object and practice of *form* (style) over both *function* and *content*.

This point leads us to the key feature of Bourdieu's sociology of culture. In chapter 1, we saw how Karl Mannheim argued that there was no reality in 'high culture' other than that it was the culture of the highest groups in society. An elite will define *its own culture* as being the best, the most refined, and intrinsically superior to other forms of culture. But the apparent superiority of that culture is purely a result of the elite defining it so. In addition, in chapter 5, we saw Roland Barthes argue that meanings never rest in things themselves. Instead, they are attributed to things by particular signifying systems. No object has intrinsic properties; rather, each thing takes its meaning from how it is defined by particular groups of people. Bourdieu takes these ideas and uses them to assert that cultural value does not reside in the cultural object itself, but is a product of a training into the dispositions of a habitus which makes a person like and desire that object. As a result, there is nothing *inherently* good or bad about so-called 'high culture'. This is simply the form of culture that the cultural bourgeoisie prefers because of its socialization into a particular habitus (Bourdieu and Passeron, 1990: 39). Because this group does not perceive its tastes to be merely the result of such socialization, it *misrecognizes* its own tastes as both *natural* and as *intrinsically superior* to other types of tastes. Group members exist inside a 'web of belief' whereby they take 'high culture' truly to exist, when actually it is only a product of the dispositions produced by their own habitus (Bourdieu, 1993a). There is nothing *intrinsically* superior or inferior about, say, a Shakespeare play or a television soap opera. The set of values that places products like these in a hierarchy is a product of the habitus of the cultural bourgeoisie. This is why Bourdieu refers to the culture and tastes of this group as the *cultural arbitrary* – it is an arbitrary culture in that it is purely the product of socialization and thus there is nothing natural or inevitable about it. But it is *experienced* by this class as if it were in fact a natural and unavoidable state of affairs. The apparent 'fact' that 'high culture' is a superior form of culture is actually based on a vast amount of social effort being expended to disguise the social origin of this state of affairs, namely that tastes for 'high culture' are purely a result of socialization into the habitus of the cultural bourgeoisie (Bourdieu, 1993a; 1996).

One of the reasons why members of the cultural bourgeoisie never regard the culture they favour as being arbitrary is that their belief in it is regularly 'topped up' by periodic reconfirmations. Just as a group of religious believers get their beliefs revitalized by regularly participating in religious rituals, so too do the cultural bourgeoisie engage in rituals that renew their beliefs as to the natural superiority of their own cultural tastes. This is achieved (but unconsciously rather than consciously) through visiting locales marked out as places where 'legitimate' culture can be accessed. These include art galleries and museums (Bourdieu and Darbel, 1991). Such places are essentially 'temples of culture', where the refined come to worship their own refinement. By being exposed to artworks and other forms of culture defined by the norms of the cultural bourgeoisie as legitimate, the practices of the habitus are evoked and reconfirmed. The cultural bourgeoisie feels comfortable in such places, because since childhood they have been made familiar with them and they know how to 'decode' (interpret) what is on offer inside. Familiarity with 'Art' means one can talk about it with confidence. By talking about the pictures viewed at an exhibition, bourgeois cultural muscles can be flexed. This can be done by giving opinions on what the paintings and sculptures 'mean'. The particular artist and his or her style can be connected to other artists and their styles. In general, members of the cultural bourgeoisie can produce a discourse that proves to themselves and others just how 'cultured' they are. Again, this is generally not being done deliberately as a way to 'show off' (although in some situations showing off is being done consciously), but is instead experienced by individuals just as a 'natural' thing to do. In this way, the capacity to produce refined judgements is constantly refreshed.

Trips to art galleries and other such places are actually ways in which the cultural bourgeoisie maintain their power. This is based on what Bourdieu takes to be the fact that the cultural bourgeoisie have the cultural resources (capital) to be able both to define their own preferred cultural objects as being intrinsically superior to other things they do not like, and to impose this definition on other groups. Taste, in fact, is a major source of elite power over the dominated. It is always, according to Bourdieu (1992a: 56), a 'practical affirmation of a . . . difference'. That is to say, taste can only ever operate negatively. A positive judgement ('I *love* that') only makes sense as a contrast to a negative judgement ('But I *loathe* that'). In modern Western societies, taste is based around a series of oppositions between the 'refined' cultural bourgeoisie and 'the people', the broad masses of the population made up of the working and lower-middle classes. Culture therefore is based around a fundamental series of oppositions, each with its roots in the fundamental distinction of elite/masses. These include culture/nature, refined/coarse, subtle/ unsubtle, worthy/unworthy, and so on. When a member of the cultural bourgeoisie condemns an object or practice as lacking in taste or refinement, they are implicitly (and mostly only semi-consciously) condemning 'the people', those who like that kind of thing. Bourdieu's study is called *Distinction* because it is an account of how each taste is based on a series of distinctions that are, in turn, based around those with high levels of cultural capital distinguishing themselves from those who lack such resources.

By accepting the views of the cultural bourgeoisie, other groups are pulled into their imaginary world too, regarding 'high culture' and bourgeois tastes as inherently better than their own cultures and preferences, the results of socialization into their own habitus. However, it is not the case that this was a knowing 'bourgeois plot' constructed deliberately to denigrate the other classes. It was the result of a whole series of unintentional and semi-intentional practices, the true nature of which cultural bourgeois individuals themselves were mostly unaware. Trips to art galleries are not generally *intended* as means of confirming cultural power. But the chatter of the 'chattering classes', as it is heard in galleries, theatres and other locales of 'high culture', is both a form of cultural superiority and an exercising of it, a set of practices only quasi-intentionally aimed at the maintenance of class power, but a reproduction of it nonetheless. The essential point here is that the contemporary cultural bourgeoisie genuinely believes in 'high culture'; what sociology reveals is that in so doing, its members have misrecognized the true nature of their own practice, which is based on the cultural subordination of other social groups.

Lower-middle-class culture

One of the groups that suffers as a result of cultural bourgeois power is the lower-middle class or the *petite bourgeoisie*. The habitus of this class is characterized by what Bourdieu (1992a: 318ff.) calls 'cultural goodwill'. This is a desire to imitate the cultural practices of the upper bourgeoisie, in order to gain the distinction that comes from being associated with such practices. For example, in the 1960s a popular activity among lower-middle-class individuals in France was photography. Such individuals collectively tried to define this practice as 'art' and therefore as something that was part of 'high culture'. But since the cultural bourgeoisie at that time defined photography as being less distinguished than the established arts such as painting, photography was still seen as the kind of thing that people with quite low levels of cultural capital are interested in (Bourdieu, 1990b).

Attempts like this by the lower-middle classes to gain distinction are doomed to failure, according to Bourdieu, for two reasons. First, the cultural bourgeoisie always manages to outmanoeuvre the lower bourgeoisie. The field of cultural consumption operates on the same basis as any other field: the odds are stacked against those with less capital, here cultural capital, because the players with most power are always able to define their own practices and favoured objects as being the most distinguished. The field of cultural consumption is like an eternal race, where it is almost a foregone conclusion that those who entered the game in a position of strength will win it (Bourdieu and Passeron, 1979: 94–6; Bourdieu, 1990a: 153). The lower-middle classes are doomed to fail to 'catch up' with their upper-middle-class rivals because they can always be subjected to the strategies whereby the latter define the practices of the former as being inferior. Moreover, even if the lower-middle classes take up a 'refined' activity, the very fact that they take it up and make it 'popular' means that it becomes regarded as vulgar by the cultural bourgeoisie, who themselves then relinquish it. For example, there are many instances of holiday resorts that were once 'exclusive', but which those 'in the know' no longer go to because they have become crowded out with 'tourists'.

Second, the lower-middle-class person lacks the apparently 'natural' ease and confidence of the upper-middle-class person, with the former always fated to feel uncomfortable and aware of potential acute embarrassments at the hands of his or her cultural superiors. The 'smoothness' of the petit bourgeois actor's practice is undercut by a constant fear of 'being found out', or made a fool of. Lacking the knowledge that is culturally valorized, he or she is compelled to compensate in ways that, to the upper bourgeois mentality, smack of *over-compensation*, such as showing off how much one knows about a particular subject. The upper-middle-class person thinks such activities rather vulgar, and this is because the lower-middle-class actor has not grasped fully the rules of the cultural game (showing off is done, but in discreet and subtle ways). In the game, the petit bourgeois is at best a mediocre player, who is not fully in control of the situations he or she finds him- or herself in, mainly because his or her training (socialization into the habitus) ill-equipped them for the competition, and because he or she is up against a team of better players, the cultural bourgeoisie. As a result, in Bourdieu's account, the petite bourgeoisie is condemned to a cultural life characterized by oscillation between pretension (trying to imitate upper-middle-class practices but failing) and retreat into admitting that they 'know their place'. This involves turning to practices defined by the upper bourgeoisie as semi-legitimate (such as photography was in 1960s France) or as outdated. The latter case refers to practices once popular among the cultural bourgeoisie but now relinquished by them (for example, listening to a classical music composer like Tchaikovsky or admiring a painter like Monet, who were once deemed part of 'high culture', but who are now defined as being rather 'common').

Working-class culture

Despite this situation of cultural subordination, the petite bourgeoisie possesses more cultural capital than the working class, and the former denigrates the latter's practices just as the upper bourgeoisie looks down upon those of the lower-middle class. In the field of cultural consumption, the working class is at the bottom of the heap, the weakest and least effective team in the overall game. It is the negative reference point against which both the cultural and the petite bourgeoisie define their cultural worth. Bourdieu (1992a: 57) considers that 'perhaps their sole function . . . is to serve as a foil' for the other groups in the field. If this is so, then the working class is destined never to escape its role as cultural pariah.

Bourdieu (1992a) characterizes the working-class habitus as involving the 'taste of the necessary'. The working class does not have a life of ease as does the upper bourgeoisie, because it is located nearer to the hard edge of social life, faced with a constant struggle to 'make ends meet'. One of the operations of habitus is to reconcile the subjective expectations of actors with what their objective life-chances are. The working-class habitus works by instilling a sense among working-class people that what society offers them is what they wanted anyway. For example, Bourdieu argues that working-class people buy less expensive forms of food, such as cheaper cuts of meat, not just because they do not have enough money to buy 'better' food, but also because it is that type of food that the habitus is orienting them towards liking. Even in a working-class household that is economically richer than others, the taste in food is still for these types of food, even though the family involved could afford to buy more expensive foods if they so wished. But they do not so wish because of the tastes instilled by their class habitus and background.

The practical sense of habitus-generated taste operates among the working class as a rejection of anything that seems 'too fancy' or seems incomprehensible and pointless. This applies to all areas of cultural life, from food to tastes in cultural goods. Much modern art is a case in point here, with Bourdieu claiming that his various forms of data indicate a widespread working-class rejection of the values of modern art, with its abstract figures and themes that are difficult to decipher ('It's just a pile of bricks . . .!'). Contrary to the upper-middle-class habitus, working-class tastes in culture privilege *content* over *form*, the *meaning* (the 'moral of the story') over the *style* (Bourdieu, 1992a: 32). On the basis of surveys designed to ascertain different class tastes in art, Bourdieu argues that working-class people like the kinds of object that those with large amounts of cultural capital dislike. These are artworks that have an immediately obvious meaning, where style does not 'get in the way' of the meaning by being non-challenging and clearly representing the subject-matter. A picture of a farmyard, for example, where you can see all the details and know immediately what the picture is about, goes down well with working-class people, whose habitus emphasizes immediately graspable meaning over form and style, whilst horrifying those above them in the cultural hierarchy ('How naive!', 'Ugh, so kitsch . . .!').

On Bourdieu's view, much of the cultural subordination of the working class stems from processes of *self-exclusion*. We mentioned above that he saw the sociology of culture as inseparable from the sociology of education. In his early work on education, he argued that the education system in modern countries operates with a systematic, but unintentional, bias against the working class (Bourdieu and Passeron, 1990 [1970]). Teachers tend to validate highly certain skills among pupils, such as the ability to 'talk well' or to 'think creatively'. But such things are the products of the habitus of the cultural bourgeoisie. As a result, teachers misrecognize as the talent of an individual pupil what are in fact the socially created habitus dispositions of the class from which they come. Conversely, because the habitus of the working class does not equip them with these skills, teachers define pupils from this class as less talented and clever. Working-class children take on this viewpoint as a self-image, coming to see themselves as 'naturally' less able than their more culturally privileged counterparts. In so doing, they *exclude themselves* from academic achievement by considering themselves as 'born failures'. Once more, most of this is unintended by both teachers and pupils, but the net effect is that the working class is kept in a condition of cultural subordination, especially because the academic qualifications that students from this group lack are an important form of cultural capital. Similar processes of self-exclusion from culture operate in other spheres, such as going to galleries and museums (Bourdieu and Darbel, 1991). It is not the monetary price of entrance that puts working-class people off from going to such places, because often admission is free or low cost. Instead, it is because their habitus has not equipped them with the skills to 'decipher' the meanings of these locales. Instead of being able 'effortlessly' to converse about art, they feel uncomfortable and out of place in such contexts. To avoid this form of cultural discomfort, they exclude themselves from attending, leaving the shrines of 'high culture' to the true believers, the cultural bourgeoisie. For these various reasons, the working class remains constantly culturally subordinated, having internalized a sense of inferiority in the face of bourgeois power, and thus remaining in a position of constantly reproduced impotence.

Assessing Bourdieu

All the various aspects of Bourdieu's writings have been subjected to criticism from a wide variety of perspectives. In this section we will give a flavour of these objections, and of the ways in which Bourdieu sought to defend himself. We will look at two main areas: the issue of 'determinism', and the nature of cultural hierarchies.

Problems of determinism

Some critics have claimed that Bourdieu's ideas are fundamentally flawed because his position is essentially a deterministic one. 'Determinism' can mean various things, most of them negative. We will here identify three main charges that have been made against Bourdieu. First, some (e.g. Martin and Szelenyi, 1987) have argued that Bourdieu, far from synthesizing 'materialist' and 'idealist' approaches to culture, is nothing other than an old-style Marxist economic reductionist, who illegitimately reduces cultural factors to economic ones. This charge, however, seems to be a difficult one to sustain. Bourdieu's defence would be that he has emphasized that there is an 'economy' of cultural forms, but that this economy is conceptualized as operating in ways different from how the *economic* economy (the field of business transactions) operates. Whereas the latter is based around economic capital, the field of cultural consumption is based around cultural capital. This field has a form and functioning of its own, irreducible to the operation of the field of the economic economy. The point of theorizing each of these areas as a *field*, in fact, is designed to overcome the base/superstructure model by insisting that culture cannot be reduced to economy, whilst simultaneously arguing that there is an 'economy' of culture with its own laws of operating, and that the operation of culture is *itself* a form of class power (Bourdieu, 1990a: 119). This is a sophisticated position that might be regarded as a distinct improvement on older Marxist models of culture.

Second, other critics claim that Bourdieu's notion of habitus is deterministic in that it seems to suggest that the habits, dispositions and tastes of particular people are created by early socialization into a class-based lifestyle, and remain fixed and unchangeable in later life. People seem to be 'programmed' to operate always in the way the habitus demands of them. Moreover, it seems that society never changes because individuals always seem to fulfil their socially designated roles (e.g. working-class persons always feel culturally inferior to others and thus remain forever in a situation of subordination). As a result, according to Jeffrey Alexander (1995), Bourdieu's vaunted balance between 'subjectivist' and 'objectivist' sociology falls heavily into the latter camp.

Bourdieu had various responses to this objection. He argued that his brand of sociology looks not at habitus alone but, rather, at how a person endowed with certain dispositions (from the habitus) operates within a given field at a given point in time. As the situation in the competition within the field changes – e.g. one 'team' becomes more successful and another team becomes less successful – the amount of success the individual may have in the competition might change (her team might be on a winning streak, as it were, so she herself may do better too). The basic point here is that Bourdieu does indeed see individuals as active and creative and not as mere passive puppets of their habitus. The different situations they find themselves in require creative responses on the behalf of individuals, so the habitus (which provides each person with a certain level of resources for the purposes of responding to events) *constrains* behaviour, but does not *determine* it.

A critic might further respond that this does not square well with Bourdieu's assertion that in all social games the winners win and the losers lose. But Bourdieu's defence would be that he had said this was a *tendency*, not an *inevitability*. Moreover, it is a tendency that can be verified with reference to empirical data. Bourdieu argues that it is a statistically provable *fact* that people with fewer forms of capital tend to lose the games they play, ending up with equally small amounts of capital and passing this disadvantage on to their children. As Bourdieu (1993b: 25) says: 'the degree to which the world is *really* determined is not a question of opinion: as a sociologist, it's not for me to be "for determinism" or "for freedom", but to discover necessity, if it exists, in the places where it is.' In other words, the sociologist's job is to show how the losers tend to lose and the winners tend to win, because that is what actually happens in modern Western societies.

While many people would agree with that view, it is not certain that the particular account Bourdieu gives of these issues is the *only* one that could be given. Although he emphasizes that his ideas are all based on empirical researches, doubt has been cast on how rigorously he has used empirical research methods such as large statistical surveys and ethnographic methods (Griller, 1996). More seriously, it is perhaps the case that Bourdieu's arguments are generally circular in form, and they fail to live up to the rigorous definition of scientific procedure he claims for them. Thus, he (1990a: 40–1) talks of his concepts as being 'open', as fluid guides to the research process rather than principles that determine in advance what one will find empirically. But the problem here may be that the key concept of habitus, with its emphasis on all practices of a class being generated by that class's habitus, might mean that empirical data are interpreted in such a way as to confirm this idea rather than in a way that might go against it. While Bourdieu attacked others for rigidly sticking to certain assumptions, he may himself actually have been even more dogmatic about the 'truth' of his own viewpoint (Verdes-Leroux, 2001). Nonetheless, this may not be a problem for other sociologists if they are of the opinion that Bourdieu's ideas are in fact useful for understanding their own particular areas of interest.

Problems of hierarchy

Similar problems about Bourdieu making very large assumptions arise in terms of what he has said about culture. In the overall conclusion to this book, we will examine the degree to which Bourdieu and other sociologists might be said to have a bias against the idea of 'high culture'. Here we can observe the various criticisms that have been made of his accounts of the class-based nature of culture. Some have argued that Bourdieu places far too great an emphasis on class as the major factor in modern Western societies. This objection takes two forms, one analytical, the other empirical. In the first instance, Brubaker (1985) argues that Bourdieu's definition of 'class' could be seen as a catch-all category, subsuming within it factors such as sex/gender, racial characteristics and age differences, and comprising an apparently homogeneous class, the individuals in which Bourdieu sees as producing practices all generated by a single habitus. A major dilemma then is how to deal with these factors: as wholly autonomous of 'class', or as related to class in some ways – but if so, in which ways? Bourdieu's work remains unclear on these dilemmas.

At a more empirical level, some claim that cultural life is not as stratified as Bourdieu makes out. He allegedly overemphasizes the cultural subordination of the lower classes (Honneth, 1986; Fowler, 1997). Frow (1987), for example, argues that Bourdieu's representation of the working class and its habitus fails to 'get inside' working-class culture, and only represents superficial elements of it. Bourdieu's analysis therefore inadvertently reproduces upper-middle-class attitudes about the working class – both that its members are more 'natural' and 'spontaneous' than the bourgeoisie, and that they are helpless victims in a vicious system – and passes this off as objective sociological discussion. For a critic like de Certeau (1984), Bourdieu's externalist analysis fails to grasp the lived experience of working-class culture, with all its ridiculing of elites and its various ways of dealing with power on a day-to-day basis. But just as Bourdieu has perhaps assumed that the working class is relatively culturally passive, critics like these assume that it is culturally active. There is no simple way to say which assumptions are more correct. In fact, as Bourdieu (1990a: 150–5) himself noted, these ideas tell us more about the academics who create them than about working-class people themselves. Moreover, in his later work, Bourdieu (1990a; see also 1998a, 1999) tended to emphasize that not all working-class people are *necessarily* condemned to the cultural scrap-heap. Some do escape this fate, through mechanisms of social mobility. Moreover, it is not guaranteed that middle-class individuals will be successful in the various games that they play because today there is also the possibility of *downward* social mobility, where individuals might end up with less economic and cultural capital than their parents had. However, Bourdieu added that the people who arise out of the working class are a minority, and that the majority of people born into the working class remain within it, and within the terms of subordination to bourgeois power which that lifestyle involves.

Other critics raise the possibility that Bourdieu's analysis might be now somewhat out-dated. In modern Western countries today, arguably, neither the cultural bourgeoisie nor high culture now enjoys as much authority as they once had. It may be the case that neither the lower-middle class nor the working class is as cowed as they were in the light of bourgeois cultural power. Some postmodernists, such as Twitchell (1992), argue that cultural distinctions of 'high' and 'low', and therefore by implication the class-based forms of power that upheld them, are now on the wane, if not in fact wholly defunct (see previous chapter). Admittedly, Bourdieu's researches were carried out before there was an explosion in the development of new communication technologies, such as satellite television, which may have appeal *across* classes. Nonetheless, Bourdieu would be able to respond to this view on the basis of empirical data. It may be the case that television and other media forms continue to be viewed and read on class-based lines, as evidenced by the fact that advertisers split audiences into socio-economic-cultural groups and pitch their wares at what are identified as 'niche' markets. Far from destroying class-based forms of consumption, new media may be appropriated into them, reproducing the older cultural hierarchies. For example, empirical researchers (e.g. Warde et al., 1999) have identified a group they define as 'cultural omnivores', who *seem* to break down older barriers of cultural taste by being interested in 'low' culture such as soccer and 'high' culture such as opera. But these are middle-class people who have both the economic capital to engage in a lot of different activities and sufficient cultural capital to allow them to feel comfortable in their cultural 'mixing and matching'. They can then use their more eclectic tastes as a way of distinguishing themselves from people whom they would regard as having rather 'conventional' tastes. This finding fits with Bourdieu's overall assertion that culture is always a means of marking certain groups off as superior to others.

Conclusion

The above controversies are about whether Bourdieu's arguments about bourgeois cultural power, first formulated in the 1960s and 1970s, are still relevant today. Similar debates have occurred which suggest that Bourdieu's model of cultural power in France does not fit other countries such as the USA (Lamont and Fournier, 1992). In the latter country, class relations have always been much more diffuse and less tightly hierarchical than in France. But Bourdieu never claimed that the model he developed in order to understand the French context was supposed to explain completely what occurred in other countries. He was quite aware that there are many different forms of social and cultural organization. He was also aware that times change, and that the model he first produced thirty years ago and more would have to be altered to fit new conditions. Therefore the question as to how useful Bourdieu's position is for us today is not about whether the 1960s and 1970s French model applies completely to Britain, America or anywhere else in the present day. Instead, the question involves asking how useful are his ideas in general in helping us to understand our own contexts. What utility do the concepts of habitus and field in particular have for us?

A point that would be conceded by many of his critics is that Bourdieu's sociological study of culture is an impressive achievement. Despite the problems set out above, it nonetheless encompasses a number of different areas – especially education and cultural consumption – that other approaches have not connected so systematically. It also bases analysis of these particular fields as they operate at particular times in a sophisticated theory of social action, which emphasizes how human beings are partly highly creative creatures responding to the contexts they find themselves in, but who nonetheless are to a large degree unconsciously shaped by their social backgrounds. It is the sheer scale of Bourdieu's endeavours that is to be admired, perhaps allowing us to forgive some of the more obvious flaws of his work. Bourdieu's main intention was to provide tools for analysing different cultural contexts in a way that drew on classical sociology but which was nonetheless new and challenging. In that regard he might be judged to have succeeded rather well.

8

The Land of the Free? Producing Culture in America and Elsewhere

Introduction

How is culture made? Who is it made by, and for whom do they make it? These are key questions for the sociology of culture. After all, sociology is (or should be) concerned with how people make the world they live in, as much as it is concerned with how that world makes and shapes those people. Since the beginnings of human history, people have been making artefacts that are expressive of the cultural contexts in which they operate. Cave paintings, religious icons, items of jewellery – all of these items and many more have been made by people in different societies, the meanings embodied in these creations potentially telling us a great deal about the ideas and values of those people. In the modern West, the variety of cultural artefacts is enormous, ranging from music recordings to adverts for soup, from teen magazines to works of visual art. The questions with which this situation confronts the sociologist are the same as those facing an anthropologist who wishes to understand the culture of a non-Western society: who makes these things? what is required to make them? why do they get made in this particular way and not another way? and for whom are they made?

In this chapter we will examine the school of thought within sociology known as the *production of culture* approach. This is a method of studying cultural artefacts which has been developed mostly by American academics. It seeks to explore the questions mentioned above, particularly through the means of detailed empirical case studies. In so doing, it provides ways of understanding culture which depart from some of the assumptions and arguments of the other paradigms covered in this book. The central claim to novelty of those who advocate the 'production of culture' viewpoint is that looking close-up at how cultural forms are actually made gets us away from making sweeping generalizations about the nature of modern culture which bear little resemblance to what actually occurs in particular social contexts. The vision of the sociology of culture can be modified by attending to the *details* of cultural production, by examining the *micro-level processes* through which specific groups of people create and recreate the cultural goods utilized by themselves and by others. This emphasis on what happens at the ground level has important ramifications for how sociology might understand both the nature of 'Art' and of 'ideology'.

We begin the chapter by setting out the basic tenets of the production of culture approach. We then move on to examine how it thinks about the distinction between 'high' and 'low' cultures. Following from this, we examine how this perspective analyses what have been called 'art worlds', particular arenas within which cultural goods, and their reputed value, are created. We then move on to consider how this approach has understood the ways in which the particular contents of specific types of cultural product are created. Finally, we raise the issue of how particular cultural products are claimed to be 'authentic' by those who either make them or use them, and how sociology challenges such ideas of 'authenticity'. We conclude with an assessment of the strengths and weaknesses of the production of culture perspective.

Producing culture

Examining how culture is made is an issue dealt with, to one degree or another, in the ideas of Karl Marx, Max Weber and Emile Durkheim (see chapter 1). Durkheim gave a very general account of how the 'shape' of a given society generates particular types of culture which express the structure of social organization. In this view, it is 'Society' itself which produces cultural forms. This is rather vague, as it does not examine which *specific* groups of people in a society actually make cultural forms. Both Marx and Weber were more oriented towards focusing on that issue. For Marx, culture was synonymous with ideology, and ideology was produced by particular groups within a ruling class. There was a division of labour within the ruling class between those who produced ideological ideas – priests, philosophers, academics, etc. – and those who were concerned with more immediately pressing and 'material' aspects of ruling class power, such as kings, soldiers and bureaucrats. Weber's focus on the major world religions pointed him towards analysing one particular set of cultural producers – in this case, priests – and the means by which they produced religious ideas. Thus within classical sociology there is already an orientation towards understanding how culture is made, and how the meanings of cultural artefacts are shaped by the social contexts of production, especially by the socially generated dispositions of the particular groups of people who produce these cultural goods.

However, the production of culture perspective, as a distinctive school of thought, is a fairly recent development. There are early traces of it in the 1960s work of the sociologists Edward Shils and Herbert Gans (see chapter 3). It has been elaborated since the 1970s by American sociologists such as Richard Peterson and Paul Hirsch (see Peterson, 1976). Such sociologists often began their careers within the sociology of work and organizations. They apply the insights of those types of sociology as to *how things are made* and *how things get done* to the specific field of cultural production. On this view, cultural forms are likened to any other type of product: cultural workers act upon 'raw materials' which are thereby transformed into 'cultural commodities' (Hirsch, 1978: 316). This is a view that has certain similarities with Raymond Williams's notions of 'cultural materialism' (see chapter 4). On Peterson's definition (1994: 165), the production of culture perspective is concerned with 'how the content of culture is influenced by the milieu in which it is created, distributed, evaluated, taught and preserved'. Hence the key focus of this approach is on 'the effects of the contexts . . . in which [cultural] products are created and disseminated' (Crane, 1992: ix). 'Contexts' here means two things. First, the *institutional* contexts in which cultural goods are produced. For example, what difference does it make to both the meaning and style of a TV programme that it is produced by a *commercial* broadcasting company, rather than by a *state-subsidized* one? Will the tone and emphasis of a television news broadcast be shaped by the fact it is made for a station that relies on advertising and therefore needs to make all its programming as appealing as possible to potential viewers? How does this impact on how news is selected and presented? In general terms, the production of culture perspective examines the 'characteristics of the media' that produce cultural goods, and attempts to show how the very nature of these media may impact upon 'the nature of the cultural products they disseminate' (ibid.).

The second meaning of 'contexts' involved here concerns the nature of the *personnel* who make cultural products. These people are in essence 'cultural workers' or 'cultural producers', for they are the people who make cultural artefacts such as TV programmes and adverts for consumer goods. The questions to be asked of them are: how do their personal dispositions and their roles within the institutions they work for impact upon the nature of the cultural goods they produce? An important aspect of this focus is that it seeks to examine the role of *all* the people involved in the making of a particular cultural good, not just the more obviously 'creative' personnel involved. For example, how is a film's content influenced not just by the 'artistic' vision of the director, but by the producer's insistence on how much money can be spent on it, the film studio managers' directives as to what type of audience the film is to be aimed at, and the production manager's advice to the director as to which scenes are possible to shoot and which are beyond the capacities of the film crew?

This focus on the *total social process* involved in producing a particular cultural good is intended to show that cultural production operates just like any other context of production. Just as making a refrigerator requires both a division of labour amongst the workers involved and forms of management structure to direct their efforts, so too does cultural production involve such forms of organization. This is the point where the production of culture perspective mounts a challenge towards conventional ways of understanding cultural creation. It is not just mass media products like films and TV programmes that are subject to processes of social organization, but also the products associated with 'high culture', so-called 'works of art'. The conventional view sees artworks as being made in a social vacuum, involving a single artistic 'genius' whose 'acts[s] of inspiration [are] inspired by unique inspiration'. Such singular artistic activity, because of its utterly unique nature, cannot be 'compared to the humdrum production of ordinary objects' (Coser, 1978: 225). The production of culture perspective, by contrast, asserts that this can indeed be done. The sociologist should home in on the 'mundane processes' that underlie even the most apparently idiosyncratic and personal acts of cultural creation, and show that the 'artist' is actually just another type of cultural worker, albeit one whom modern societies tend to label as being somehow 'special' and different from other such workers, such as newspaper editors. Both 'artists' and newspaper editors carry out their roles within complex divisions of labour; they rely on a social organization of many other workers, each with their assigned roles. These other cultural workers can be doing their jobs at the same time as the artist or editor, or could have already provided the conditions for the artist or editor to be able to do their jobs. One of the key figures in applying a production of culture perspective to the creation of 'art', Howard Becker, phrases it like this:

> Think, with respect to any work of art, of all the activities that must be carried on for that work to appear as it finally does. For a symphony orchestra to give a concert, for instance, instruments must have been invented, manufactured and maintained, a notation must have been devised and music composed using that notation, people must have learned to play the notated notes on the instruments, times and places for rehearsal must have been provided, ads for the concert must have been placed, publicity arranged and tickets sold. (1974: 767)

The effect of this approach is to show that 'art' is always collectively rather than individually produced. Even the painter or writer working alone is dependent on a whole series of other people, both those who make his or her creativity possible in the first place, and those who disseminate it so that others can have access to it. From this viewpoint, cultural production *of any type*, be it of 'artworks' or of mass media goods, is always wrapped up in the social relations characteristic of the contexts of production.

Creating 'high culture'

The outcome of looking at cultural creation this way is to show that the distinction between a 'sacred' realm of 'high culture' and a 'profane' realm of mass culture is itself produced, a social fabrication that operates in the interests of those groups that have something to gain from making this distinction. Sociology, on this view, is concerned with a 'desacralization' of cultural production, illustrating the production of both 'high culture' itself, and the belief that it is somehow 'removed' from social relations and superior to other forms of culture (Coser, 1978: 225). This outlook places the production of culture perspective close to that of Bourdieu, who likewise saw 'art' as a fabricated label that operates in the interests of certain social groups (see previous chapter).

Bourdieu related the erection of a belief in 'art' and 'high culture' as superior to other forms of culture to the habitus of the cultural bourgeoisie. Production of culture scholars have tended more towards locating such beliefs in the creation by upper-middle-class groups of particular material contexts. The most cited case study here is that offered by Paul Dimaggio of the cultural conditions of the city of Boston in the nineteenth century. Dimaggio (1986: 195) argues that in the early years of the century, there was no clear distinction between high and popular culture, for all sorts of cultural goods were available in a single, as-yet undifferentiated cultural marketplace. What were later defined as works of fine art appeared alongside 'grotesque' forms of 'popular' culture such as bearded ladies and mutant animals. However, by the end of the century, the Boston upper class had marked off a distinctive cultural territory, largely by removing what were now defined as the 'high arts' from the commercial marketplace, and placing them within an organizational network of non-profit corporations. By contrast, popular entertainment remained within the strictly commercial realm and was sold as a purely economic commodity.

Tied up with this development, as both cause and effect of it, was the creation of two separate publics of cultural consumers, an upper-middle-class public that went to classical music concerts and art galleries, and a 'popular' audience drawn from the working and lower-middle classes. The 'high arts' were 'tamed' so as to be brought into line with the behavioural standards of the upper-middle class. 'Art' was seen to be a decorous and genteel realm, that fitted perfectly with the lifestyle of refined gentlemen and ladies. By contrast, the tastes of the popular audience were oriented towards entertainments such as the forms of variety theatre known as 'vaudeville' and 'burlesque', where sentimental songs, risqué comedians and strippers such as Gypsy Rose Lee were the order of the day. Two cultural worlds were thereby created, one 'sacred' and the other 'profane', these in turn mirroring and confirming the increasingly rigid social division between the 're-fined' middle class and the 'vulgar' wider populace. This evolution of 'taste cultures' was the basis for the different class-based forms of cultural consumption in large American cities analysed by Herbert Gans (see chapter 3).

According to Dimaggio, the Boston upper-middle class was successful in erecting and maintaining a separate realm of 'high culture' because it created new social institutions through which this form of culture could be both produced and controlled. Crucial to this development was a group within this class whose members Dimaggio refers to as *cultural capitalists*. These entrepreneurs were able to channel the overall wealth of their class – derived from 'mundane' activities such as trading and owning factories – into the production of forms of 'high culture', which were seen as aesthetically and spiritually superior to such everyday activities. Such individuals were the guiding lights behind the development of 'cultural enterprises' such as the Museum of Fine Arts and the Boston Symphony Orchestra, institutions that both provided the middle-class audience with the kind of cultural goods they wanted, and also served as mechanisms that defined what was true 'art' and what was not. It was institutions like these that maintained and policed the divide between 'high culture' and 'popular culture', ensuring that the production of *legitimate* culture was controlled and circumscribed in line with upper-middle-class tastes (Dimaggio, 1986: 209). But this institutional basis, which guaranteed the divide between 'high' and 'low' culture, was not perceived as such either by the people who ran it – gallery directors, concert hall managers – or the bourgeois public for whom it was operated. Both producers and consumers saw such a situation as wholly 'natural', rather than as the result of a huge amount of collective effort and wealth being expended to disguise the fact that this divide was purely a social fabrication.

There are both empirical and theoretical implications of Dimaggio's analysis of the specific case of Boston. At the empirical level, it would be possible to trace out similar processes not just in other American cities at this time, but all across the Western world. In cities such as Manchester in England and Sydney in Australia, the upper-middle classes were busily converting *economic capital* into *cultural capital*, by financing the erection of concert halls, art galleries and other temples of culture. From this viewpoint, we can see a spread across the whole Western world in the later nineteenth century of a whole series of institutions upon which the activities of 'high culture' were erected. Moreover, from the very beginning, this was in some senses a 'global' process, with cultural institutions in different countries supporting and confirming each other. For example, the composer of a symphony that had been well received by upper-middle-class audiences in Paris or Berlin might get invited to New York, where his works would be played to an equally appreciative audience. Since World War II, this network of association and mutual support between cultural institutions has spread outside the narrow compass of the Western world to countries such as Japan and South Korea. The international market in the goods of 'high culture' that we see today is to a large degree the outcome of the activities of the Victorian upper-middle classes, who from this point of view laid the foundations for the continuing power of those who believe in, and draw upon, 'high culture'.

At the theoretical level, implicit in Dimaggio's analysis is an important criticism of all analyses that see the products of 'high culture' as somehow perfect, timeless and 'beyond' social relations. From this point of view, anyone who based their analysis of cultural matters on such ideas would be ignoring the fact that 'high culture' is only possible under certain institutional conditions. Moreover, those foundations were from the very beginning laid by a social class that wished to see itself, and have itself seen, as being morally and aesthetically superior to everyone else. From a production of culture perspective, analysis that separates 'art' and 'mass culture' does exactly what the bourgeoisie of Boston and elsewhere did more than a hundred years ago. Such analysis therefore utilizes as its central distinction one which is thoroughly wrapped up in relations of class power. This much Pierre Bourdieu has already pointed out. But the production of culture perspective can take this kind of critique further. Adorno, for example, lamented what he saw as the characteristic cultural movement of the twentieth century, namely that the profit motive was increasingly colonizing the realm of 'true' art (see chapter 2). But, given Dimaggio's outlook, it could be pointed out that in actual fact the relationship between 'art' and commerce also has had another dimension to it, in that middle-class groups created an institutional sphere of art that was in some senses *beyond* the sphere of immediate profit and money-making. They used (in Bourdieu's terms) their economic capital to make cultural capital for themselves, and this legacy is just as important an aspect of cultural life in modern societies as is the search by the captains of the culture industries to make money out of cultural forms. In essence, the effect of Dimaggio's analysis is to alert us to the fact that any attempt at 'preserving' the products of 'high culture' from the depredations of the capitalist market is also in some ways a form of bourgeois class power, rather than the purely 'humanitarian' and 'disinterested' effort it is sometimes presented as.

Cultural worlds

The key point of Dimaggio's argument is that it is the existence of particular institutions that makes the production of certain types of culture possible. Institutions create their own 'worlds' in which cultural creators operate. This situation has been examined in two main ways. First, one can look at how particular institutional contexts give rise to particular types of cultural product. Here, the focus is on the object, the cultural good, itself. This approach will be the focus of the next section. In this section we will examine the other major way of thinking about the effects of institutional contexts on cultural production. This concerns the ramifications that the institutional setting they work within has for the *reputations* of cultural producers. How do different types of 'artist' fare within the contexts that they are constrained to work within if they wish to create things at all? What institutional forces do they have to contend with, and how does the institution affect their chances of being recognized as successful or not?

Sociologists who adopt the production of culture perspective have examined different 'cultural worlds' in what are defined in modern Western societies as both 'artistic' and mass media cultures. In terms of the study of 'art' and 'artists', a key contribution has been made by Howard Becker. We saw above that he stresses the *collective* nature of artistic production. In his book *Art Worlds* (1984: x) he defines an 'art world' as a 'network of people whose cooperative activity, organized via their joint knowledge of conventional means of doing things, produces the kind of art works that art world is noted for'. The focus is on seeing the art world as a sociologist of work would see it – as a conglomeration of different people carrying out specialist tasks. Becker's point is that *all* of them are crucial in the making of artworks. This displaces the individual 'genius' from the centre of the picture. Instead, Becker's point is that once all of the various contributions towards making a given work of art are taken into account, it becomes difficult to decide 'which of all these people is *the* artist . . . [rather than just] support personnel' (ibid.). The aim of such an analysis is to treat 'people defined as artists as not so very different from other kinds of workers, especially the other workers who participate in the making of art works' (ibid.).

The fact that some people are defined as 'artists' and others not is the process to which Becker wishes to draw attention. Whether someone is so defined or not depends on their standing within the set of institutions – art schools, galleries, museums, newspaper reviews – that make up the art world. Becker seeks to analyse the processes of definition within this institutional framework of who is said to be an 'artist' and who is not, who is defined as 'innovative' and 'original', and who is said to be 'derivative' and 'unoriginal'. He does this in the manner of the symbolic interactionist school of sociological thought. This position is based on the idea that apart from the intention that an individual had in carrying out a particular act, there is also a socially recognized meaning of the act. This meaning derives from the 'label' put on the act by other people. The act itself does not have any social meaning apart from the meaning ascribed to it by other people in the process of labelling (Becker, 1963). Quite clearly, some people have more power than others to make their label 'stick', and thus to define the meaning of the act.

Becker applies this model to the activities of artists in the institutional context of the art world. The success or otherwise of an artist in this world is largely a result of the labels placed on his or her work by others in the same business, such as other artists, gallery owners, newspaper columnists and so on. Some of these groups have more power than others to define what is 'good' or 'true' art, and what is not. The 'artistic' nature of cultural goods known as 'art' does not lie in the objects themselves, but in the definitions given of these by the members of the art world, some of whom enjoy high levels of institutional power, which in turn enable them to cast 'definitive' judgements on the qualities of these artworks. For example, curators of art galleries can decide which works of art go on public display or are included in particular exhibitions. Similarly, judges of art competitions such as the Turner Prize have the power to define as legitimate or illegitimate not just particular works of art but also the other activities of the artists who made them. In these ways are reputations made and broken, as different people get lauded with all the praise that the institution of the art world has at its disposal to proffer, or get condemned as not being fit enough to be part of the world of art.

Becker claimed that this kind of analysis could be applied to any other form of cultural production, because the mundane processes of labelling cultural products and their producers go on in other areas beyond that of the production of so-called 'high culture'. Wherever there is an institution involved in a particular type of cultural production, there is a 'cultural world' where these kinds of process are at work. Richard Peterson (1978) has produced a series of analyses of one such world, the realm of country music production, an area defined by those who exist within the 'high art' world as part of an inferior mass culture. Peterson's point, however, is to show that the same kinds of struggle over cultural legitimacy and illegitimacy as in the world of 'art' go on within the world of country music production, centred around Nashville, Tennessee. He looks at the institutional context of country music production in order to ascertain why certain singers are successful and others not in this particular cultural milieu.

Peterson's case study of country music production in the late 1960s and early 1970s hinges on his identification of a crucial institutional aspect of this type of musical production, namely the close connections between record companies and radio stations. Country music grew in popularity throughout the United States in the late 1960s. As a result, there was also a growth of radio stations specializing in this type of music. However, the rapid growth of country music radio meant that there were not enough disc jockeys who were thoroughly familiar with this kind of music. As a result, many who had little or no knowledge of, or interest in, country music were hired by radio stations. They sought to modernize country music by promoting records that removed what they perceived as the 'raw edged' sound associated with traditional country music, replacing this with a 'smoother' type of music involving 'easy listening'-style crooning and light orchestral string arrangements. This musical preference was promoted as a 'new' country music, a 'progressive, mellow [and] metropolitan' type of music (Peterson, 1978: 302). Recording industry executives, feeling that this was the way country music was going, accommodated this stylistic change by demanding records be produced that fitted this new template. Singers and other musicians were forced to adapt to this new style. Those that would not, or could not, were locked out from the recording industry. As Peterson (ibid. 309) puts it: 'in a short space of time the greater part of a generation of entertainers who played conventional country music found themselves cut off from making records, the most important tool of their artistic production.'

In the cultural world of country music, changes in the institutional context – in this case the relations between recording companies and radio stations – led to processes of labelling that both compelled new types of cultural good to be produced and also delegitimated those cultural producers who refused or were unable to make their products in this novel way. They were defined as being unacceptably old-fashioned and unappealing to what record producers saw as a new, more affluent urban audience. As a result, they were prevented from having access to recording facilities, and were deprived to a large extent of the power to create cultural goods. This example shows how institutional power can operate to prevent cultural production, as well as to enable it.

Institutions and contents

In the section above, we have considered how a production of culture perspective can illuminate the ways in which power is located within particular institutional contexts of cultural creation, and how it can affect the reputations of the cultural producers involved in a particular 'cultural world'. In this section we will examine how this perspective can also be used to account for the very nature of cultural goods themselves. We will do so by looking at different 'cultural worlds' underpinned by institutions and organizations, especially those involving the mass media. The crucial question that production of culture scholars ask here is: 'how do the media shape and frame culture'? (Crane, 1992: ix). In other words, in what ways does the very nature of a media organization *itself* contribute to the content of the cultural goods it produces?

This question had already been asked by Adorno and Horkheimer in their analysis of the Culture Industry (see chapter 2). They reflected on the 'industrial' production of culture under assembly-line conditions. However, most of their account was speculative, as they mainly conjectured how such products were made, rather than carefully investigating this process empirically. This led them to assume that all Culture Industry production involves a constant churning out of the same sorts of product, time after time. The production of culture perspective tries to avoid this assumption in two ways. First, by investigating what actually occurs in *particular* contexts of production – that is, in specific organizations at specific times – rather than theorizing about a homogenous Culture Industry in which all particular organizations are alleged to be exactly like every other. In other words, different culture *industries*, and specific companies within them, are examined rather than the monolithic leviathan imagined by the early Frankfurt thinkers. Second, Adorno's and Horkheimer's stress on the repetitive nature of what the Culture Industry produces is replaced by an emphasis on cultural production as potentially involving processes of *innovation*, which are both facilitated and organized by particular contexts of production (Hirsch, 1972). This emphasis is also aimed at avoiding a crude economic reductionist view, which sees 'culture' purely as the product of the socio-economic 'base' (see chapter 1). In its place, the production of culture perspective stresses that culture is produced by active social agents – cultural producers – who come together in organizational networks which are dynamic and oriented towards change. Clearly not all contexts of production are fully oriented towards innovation, but nonetheless the sociologist has to be aware that certain contexts *might* be like this.

Such an approach potentially reveals aspects of cultural production that hitherto had gone unexamined. A case in point here is the creation of news reports, both in newspapers and on television. It is something of a sociological truism that news broadcasts are 'framed' in ways which serve the interests of dominant groups in a society. For example, groups and organizations which are opposed to the government of a particular country are labelled in highly negative ways – for example, designated as 'terrorists'. In doing this, news media are said to serve the interests of those in power, by helping to promote dominant ideologies amongst the general populace (Glasgow University Media Group, 1976). The problem with this view is that it treats the news media as a 'black box', refusing to look into the details of how and why particular news stories get selected for printing or broadcasting, and the ways in which certain ideological slants are built into the presentation of them. A production of culture perspective reveals the mundane processes by which 'news' is gathered and constructed. Gaye Tuchman's (1978) study of the work practices of newspaper offices is a good example of this approach. She observed the ways in which the editing process of a particular American newspaper was shaped by the everyday interactions of journalists. It was their 'feel' for the newsworthiness of a story that was a major factor in whether it got printed or not, and, if it was printed, how it was written up and how much priority it was given over other stories. In a similar fashion to Bourdieu's account of how social actors operate through *practical*, semi-conscious rather than fully reflective forms of reasoning (see chapter 7), Tuchman emphasizes that the ways in which stories are selected and framed depends on editors implicitly drawing on their practical sense of how 'good' a story is, a sense born of years of experience in the newspaper business. For example, an editor of the newspaper she studied would 'sense' when a particular story had run long enough, reasoning that readers must be getting bored with the same story getting large amounts of coverage over several days. According to the editor's 'feeling' of what makes for interesting copy, he would either continue the coverage, believing there was still some mileage in it, or relinquish it in favour of another story. The decision to continue with a particular feature or not was made on the basis of how 'right' it felt to the editor to take a particular course of action.

This kind of micro-level analysis of why certain stories get covered and others not challenges the more 'theoretical' view that stories are selected for purely 'ideological' reasons. Instead, a production of culture perspective highlights how some issues are covered and others not due to the actual ways in which cultural producers, in this case editors, operate practically in doing their jobs, and in negotiating means of doing those jobs in ways that they are comfortable with. The three editors who were responsible for selecting stories for one newspaper Tuchman studied (1978: 270) had 'worked out a *modus vivendi*, a living compromise, for the three men were doomed to sit next to one another, assessing stories together, until one of them was promoted or left the organization'. The editors were forced to work together, compromising with each other in terms of stories selected for publication, with each being mindful of not pushing his own preferences so strongly that it would upset the norm of cooperation and mutual tolerance that had evolved in their daily working lives. To a large degree this norm of 'getting along' with each other shaped both what was printed and how it was represented. This sort of analysis reveals the minute details of cultural production, and brings to light the prosaic, everyday practices involved, in ways that more macro-level analyses of 'ideologies' downplay or ignore altogether.

Similar studies which examine the often rather prosaic reasons why certain cultural goods turn out the way that they do have been carried out in the world of publishing. For example, Powell (1978) reveals the often rather chance reasons why academic publishers choose to publish certain authors and not others. Rather than being due to any grand 'ideological' commitments to certain political viewpoints, selection of an author's manuscript for publication can depend on such arbitrary factors as a publisher meeting an author by chance at a conference and developing a personal rapport with him or her. Crane's (1979) study of why the work of certain academics gets published in particular scientific journals, while the work of others does not, excavates the often tacit assumptions upon which journal editors base their assessments of papers submitted. Instead of being biased towards one theoretical perspective and eliminating authors who do not conform to it, the editors Crane studied were more likely to have a (mostly unintentional) positive disposition towards authors who already had famous reputations or were attached to what were labelled as 'good' universities. Unknown authors and those affiliated to institutions with a low status were more likely to get eliminated by the editors in their role as 'cultural gatekeepers'. For the most part, this tendency was unintended by the editors, who generally regarded themselves as neutral arbiters of 'good' and 'bad' research and scholarship. Like the newspaper editors above, they had a practical rather than fully reflective 'sense' for what was publishable and what was not, learned from past experience in selecting articles that felt 'right' for their journal.

An important part of this sense of rightness and wrongness with which cultural gatekeepers such as newspaper and journal editors operate is their attempt to produce publications that will appeal to the particular readership they are aiming at. It is part of the job of such cultural workers to try to second guess their public, that is, to attempt to anticipate what will prove suitable for the kinds of people who purchase their publication. The ways in which producers shape their products in light of their understanding of their public's taste can have great ramifications for both the content and style of those products. A production of culture perspective stresses that these dynamics occur in the 'cultural worlds' that are defined as the 'high arts' as much as in more obviously commercial cultural sectors such as newspaper publication. In the world of opera production, for example, Rosanne Martorella (1977) shows how the ideas held by the board members of opera companies about what the public will and will not accept can have great effects on both the operas selected for production and the style in which they are presented. The 'artistic' personnel – directors, actors, designers – of the opera companies she studied were under great pressure by management to put on operas that the latter group saw as being already well known to the public, and which were relatively 'unchallenging', such as *Carmen* and *Aida*. Nineteenth-century operas were particularly favoured by management as they were both part of an acknowledged repertoire of works that audiences had already seen and would come back to see again, and could be staged using sets and props that were easily available and did not have to be made from scratch. Given the high overheads for opera companies in staging new productions, there was obviously a pure economic rationale involved here: well-known operas were cheaper to stage than new ones, and because they already had an almost guaranteed audience, they were likely to turn a profit for the company.

But there was another, more hidden 'cultural' element in why management favoured staging this kind of opera. Individuals in senior management and on company boards tended to like more old-fashioned, artistically 'safer' operas which were staged in traditional ways. This was because they were part of a section of the upper-middle class which had rather conservative artistic tastes. By contrast, the 'artistic' personnel were more oriented towards new operas staged in more avant-garde ways. There was thus a tension between two sections of the middle class, the 'artistic' and the 'managerial', with the latter group ultimately having the final say in what was offered and how it was presented. This group's aesthetic conservatism coloured their view of what the audience would enjoy and would pay for, this image squaring with their own tastes. In this case, the organization of cultural production worked in favour of an inhibition of innovation rather than the encouragement of it. Here we have a 'high art' organization turning out the same 'safe' products time after time in ways rather reminiscent of how Adorno and Horkheimer described the production of mass culture. But while the Frankfurt theorists would have seen this situation in opera production purely as a result of profit motives colonizing a cultural world of 'art', the implication of Martorella's study is that the tendency towards producing the same kinds of aesthetically 'unchallenging' opera was also in part due to the tastes of the group of managers, who disliked any other types of opera. Once more we can see how an analysis of the *details* of the operation of particular contexts of cultural production can reveal factors that a more macro-level, non-empirical style of analysis cannot.

Understanding Hollywood:
ideology or managerial structure?

Other contexts have been identified by production of culture scholars which are in fact more oriented around innovation than the constant fabrication of the same. On the face of it, television and film production would seem a very unlikely locale for innovative forms of cultural production. After all, it was film production in particular that Adorno and Horkheimer had been thinking about when they argued that Culture Industry production was wholly standardized. In addition, we only have to look at what is on offer at the local multiplex cinema to realize how much of Hollywood film production conforms to fairly rigid genres: the romance, the thriller, the teen pic, the war movie, and so on. Television also offers products that fit into standard categories: soap operas, situation comedies, cop shows, etc. However, a closer look at film production in particular perhaps tells a different story. Production of culture scholars emphasize that the Hollywood film industry has gone through phases characterized by either higher or lower levels of innovation. Whether Hollywood studios are oriented in one direction or another at any one particular time seems to be dependent on two factors: how film production is actually organized, and how management perceives the market for films of a certain type.

In terms of the first factor, the ways in which decisions are made in the film production organization seems to play a large part in the process whereby some films are given the go-ahead to be made while others never leave the script stage. At certain periods, Hollywood studios have been based around an organization whereby 'responsibility without authority is spread through a lengthy chain of command; . . . [this] is a system that encourages the manufacture of safe, highly saleable pictures. It is not a system that encourages risk or diversity' (Pryluck, 1986: 131–2). Highly standardized films that are not at all innovative tend to get made in periods when a whole series of managers have a certain amount of say as to what gets made, but there is no one individual or group at the top demanding innovation. Instead, no single middle-ranking manager wants to 'rock the boat', so he or she sanctions the making of films that are perceived to be highly marketable precisely because they conform to a tried and tested formula. In such a situation, 'artistic' personnel, especially directors, are rewarded by managers for making standardized films that make large profits, and are discouraged or prevented from making more 'risky' films that are seen by managers as too different from the accepted norm (Faulkner and Anderson, 1987). Directors with a track record of producing movies that conform to a formula, did not go over budget and did well on release are given contracts to make other films – which conform to the same 'winning' formula (Faulkner, 1983). By contrast, directors with a track record of 'failure' – those who have achieved exactly the opposite of those factors just described – get marginalized or shut out from film-making altogether. Examples of this type of director include Orson Welles and Peter Bogdanovich, who were shut out from mainstream film-making in the 1940s and 1980s respectively. Both had angered studio executives by failing to produce films which met the demands of the studio for a 'safe' product.

Adorno and Horkheimer argued that the standardized nature of Hollywood films was due to the very division of labour between 'artistic' personnel – the director was merely a manager of a whole series of specialists like set designers and composers. A production of culture perspective argues that in fact the standardized nature of production occurs not as a result of the division of labour between 'creative' workers but because of a certain form of organization at the *management* level. If management is organized differently, then *exactly the same* 'artistic' division of labour can be directed towards more 'innovative' movie production. It is not the 'creative' element that lies at the basis of greater or lesser levels of innovation, but the managerial structure.

From this perspective, Hollywood film production is not an unchanging monolith but, rather, varies in its output depending on how the managerial level of studio executives is organized, and, as a result, how decisions are taken and how creative personnel are rewarded. At certain periods Hollywood has been more rather than less innovative. The reasons for this lie in how managers have perceived the buoyancy or otherwise of the market for films, competition between studios and between film and other entertainment media being another factor Adorno and Horkheimer did not examine because of their assumption that there was one big Culture Industry, the parts of which were not in competition with each other. At particular times Hollywood studios have been compelled to innovate by what studio executives saw as a threat from another medium. One such period of innovation was the late 1950s and early 1960s, when the fear of a major loss of audiences to television stimulated studio executives to produce grand spectaculars such as *Ben-Hur* (1959) and *Cleopatra* (1963). These vast and lavish entertainments, involving hundreds of extras and elaborate recreations of past times, were put into production in the hope of luring audiences back into cinemas, through offering a kind of viewing spectacle that could not be seen on TV.

In the late 1960s, with the rise of the counter-culture and student protests, Hollywood again innovated, making films that were geared to what was seen by executives as the lucrative 'alternative' youth market. Larger studios copied youth-oriented 'drugs' movies made by smaller, independent studios, such as *The Trip* (1967), funding explicitly anti-establishment films such as *Easy Rider* (1969). From a Culture Industry perspective, this is yet another instance of the powers-that-be taming the counter-culture by packaging and commodifying it, and selling it back to youth in a 'safe' and politically neutralized fashion. But from a production of culture perspective, something more mundane was going on. Studio managers, fearing for the profitability of their companies – and thus, ultimately, for the security of their own jobs – abandoned old formulae in a rather desperate bid to capture a newly emerging youth market, in order to compensate for the shrinking of a 'family' audience that had migrated to television viewing. Decision-making structures were loosened, in a bid to encourage more innovation in the movie-making process – although that innovation still had to be channelled in profitable ways. If there were political ramifications of this process, they were unintended by Hollywood producers, who were merely aiming at preserving the financial status of their organizations. Once again, we are being oriented away from seeing cultural production as some kind of conspiracy by the powerful, towards seeing how the apparently powerful are in the grip of social and market forces they seek to, but can only partially, control.

According to Dominick (1987), Hollywood production was at its most innovative and varied in the period from the late 1960s to the mid-1970s, as a result of the changes in markets and perception thereof by studio executives described above. After that period, smaller-scale films, often 'personal' projects of the directors involved, were relinquished in favour of 'blockbusters', the first of which was *Jaws* (1975) and the initially most successful of which was *Star Wars* (1977). This marked a return to more formulaic film-making, with production being more and more geared to sequels with guaranteed appeal on the basis of the success of the first movie – e.g. the various sequels to *Star Wars* – and movies that fitted a well-known formula, such as the 'action' genre films of Arnold Schwarzenegger. This type of production continues today. Such a change can be marked in terms of the careers of particular actors who have worked in Hollywood since the late 1960s. For example, in the early 1970s Jack Nicholson acted in medium- to low-budget, rather low-key films made as 'personal' projects by their directors, such as *Five Easy Pieces* (1970) and *The Last Detail* (1973). But by the 1980s, he was starring in films that executives thought had built-in audience appeal, either because they had an all-star line-up – e.g. *The Witches of Eastwick* (1987) with Cher, Susan Sarandon and Michelle Pfeiffer – or because they could be heavily pre-sold to a primarily teenage audience, such as *Batman* (1989).

As studio executives came to believe that financial success lay in winning over younger audiences with 'blockbusters' released in the summer months, the type of small-scale production that had characterized a lot of Hollywood's output in the early 1970s fell into disfavour, at best being occasionally produced for what was seen as a small niche market of older viewers (films such as *Driving Miss Daisy* (1989) fall into this category). As we saw in chapter 6, Fredric Jameson (1992) argues that the 'nostalgia films' of the mid-1980s – such as *Blue Velvet* (1986), *Back to the Future* (1985) and its sequels, and *Peggy Sue Got Married* (1986), which recreate idealized versions of America's past, especially the 1950s – were indicative of postmodern art's obsession with façades and cultural pastiche. While this may have been part of the driving force behind writers and directors wanting to create such movies, the reason why managers gave the go-ahead for these films to be made lay more in the desire to reach out to particular types of consumer, primarily teenagers in the case of *Back to the Future* and couples of all ages with the romantic story of Peggy Sue. By ignoring the economic and managerial reasons behind such productions, Jameson can be accused of both concentrating too much on 'cultural' factors, which he isolates from other factors, and ignoring the motives of different groups of cultural producers. Only by looking at the minutiae of contexts of cultural production, runs the production of culture argument, can the true reasons for cultural change – as well as cultural stasis – be truly discerned.

Making television

This argument may also hold true for television production. Like Hollywood film, American network television on the surface seems to conform to a Culture Industry kind of model. Writers and directors are generally under the tight supervision of managers, whose primary aim is making money through already established genre products rather than making programmes that in any sense 'break the mold' (Cantor, 1971). This gives rise to clashes, like the ones described in terms of opera companies above, between management and creative personnel, because the latter group has an interest in flexing their cultural muscles and producing scripts and programmes that are different from the norm. Managers, by contrast, who often have little interest in or knowledge of the aesthetic elements of the products they are supervising, are focused on 'audience demographics', and attempt to create shows which are geared towards a particular audience. Large audiences mean advertisers will want to lodge adverts at the time that a successful show is scheduled, increasing the profits of the networks and keeping shareholders happy. Although American television seems to be more rigidly organized than cinema, and thus has historically had a greater tendency towards standardized output, different television companies have nonetheless still sought to remain ahead of their competitors by – mostly cautious – forms of innovation. In some cases, such changes have resulted from managers perceiving cultural shifts in American society and allowing creative personnel to innovate to some degree in the hope that the resulting programmes will capture a new audience or appeal to the changing sensibilities of a mass audience composed of a wide range of all social strata. For example, *Hill Street Blues* was commissioned by executives at the NBC network in the early 1980s on the basis of their feeling that mass audience tastes were shifting in favour of more 'realistic' and 'gritty' cop shows than had hitherto been shown. The reason behind the 'daring' introduction of a central character who was gay into the situation comedy *Will and Grace* in 1998 was that managers at NBC were seeking to woo a specific audience, in this case an affluent gay and gay-friendly urban grouping of young professionals.

This kind of 'innovation' is in fact rather timid, because all it does is to place a character with an 'unusual' (for American network TV, that is) characteristic into a standard issue comedy series. But it would be wrong to suggest that American television companies *must* be oriented towards generally standardized forms of production. The HBO company has scored various commercial coups over its rivals with the series *The Sopranos* (everyday life in a mafia family) and *Sex and the City* (the risqué sexual adventures of four young women). Both series would probably not have been commissioned by other networks, oriented as they are to more tried-and-tested formulae, especially since *The Sopranos* went down badly with focus groups of 'representative' audience members, one of the main techniques by which television executives seek to assess what will sell and what will not. The more fluid management structure within HBO compared with that of other broadcasters, plus its increasing reputation for producing 'hip' programming, meant that these shows found their way onto TV screens when otherwise they might never have passed the script stage. At the time of writing HBO remains the exception rather than the norm of American television production. Yet in the future other broadcasters may be forced to follow suit as the pursuit of specific audiences means that programmes have to be increasingly tailored to fit what producers see as the tastes of minority groups rather than having to appeal to a very wide-ranging mass audience by being blandly standardized and inoffensive. The dynamic effect of the perceptions that cultural gatekeepers and producers have of the changing nature of audiences backs up the production of culture scholars' view that empirical analysis of trends within the culture industries is required if the true nature of cultural production today is to be grasped.

Desperately seeking the real

According to postmodern theory, in the contemporary cultural situation 'reality' has been obliterated by 'hyperreality', an ever-changing constellation of signs and symbols whose meanings remain opaque (see chapter 6). In this situation, all forms of 'authenticity' melt away into ambiguity, where nothing is as it seems, and people are fundamentally alienated from the real. A production of culture perspective, with its emphasis on how culture is always *fabricated*, puts a different spin on these themes. In *all* cultural contexts, not just those that are allegedly postmodern in character, culture is *made* by people. As a result, no form of culture is 'natural' or 'authentic', because it is always fabricated in one way or another. The point is then to examine how groups of people in different cultural contexts hide this fact from themselves, and use ideas of cultural 'authenticity' both to justify themselves and to denigrate the cultural habits of other groups.

We may again take the example of country music to illustrate these issues. According to Peterson (1997), there exist today two main types of country music fan in America – and elsewhere in the world. On the one side there are 'hard-core' fans who celebrate and identify with the 'harder-edged' style of country music that we mentioned above and which was threatened by the relationship between record producers and radio station disc jockeys from the 1970s onwards. On the other side, there are 'soft-shell' fans who enjoy the more easy-listening, 'pop' style of country music that the contemporary Nashville record companies are keen to sell. The 'hard-core fans' fight back against this process, and denigrate what they see as the 'inauthentic' tastes of 'soft-shell' fans, by claiming that they are the true inheritors of *the* authentic country music tradition. They appeal in particular to the iconic figure of the singer Hank Williams, who they take to be a prime representative of the true, more 'hard-edged' country sound. But what this strategy ignores is that Williams *himself* was part of a process of making a certain style of country music seem 'authentic'. Both he and his producers back in the 1940s were engaged in a fabrication – partly conscious, partly unconscious – of the authenticity of his type of music. In the 1940s, his musical style was regarded by older country fans as shockingly new, and therefore 'inauthentic'. But as time went on, this inauthenticity was replaced by a veneer of authenticity. Williams was publicized in ways that accentuated that he was a true 'son of the soil' rather than the manufactured product he in part was. By attaching his persona to a mythical *Gemeinschaft* type of community (see chapter 1) of the 'old West', Williams was transformed into an apparently 'true' spokesman for the 'real' country music. As the audience for country music became more urban in character, the rural nature of Williams's persona became more accentuated, especially after his death in 1953 when he was canonized as a kind of secular musical saint, who seemed to lend 'grass-roots' authenticity to what was increasingly a multimillion-dollar industry. Thus when contemporary hard-core fans invoke his name as a guarantor of the 'real' country music, they misrecognize the fact that they are buying into a form of fabricated authenticity. This is the same situation that pertained, according to Dimaggio (see above), with the nineteenth-century middle classes who created the conditions for the propagation of 'high culture' but who then took this condition as being 'natural' rather than being fabricated by themselves. All such groups have become alienated from their own acts of cultural creation, seeing things they have produced as if they have a life of their own (see chapter 1).

This process is emphasized by production of culture scholars as being at the heart of many cultural phenomena. In terms of music more generally, Taylor (1997) argues that a key struggle amongst fans of many different types of music is one which involves tension between those who construe themselves as 'true' fans and the others they denigrate as mere amateurs (see also Thornton, 1995). For the former group, great respect is accorded to performers who have not 'sold out' to major record corporations. But their beliefs are based on an identification of a true and inviolable 'essence' of the type of music they like, and in so doing they fail to see that there is no such essence, merely different ways in which such authenticity has been created by complexes of cultural producers.

This situation perhaps applies to all forms of cultural production. For example, MacCannell (1974) argues that contemporary tourism relies on forms of 'staged authenticity', with particular tourist locations being manipulated by tourist officials so as to *seem* authentic to visitors. For example, the Scottish tourist industry ensures that American, Japanese and other tourists get a taste of the 'true' romantic and mystical nature of Scotland by laying on trips to 'haunted' castles and houses. Because 'real' ghosts are rather unreliable in turning up when a tour party is present, actors are hired to impersonate them, giving the tourists both a mild thrill and ensuring that they have experienced the 'real' Scotland of ghouls and other spooky happenings (Inglis and Holmes, 2003). Needless to say, such phantoms have very little to do with the everyday lives of most Scottish people, but the prosaic nature of the 'real' Scotland is hidden by the fabrication of the ghost, a token of 'authentic' Scottish history. Such examples, which have been occurring for the whole duration of modernity, perhaps show that the fabrication of, and concomitant search for, 'authenticity' are not limited to an alleged period of postmodernity. (For a further twist on such issues, see the idea of 'post-tourists' in chapter 6.)

Conclusion

The production of culture perspective is one which has created a great many interesting case studies of how people create forms of culture, and how, in some cases, they then understand their own fabrications as being somehow authentically 'natural'. Nonetheless, it would be wrong to claim that this is a way of analysing culture without there being limitations or problems attached. It is, by its very nature, oriented more towards contexts of production of cultural goods, rather than being concerned with how those goods are then interpreted and reinterpreted by the people who buy or otherwise use them. In this way, it might actually be misnamed. Sociologists who use this approach 'assume they study the production of "culture". They do not. They study the production of cultural objects, and these objects become a part of and contribute to culture. But they are not culture as such' (Mukerji and Schudson, 1991: 32–3). It is true that the production of culture perspective does not have a fully worked-out approach to the study of cultural *consumption*. Nonetheless, the above critics ignore the fact that the production of culture approach allows analysis of the ways in which fans draw upon the fabrications of authenticity provided by cultural producers such as in the music industries. Moreover, although this perspective generally does not look at the nature of media audiences directly, it does so indirectly by examining the ways in which cultural producers such as television executives construct images of the audience and create cultural goods on the basis of those images.

This is one of the main reasons why cultural production in modern capitalist societies is not wholly unchanging and static, as Adorno and Horkheimer alleged. As cultural producers perceive the nature of audiences to be changing, the nature of the products they conceive changes too. This is why Mukerji and Schudson are only partly correct when they allege that this perspective is 'much better at explaining the normal mechanisms for creating "normal" culture than it is at explaining what happens when culture changes' (ibid.). It is in fact one of the strengths of this approach over the Culture Industry thesis that it can map empirically what occurs when cultural producers innovate.

More of a problem is precisely *how* innovations are explained. There is a tendency to see all changes as a result of alterations in the division of labour, especially at the managerial level, within contexts of production. But there may be other 'external' factors involved. For example, Friedberg (2001) takes issue with Peterson's (1990) account of why rock 'n' roll music took off in America in the mid-1950s, which stresses that internal changes within the music industry itself were responsible for this new style of music. Friedberg argues that this ignores the fact that for many years before such changes, blues and country music styles were being blended together by musicians in ways that would eventually give birth to rock 'n' roll. This trend in turn produced musicians who wanted to extend this new musical style, including singers like Elvis Presley and Chuck Berry. Peterson's downplaying of cultural forces that were occurring *outside* the immediate context of record company production can be taken as a more general problem with production of culture perspectives, which perhaps home in on too narrow a range of factors. They focus on how certain forms of culture are *commodified* – for example, turned into records – and downplay or ignore where these forms of culture came from and, ironically, who made them in contexts outside of the formal contexts of cultural production (e.g. in clubs, bars and other 'unofficial' locales of cultural production). This omission fits with the above criticism that this perspective looks at cultural goods, rather than at the whole set of phenomena we might want to classify as comprising 'culture' in a more general sense.

Moreover, there is a reluctance to relate the specific contexts of production analysed to wider sociological entities such as 'modernity' or 'capitalist society'. This perspective certainly gives one a view of what happens in (some parts of) cultural life as if through a microscope. But so oriented are scholars in this school of thought towards the empirical and the particular that they rarely rise to a more general level of connecting specific contexts to more general trends, which, for all their faults, the early Frankfurt thinkers attempted to do. Perhaps when looked at from a more bird's eye perspective, the nature of cultural production today does indeed look rather more like the situation that Adorno and Horkheimer described.

Nonetheless, the benefits of a production of culture approach are clear. The careful, empirically informed analysis involved in this type of study, with case studies being a particularly favoured means of getting to grips with particular contexts, allows one to challenge and recast the more speculative philosophical approaches to cultural life apparent in both the Frankfurt School and postmodern theory. A fully rounded approach to the study of *all* aspects of cultural production would involve looking at a 'circuit of culture' which includes production, consumption and the identities thus created amongst the consumers of cultural goods (Johnson, 1986). For such an approach to be satisfying, the production aspect would have to draw on some of the ideas and methods proposed by the sociologists mentioned in this chapter.

Conclusion:
Globalization, Reflexivity
and the Future

Throughout this book we have reviewed and subjected to scrutiny the various ways of thinking about culture developed by sociologists and cognate others. We have seen that there is a great diversity both as to how different types of sociology define 'culture', and what conclusions they draw from their analysis of cultural life in the modern world. In this conclusion, we will attempt to draw together many of the threads we have unpicked in the previous chapters.

We will consider three main topics, all of which are crucial for how the sociology of culture might operate now and in the future. The first concerns the question of how *useful* the ideas outlined in this book might be. To what uses can they be put in understanding important issues in the world today? We will seek to show how the styles of sociology we have examined can be put to use in understanding particular issues that are today of pressing importance. We will take the example of *globalization* and show how the processes associated with making the world an ever more interconnected place can have light thrown upon them by the sociological paradigms covered in this book. We will endeavour to show how the different types of the sociology of culture can be very helpful in understanding our place in the contemporary world.

The second topic we will turn to is the issue of *reflexivity*. This is the idea that anyone putting forward a certain position on a particular issue must think about why they hold such ideas and where their notions come from. In essence, reflexivity involves casting a critical eye over one's own ideas, interrogating them in such a way that one is no longer caught up in the naive belief that one's own views must be the only possible correct ones. Being reflexive about our own opinions is especially important in the sociology of culture, because opinions about cultural matters generally involve, in one way or another, political beliefs about how we ourselves, and other people, should live (Bourdieu and Wacquant, 1992). Thus it is absolutely crucial that anyone studying culture sociologically is aware of the often hidden assumptions we all make about what 'culture' is and what it should be like.

The third topic we will investigate here concerns the question of what the sociology of culture might look like in the future. We will consider how the sociology of culture might address some of its current deficiencies by learning from other disciplines, as well as how its core concerns can be built upon in the future.

Thinking the global

Globalization is an increasingly central topic in the social sciences. This is in large part due to academic analysts responding to what seem to be processes overwhelmingly oriented towards making the world a thoroughly *interconnected* place (Waters, 1995). Economic transactions are now 'global' in scale, with, for example, companies located in one country having subsidiaries throughout a host of others. Politics seems to be increasingly played out on a world stage, with the political decisions made in one state often being due to the pressure of economic and political forces that originated outside of that state's national boundaries. Social relations too can be seen in many cases as increasingly detached from local contexts. For example, for most people in Western countries today, it is no longer an occasion for wonder or reflection that one can pick up a telephone and converse with a friend or family member on the other side of the world. Given these sorts of economic, political and social transformations, how are globalizing processes changing the nature of 'culture'? We will here identify three main themes which can be explored using the ways of thinking outlined in this book.

Alienation and solidarity

These have been key themes in sociology since the time of the classical sociologists. They refer to two possible conditions of modernity. On the one hand, 'alienation' refers to a situation whereby individuals feel socially dislocated and culturally disorientated. On the other hand, 'solidarity' refers to a situation where people feel socially and culturally part of some form of community. Modernity can be regarded under either of these terms, as either a society characterized by incoherence and disorder, or as a social order where novel forms of community are forged.

Many of the classical sociologists were particularly oriented towards diagnosing the alienating conditions of modernity as these occurred in the nineteenth century. These diagnoses could be applied to the world as it is in the early twenty-first century. The sheer rapidity of a global order, based around rapid flows of communication through the mass media, email and the internet, was pointed to by Marx 150 years ago when he described the social and cultural effects of capitalism:

> Constant revolutionizing of production, uninterrupted disturbance of all social relations, everlasting uncertainty and agitation . . . All fixed, fast-frozen relationships . . . are swept away, all new-formed ones become obsolete before they can ossify. All that is solid melts into air, all that is holy is profaned. (1983 [1848]: 207)

On this view of modernity, older cultural traditions are cast aside in favour of new ones, and novel ideas and ways of doing things are created only to be destroyed again in constant surges of innovation and change. Today's global order could be seen to work in this way, with frequent technological and economic transitions compelling vast alterations in the ways people both think and act. Insecurity and risk (Beck, 1992) characterize not only material factors like job security (Sennett, 1999), but also how individuals feel about their own place in the world, as they become more and more subjected to disruption and unexpected agitation (Giddens, 1991). A 'culture' of *insecurity* and *unease* may be an increasing characteristic of the everyday lives of people all over the world today.

A similar feeling of alienation and disaffection may characterize 'culture' today not just in terms of how people in different places feel about their place in the world, but also how they deal with the world of objects around them. In the early twentieth century, Georg Simmel argued that modern cultural life was characterized by

> the feeling of being surrounded by an immense number of cultural elements, which are not meaningless, but not profoundly meaningful to the individual either; elements which have a certain crushing quality as a mass, because an individual cannot inwardly assimilate every individual thing, but cannot simply reject it either, since it belongs potentially . . . to the sphere of his or her cultural development. (1997: 73)

Simmel's point was that there is so much today to choose from in terms of cultural objects – from multiple television channels, to hundreds of thousands of books, to a multiplicity of musical styles and recording artists – that there can be a sense of the individual being overwhelmed by *so much culture*. This is a situation arguably increased by the globalization of cultural production, whereby one can now choose from a vast array of films, music and other cultural goods from across the world.

This situation could of course be regarded in a much more positive light. It may well be the case that older patterns of cultural interest and consumption are being eroded in favour of new permutations of taste and disposition. Whereas people may once have been more constrained to fit in with the cultural preferences of the group to which they belonged – a particular nation or a specific social class – the sheer variety of goods now on offer may be forcing changes towards more heterodox, varied and open forms of taste. This is not to deny that cultural preferences are still to an extent shaped by 'local' and particular factors such as class membership, as Bourdieu has pointed out (see chapter 7). But it does open up the possibility of turning Simmel's original insight upside down: that perhaps some groups of people, when faced with a great diversity of different cultural goods, actually *revel* in that situation rather than being disturbed by it. This example shows how we can use the ideas of the classical sociologists to think *against* their original intentions as well as in line with them. Attending to the history of sociological thought allows one to use certain ideas in ways that are not slavishly faithful to the intentions of their originators.

In the same more 'optimistic' vein as that just now opened up, we can see processes of globalization as generating new opportunities as well as new challenges. A focus on the alienating aspects of globalization tends to allow us to think about a situation whereby the world itself seems now to be *out of control*, beyond both human understanding and authority. But there are parts of a globalizing world that *are* the results of conscious human planning, and these might be seen as encouraging new forms of global solidarity. Durkheimian sociology examines the ways in which modern societies enact rituals to refresh people's beliefs in the highest cultural values of those societies (Alexander, 1988). Global events like the World Cup in soccer and the Olympic Games can be seen in this light, as attempts to foster novel forms of social unity across national boundaries by bringing different groups of people together under the ideals of sportsmanship, participation and fair play. Events like Live Aid, televised all across the world, are attempts to right some of the ills of the world, such as endemic poverty in Africa, by fostering a global consciousness (Robertson, 1992), a conscious awareness amongst the people of the earth that they are all responsible for each others' welfare and well-being. Although such events have to fight against both the inequalities built into the world economic and political system(s), and tendencies towards divergence, conflict and warfare, they nonetheless point towards a more beneficial notion of 'world culture', which involves consciousness of how one's own individual actions can have adverse or more positive consequences for the lives of others in completely different parts of the globe.

Homogeneity and heterogeneity

The possibility of a 'world culture' brings us to the second main theme we will address here. This concerns tendencies towards both global homogeneity and heterogeneity. Under conditions of globalization, are cultural differences across the world being eroded or accentuated? The perspectives we have examined in this book can be used to investigate both possibilities. Any outlook that sees one of the main characteristics of modernity as being fabricated 'mass culture' can be deployed for thinking about the ways in which the world might be moving towards increasing cultural sameness. The thinkers associated with the early Frankfurt School (see chapter 2) and the American mass culture theorists (see chapter 3) both developed ideas about how 'factory-produced' culture on the lines of Hollywood films was increasingly becoming the major form of entertainment in Western countries. Just because an idea was formulated a long time ago does not invalidate its potential usefulness for us today. Consider these comments of one of the mass culture theorists, Clement Greenberg, from the 1930s:

> Kitsch has not been confined to the cities in which it was born, but has flowed out over the countryside, wiping out folk culture. Nor has it shown any regard for geographical and national-cultural boundaries. Another mass product of Western industrialism, it has gone on a triumphal tour of the world, crowding out and defacing native cultures in one . . . country after another, so that it is now by way of becoming a universal culture, the first universal culture ever . . . Today the native of China, no less than the South American Indian, the Hindu, no less than the Polynesian, have come to prefer to the products of their native art, magazine covers . . . and calendar girls. (1986 [1939]: 13–14)

Here Greenberg makes an argument the like of which is often heard today. On this view, 'mass culture', especially in its American forms, spreads out all across the world, transforming in its wake the cultural practices and preferences of different national groups, even people living in those places apparently out of the reach of such influences. Labels and trade-names such as Nike, Coca-Cola and Gap radiate out from the epicentre in the United States, inexorably spreading everywhere, such that they and the consumerist mentalities they bring with them eventually become dominant forms of culture in all parts of the globe (Klein, 2001). On this view, the idea of Adorno and Horkheimer that a single, monolithic, propagandistic Culture Industry comes to dominate life in Western countries could now be applied to situations all across the world.

Seeing matters in this light may be politically useful for those opposed to what they see as the worldwide domination of rapacious American capitalism. There may indeed be a great deal of truth in the notion that 'mass culture' oozes everywhere across the face of the earth. But it should be plain from much of the discussion in this book that making such assertions is not enough. They have to be backed up by some form of empirical evidence. It is sometimes the case that an empirical focus can challenge the more simplistic versions of these sorts of views. For example, in chapter 8 we saw how an empirical analysis of how and why certain cultural goods – such as Hollywood films – actually get made can reveal that cultural producers, for example, film studio executives, are not really engaged in some dastardly plot to take over the world. Instead, they are as much prisoners of an uncertain and risky economic environment as are the people they sell their products to. On this more empirical view, films, television programmes and other products are commissioned *in the hope* they will sell, rather than in the sure and certain knowledge they will do so. By looking at the actual conditions of production of culture, it can be seen that sometimes those who seem to be in control of global forces are actually as helpless to some degree as everyone else.

In addition, despite the undoubted global reach of American film, television and music production, different national contexts still produce 'local' forms of culture, such as the thriving film industries in India and Hong Kong, which produce entertainments primarily for domestic markets. In fact, the increasing popularity in the West of films from these contexts shows that the traffic in cultural goods is not all one-way in the direction of increasing Western dominance. This can also be witnessed of terms of the growing phenomenon of 'cultural hybridity' in cultural products. Certain forms of music, for example, such as those going under the title 'world music', bear traces of influence from many different 'cultures', combining such hitherto unconnected styles as African drumming and Buddhist chants

(Erimann, 1996). The very content of cultural products may become in future more and more disconnected from particular national and geographical cultural traditions. Thus cultural goods sold in different places around the world may increasingly involve 'fusions' of previously separated cultural phenomena, rather than simply be vehicles for the propagation of 'American' or 'Western' values. However, we would have to enquire of these new cultural forms whether they truly were 'organic' and 'spontaneous' outcomes of 'global' forms of transcultural consciousness, or merely the fabrications of Western culture industries seeking to exploit new markets, such as that which involves wealthy, middle-class Westerners seeking a 'spiritual fix' from 'Eastern' mystical philosophies. If the latter were the case, then we might be returned to accepting in some senses the mass culture model which emphasizes Western cultural power.

Nonetheless, if one also looks in more empirical ways at contexts of cultural *consumption*, a more nuanced picture may emerge than that proffered by theories of 'mass culture'. Some of the accounts of tastes and preferences we have examined in this book can be used to think about ways in which people outside of the West may retain dispositions towards forms of cultural goods *not* produced by Western culture industries. In chapter 3, we saw how Herbert Gans argued that different groups in big American cities, such as Italian-Americans, possessed their own specific criteria of what they were interested in and what entertained them. They had their own 'taste culture' that filtered out the products of the culture industries that the group took no interest in. In like fashion, the implication of the arguments of Karl Mannheim (chapter 1) and Pierre Bourdieu (chapter 7), that each social class has both its own particular forms of cultural taste and specific way of understanding the world, is that different groups of people do not respond uniformly to the things that they are offered. The 'culture' of each group (its tastes, its 'worldview') dictates how its members respond to objects and situations that globalizing forces lay in their path. Thus, how a middle-class Korean reacts to advertisements for Benetton clothes or Pepsi may differ markedly from how a working-class Argentinean may respond. Different national and group traditions will, on this view, mean that there will never be anything other than *heterogeneous* sets of responses to the primarily (though not exclusively) *homogeneous* set of cultural goods being created in, and disseminated from, the United States and other locales of global cultural production. From this perspective, even *within* Western countries, the audiences for cultural goods are always disparate and differentiated, rather than forming a uniform 'mass audience'. This is the sort of analysis that has long been offered by the 'culturalist' approach to cultural matters (see chapter 4). The ability of ordinary people to some degree to resist the powerful forces that attempt to shape their lives is here foregrounded, a style of thinking that could be applied to working-class English youths or peasants in the hinterlands of Malaysia (Scott, 1985).

As we have seen, the danger of this approach is that it can over-emphasize the 'resistive' capacities of people, and thus underestimate the extent to which they can be imposed upon by the powerful. Globalizing forces, after all, potentially have the power to transform local contexts, perhaps changing them beyond all recognition. Under conditions of globalization, it might in fact be argued that the 'local' is disappearing under the pressure of compulsions to become like everywhere else. Certain forms of spatial location, for example air-port departure lounges, are increasingly similar across every part of the world (Augé, 1995). The architecture of tower blocks in the financial districts of large cities often looks very similar, whether you are in Frankfurt or Kuala Lumpur.

Nonetheless, there is evidence to suggest that even if 'local' con-texts are increasingly brought under the influence of global forces, the effects of these forces need not lead to increasing homogeneity. In place of seeing local and national traditions as wholly unchanged by global situations, we can see them as adapting to new circum-stances in their own particular ways. We noted above the possibility of seeing some cultural products, such as 'world music' recordings, as 'hybrid' entities, involving disparate cultural influences. So too may identities today be seen as 'hybrid', involving interwoven pat-terns of belief and value from previously separated sources (Werbner, 1997). This idea is particularly associated with post-structuralist and postmodernist notions of the self (see chapter 6), which see identity as shifting and open to change. Although we have seen that this position perhaps overemphasizes the degree to which ways of think-ing and feeling are fluid and open, nonetheless it does point to the possibility that global forces can shape the ways in which people think without altering completely their adherence to the cultural traditions within which they were raised.

The nature of boundaries

At a fundamental level, issues surrounding the notion of globalization are oriented towards understanding the nature of boundaries, the third and final topic we will deal with here. Many contemporary sociologists (e.g. Urry, 2000) argue that under the conditions of globalization which we are now faced with, the original ideas of the classical thinkers, from Herder to Durkheim, have to be rethought, because they saw both 'society' and 'culture' as bounded entities, tied to particular geographical areas and a single state's territory: 'French' culture, 'British' society and so on. The challenge of globalization is to think how social and cultural forms of life today may transcend these national boundaries in certain important ways. Some of the perspectives we have looked at in this book do go some way to meeting this challenge.

Postmodernist ideas, in particular, operate around a vocabulary of boundaries being transgressed, overcome and overthrown. We noted in chapter 6 that Baudrillard's account of hyperreality, while overstated in some senses, highlights some of the important aspects of cyberspace, a locale where signs proliferate, and where there are whole 'virtual' worlds of meaning. Use of the internet, either by a private individual or by a member of a chat-group, has implications not only for how people think about their place in the world – not just as 'American', for example, but also as part of a worldwide community of Star Trek fans – but also for the ways in which national authorities seek to control them. If information can be sent by email from one country to another without much official hindrance, this obviously affects the capacities of national governments to control the ideas that are penetrating their putative realm of control.

Semiotic approaches to culture may also be a valuable resource here, in that they can allow us to track the proliferation of meanings across national boundaries. For example, it is possible to identify *worldwide systems of signs*, the meanings of which can be deciphered everywhere. For example, the logo 'Coca-Cola' is increasingly becoming a sign that can be comprehended in every corner of the globe. The *lexicon* of a uniform 'world culture' that exists above and beyond delimited national territories, if such a thing indeed exists, can be discerned using semiotic means. But any naive belief in a wholly homogeneous mass culture that affects every part of the world equally can also be challenged by semiotic approaches. The newer forms of 'social semiotics' we examined in chapter 5 insist, unlike some forms of postmodernism, that the meanings of signs are 'decoded' by people in particular social contexts, these contexts potentially having a powerful effect on how the signs are understood.

Once again, the empirically sensitive nature of most forms of the sociology of culture point us towards not uncritically accepting the idea that the existence of a 'world culture' necessarily means that it compels people everywhere to think, act and feel in exactly the same ways. It may, in fact, be more profitable to think not of 'globalization', where that means tendencies towards increasing homogenization and sameness, but of 'glocalization', which points to a condition where forces of homogenization are always intertwined with forces of heterogenization (Robertson, 1992). Culturally, as well as socially, economically and politically, the contemporary world can be characterized as involving dialectics of sameness and difference. If this is so, then many of the ways of thinking covered in this book can aid us in uncovering the often unpredictable aspects of a globalizing world.

The drive to reflexivity

Being a sociologist brings with it certain responsibilities. In return for possessing what might be seen as certain valuable types of knowledge of the human world, the ways in which those knowledges are used must be reflected upon. This demand applies to the sociologist who wishes to understand cultural matters as much as it does to any other type of sociologist. Whatever an individual's beliefs on a particular issue, good sociology might be said to rest on trying to control one's own biases and attempting to see the situation being examined in as fully rounded a way as possible. If your conclusions on a particular topic are wholly a reflection of your own pre-formed ideas, then you have succeeded not in analysing your subject matter sociologically, but merely in having dogmatically stuck to your own attitudes, and having learned nothing from the experience of research. It is out of these sorts of concern that the American sociologist Lewis Coser (1978) counselled that the sociologist of culture must do what the sociologist of religion should do: put aside as much as possible his or her own personal attitude towards the religious beliefs being studied, and become, for the purposes of that study, a *sociological agnostic*. Whether you believe the religion under study or not should make no difference. The point is to *study* it, not *moralize* about it. If applied to the study of culture, this rule can be taken to mean: it should not matter whether you like a particular type of culture or not. You are meant to be studying it sociologically, not judging it from the point of view of your own values.

This injunction is complicated by the fact that different types of sociology have different purposes. A sociology that sees itself as rigorously 'scientific', as did Durkheim's (1982 [1895]) positivist version of sociology, believes that the researcher's own values can be purged in favour of a wholly 'neutral' outlook. This kind of view is anathema to (certain kinds of) Marxists, who regard sociology as being a critique of capitalist society; as such, it is not, nor should be, a 'neutral' endeavour. A third position was adumbrated among the classical sociologists by Max Weber (1989), who held that sociologists should *try* to be 'neutral' but, inevitably, their own personal attitudes, and the values of the culture they had been reared in, would shape both what they thought was important in the thing they were studying and what conclusions they would draw about it. The best that could be done, on Weber's opinion, was for the sociologist to reflect on what kinds of bias he or she might be bringing to their sociological study, *even when they think they are being 'neutral' and 'objective'*. Weber's position is one of the main roots of the notion of *reflexivity*, the idea that sociologists must interrogate themselves to find the hidden dispositions and biases they bring to their sociological work.

This is a particularly important exercise for sociologists of culture. As has been seen time and again in this book, what one person says about the 'culture' of another group or individual is often a disguised (or not so disguised) form of social power. Cultural evaluations are often tacit forms of creating and recreating forms of social superiority and inferiority. If that is true for how social actors behave, then it is also true for the sociologist, for sociologists are also social actors. We too are members of classes and of interest groups, we too have political axes to grind, we too like some types of people and dislike others. What 'culture' is and how it should be are never just purely 'academic' matters. Instead, they are of pressing importance inside and outside the university. This is because by pronouncing on cultural issues, we are implicitly – whether we like it or not – committing ourselves *politically*, through identifying how we think cultural life should be lived. In particular, apparently 'neutral' academic 'identifications' of whether 'high culture' is better than 'popular' culture, or whether it is just a form of elite power, hide profound and deeply held political visions as to how people should live, in this case either venerating 'art' or rejecting it as a middle-class con trick.

We are not neutral observers of social and cultural life, with all their struggles, battles and controversies, but we *can* strive to be more thoughtfully aware of the kinds of bias we bring from our own personal backgrounds. In addition, we have to think about what we gain *academically* by adopting one type of position or another. Arguing in a particular way can bring the sociologist a lot of prestige from some quarters, and damn her utterly in the eyes of other groups. As Bourdieu (1990a: 150–5) argued, how we construct sociological understandings of people 'out there' in the 'real world' – the ways in which we comprehend their social and cultural existences – are always bound up with both our own personal dispositions and the politics of academic life. Thus if we are not to be prisoners of tacit assumptions and covert biases, we must seek to bring these factors out into the open as fully and honestly as possible, and to expose them to the light of reflexive self-questioning.

This much has been done to some degree by many of the sociologists whose ideas we have looked at in this book. This is particularly so in the case of those who have been sceptical about the allegedly superior qualities of 'high culture'. In their own respective ways, Mannheim (chapter 1), Shils and Gans (chapter 3), Hoggart and Williams (chapter 4), Barthes (chapter 5), Lyotard and Baudrillard (chapter 6), Bourdieu (chapter 7) and 'production of culture' scholars such as Dimaggio and Becker (chapter 8) have all criticized those who have averred that 'art' and 'high culture' are just naturally superior to 'mass' and 'popular' culture. The general sociological consensus has been that there is no such superiority. Instead, the alleged superiority of 'high culture' comes merely from it being the 'property' of elite groups, who define and label it as superior to the cultures of other groups, and in so doing retain social power for themselves. Those who argue in favour of 'high culture' have failed to question reflexively their own cultural dispositions, which generally are those of the educated and 'refined' upper-middle class, blinding them to the true, arbitrary nature of 'high culture'.

While this critique of the defenders of 'high culture' is compelling, most of the sociologists mentioned above have failed to think through *their own* hidden assumptions that led them to this position. There are two main issues that on the whole they have not uncovered. First, this viewpoint fails to consider what might be gained in making such claims *for the sociologist's position in society*. By saying 'high culture' is nothing more than a fabrication of the powerful, a political blow might be said to be struck against elite groups. Clearly this view is in part a product of the political ideals of certain sociologists. But making such claims can also have the effect of making sociologists seem more informed and clever than those groups who 'believe in' high culture, groups which in the view of certain sociologists are living in a world of illusions, whilst the sociologist has seen the real 'truth' of the situation. In so doing, we have to account for the possibility that the sociologist – individually, or collectively as part of the group known as 'sociologists' – is intentionally or unintentionally attempting to win social prestige over other people, by claiming he or she knows more about their lives than they do. The sociologist is also involved, again perhaps un- or semi-intentionally, in winning power over other *types of academic*, such as art historians, whose entire professional careers are based on interpreting and evaluating the worth of 'art'. But if 'art' and 'high culture' are revealed by the sociologist to be mere fictions, then at a stroke the sociologist seems to have gained the upper hand against these other academics. In essence, what sociologists say is always part, whether intended or not, of *academic politics*. The phenomenon of 'sociological imperialism' (Strong, 1979), whereby sociologists claim to have all the answers and everyone else is seen to be wholly deluded, is a problem that we constantly have to be on reflexive guard against. Sociology does not have *all* the answers, but it may have *some* of them. The views of others – inside and outside the academy – have to be respected, listened to and learned from. Only in that way will potential tendencies towards high-handed arrogance on the behalf of sociologists be avoided.

A second hidden aspect of the critique of 'high culture' is that being seen to be on the side of 'the people' allows one to be seen to be an advocate of 'democracy' and 'openness' against stuffy convention and tradition. Self-confessed populists like Willis and Fiske (see chapter 4) and some postmodernists (see chapter 6) can gain prestige for themselves both inside and outside the university by presenting themselves as 'champions of the people'. But this is as tendentious and politically charged a position as that of someone such as Adorno (see chapter 2), who denounced 'mass culture' in favour of a defence of 'autonomous art'. Both 'elitism' and 'populism' are politically oriented *ways of seeing* the world, and both may have valuable things to say. But neither has a monopoly on the 'truth'.

Many students that the present authors have taught tend to side with the 'populists' over the 'elitists'. But if you are of that persuasion, you have to stop to think *why* you are attracted to that position. You must also reflect on how this is not just simply *the* way of looking at cultural issues, but is rather just *one* possible perspective. What evidence can the other side bring to bear on these issues, and how should one evaluate that evidence so that it is given a fair hearing? The same caveats apply if you side more with the 'elitists'. Neither of these positions is just simply 'true'. Instead, what you must do is try to think why your own personal background might be at the root of your predisposition towards one position or the other. In what ways might your upbringing and your own current lifestyle orient you towards liking certain forms of culture and not others, and favouring one particular kind of explanation of cultural matters? If you address these questions, you will be doing what a rigorous sociological approach demands: turning the gaze of sociological enquiry back upon *yourself*.

The future of the sociology of culture

The question of reflexivity also involves us thinking about the strengths and limitations of sociology itself. If we are not to fall into the trap of 'sociological imperialism', thinking that sociology has all the answers and other disciplines have none, then we must reflect on the limits of the sociological gaze as well as its benefits.

One particular problem is that of disciplinary blindness. This is a situation where certain things are downplayed or ignored altogether, because the disciplinary lens through which we look at the world is not able to see these things or grasp them adequately. Sociology *is* able to deal with social and cultural issues – that is its very reason for existing. But it is, in our opinion, not so good at thinking about how these aspects of human life intersect with 'nature', with all those things such as plants, animals and the earth itself which together constitute the 'natural' environment in which humans live. Most forms of sociology in the twentieth century chose to ignore such factors, because they were seen to be outside of sociology's disciplinary boundaries. Some of the classical sociologists, especially Spencer and Marx (see chapter 1), were not so narrow in their focus, for they sought to understand both how 'nature' is shaped by human social and cultural life and, vice versa, how these latter are affected by 'nature'. In our opinion, a really satisfactory account of 'culture' would see it not as something wholly different from 'nature' but as connected to, and involved in interplay with, 'natural' factors. Most of the paradigms covered in this book have shunned this task. But there are signs that sociology will in the future be more open to addressing the vastly complicated – but also hugely stimulating – issues of how 'society', 'culture' and 'nature' all fit together (Benton, 1996).

Challenges to sociology in general, and the sociology of culture in particular, have been mounted in recent years from within the social sciences and humanities. In particular, the discipline of 'cultural studies' has arisen as a way of studying culture that departs in some ways from sociology's key concerns. There has been a series of 'turf wars' as to which sort of approach is superior in understanding cultural phenomena (Long, 1997; McLennan, 1998). These sorts of dispute have been based on rather superficial identifications of what both 'sociology' and 'cultural studies' are or could be. It should be quite clear from reading this book that there are many different *types* of sociology of culture, each with its own emphases and interests. In addition, there is a lot of overlap between some of these forms of sociology and the intellectual components of 'cultural studies'. In particular, 'culturalism' (see chapter 4) was the basis for the earliest types of cultural studies, as well as being sociologically informed in certain ways. Later versions of cultural studies tend to be informed more by semiotic and postmodernist ways of thinking (see chapters 5 and 6). These, too, have intimate connections with sociology, even if postmodernist thought challenges some of classical sociology's assumptions.

Sociology and cultural studies would do well to learn from each other rather than exist in a state of permanent conflict. Sociology can take from cultural studies the imperative to attend closely to particular cultural 'texts' (rather in the way suggested by Richard Hoggart in chapter 4). Cultural studies can show sociology how to focus on the *details* of cultural phenomena, rather than remain mostly at the level of rather abstract generalizations (Wolff, 1999). Conversely, cultural studies can learn from sociology how to overcome one of its own forms of disciplinary blindness, namely that 'social' factors are downplayed or ignored in favour of an exclusive focus on the 'cultural'. By relating 'culture' and 'society' to each other, and by thinking about 'culture' in terms of the problem of social structure and social action, sociology has not remained caught within the assumption that 'culture' exists as a realm unto itself, disconnected from sources of social power and untouched by how people actually act and think (Rojek and Turner, 2000). By learning from each other, cultural studies and sociology would be mutually enriched, and able in the future to provide accounts of culture that are less stricken by forms of disciplinary myopia.

This book has attempted to show that sociology has, over the years, provided a rich source of ways in which to understand cultural matters. We have shown both the limitations and the benefits of each way of thinking about culture sociologically. We believe that the strengths more than outweigh the drawbacks, and that, overall, the sociology of culture is a very important contribution to comprehending the nature of human life. By reflecting upon what deficiencies it has, by seeking to overcome them, and by augmenting its strengths, we believe that the sociology of culture will continue throughout the twenty-first century to be a very fruitful way of understanding fundamental aspects of the human condition.

References

Adorno, Theodor W. (1950) *The Authoritarian Personality*, New York: Harper and Row.

—— (1967a) 'Cultural Criticism and Society', in *Prisms*, London: Neville Spearman.

—— (1967b) 'Perennial Fashion – Jazz', in *Prisms*, London: Neville Spearman.

—— (1973) *Negative Dialectics*, London: Routledge.

—— (1976a) 'Sociology and Empirical Research', in idem et al., *The Positivist Dispute in German Sociology*, London: Heinemann.

—— (1976b) 'On the Logic of the Social Sciences', in idem et al., *The Positivist Dispute in German Sociology*, London: Heinemann.

—— (1994a) 'The Stars Down to Earth', in *Adorno: The Stars Down to Earth and Other Essays on the Irrational in Culture*, London: Routledge.

—— (1994b) 'Theses Against Occultism', in *Adorno: The Stars Down to Earth and Other Essays on the Irrational in Culture*, London: Routledge.

—— (1996a) 'Culture Industry Reconsidered', in *The Culture Industry: Selected Essays on Mass Culture*, London: Routledge.

—— (1996b) 'Free Time', in *The Culture Industry: Selected Essays on Mass Culture*, London: Routledge.

—— (1996c) 'Freudian Theory and the Pattern of Fascist Propaganda', in *The Culture Industry: Selected Essays on Mass Culture*, London: Routledge.

—— (1996d) 'How to Look at Television', in *The Culture Industry: Selected Essays on Mass Culture*, London: Routledge.

—— (1996e) 'On the Fetish Character in Music and the Regression in Listening', in *The Culture Industry: Selected Essays on Mass Culture*, London: Routledge.

—— (1996f) 'Resignation', in *The Culture Industry: Selected Essays on Mass Culture*, London: Routledge.

—— (1996g) 'Transparencies on Film', in *The Culture Industry: Selected Essays on Mass Culture*, London: Routledge.

—— (1997a) *Aesthetic Theory*, Minneapolis: University of Minnesota Press.

—— (1997b) *Minima Moralia*, London: Verso.

—— (2000) *Introduction to Sociology*, Cambridge: Polity.

Adorno, Theodor W. and Horkheimer, Max (1992 [1944]) *Dialectic of Enlightenment*, London: Verso.

Adorno, Theodor W. and Eisler, Hanns (1994 [1947]) *Composing for the Films*, London: The Athlone Press.

Alexander, Jeffrey C. (1982) *Theoretical Logic in Sociology*. Vol. I: *Positivism, Presuppositions, and Current Controversies*, Berkeley: University of California Press.

—— (1983) *Theoretical Logic in Sociology*. Vol. III: *The Classical Attempt At Theoretical Synthesis: Max Weber*, London: Routledge.

—— (1988) *Durkheimian Sociology: Cultural Studies*, Cambridge: Cambridge University Press.

—— (1995) *Fin de Siècle Social Theory: Relativism, Reduction, and the Problem of Reason*, London: Verso.

Anderson, R. J., Hughes, J. A. and Sharrock, W. W. (1987) *Classic Disputes in Sociology*, London: Allen and Unwin.

Andrews, David L. and Loy, J. W. (1993) 'British Cultural Studies and Sport: Past Encounters and Future Possibilities', *Quest*, 45, 255–76.

Arnold, Matthew (1995 [1869]) 'Culture and Anarchy', in Stefan Collini (ed.), *Culture and Anarchy and Other Writings*, Cambridge: Cambridge University Press.

Augé, Marc (1995) *Non-places: Introduction to an Anthropology of Supermodernity*, London: Verso.

Barnard, F. M. (1965) *Herder's Social and Political Thought, From Enlightenment to Nationalism*, Oxford: Clarendon Press.

Barthes, Roland (1977 [1964]) *Elements of Semiology*, New York: Hill and Wang.

—— (1983 [1970]) *The Empire of Signs*, London: Jonathan Cape.

—— (1985 [1967]) *The Fashion System*, London: Jonathan Cape.

—— (1988 [1964]) 'The Kitchen of Meaning', in *The Semiotic Challenge*, Oxford: Basil Blackwell.

—— (1988) *The Semiotic Challenge*, Oxford: Basil Blackwell.

—— (1993 [1957]) *Mythologies*, London: Vintage.

Baudrillard, Jean (1975) *The Mirror of Production*, St Louis: Telos Press.

—— (1983a) *In the Shadow of the Silent Majorities or The End of the Social*, New York: Semiotext(e).

—— (1983b) *Simulations*, New York: Semiotext(e).

—— (1987) *The Ecstasy of Communication*, New York: Semiotext(e).

—— (1990a) *Fatal Strategies*, New York: Semiotext(e)/Pluto.

—— (1990b) *Seduction*, London: Macmillan.

—— (1994 [1986]) *America*, London: Verso.

—— (1996a) *The Perfect Crime*, London: Verso.

—— (1996b [1968]) *The System of Objects*, London: Verso.

—— (1998 [1970]) *The Consumer Society: Myths and Structures*, London: Sage.

Bauman, Zygmunt (1992) *Intimations of Postmodernity*, London: Routledge.
Beck, Ulrich (1992) *Risk Society: Towards a New Modernity*, London: Sage.
Becker, Howard (1963) *Outsiders: Studies in the Sociology of Deviance*, New York: Free Press.
—— (1974) 'Art as Collective Action', *American Sociological Review*, 39, 6.
—— (1984) *Art Worlds*, Berkeley: University of California Press.
Bell, Daniel (1996 [1976]) *The Cultural Contradictions of Capitalism*, New York: Basic Books.
Bellah, Robert (et al.) (1988) *Habits of the Heart*, London: Hutchinson.
Bendix, Reinhard (1966) *Max Weber: An Intellectual Portrait*, London: Methuen.
Benjamin, Walter (1970 [1936]) 'The Work of Art in the Age of Mechanical Reproduction', in Walter Benjamin and Hannah Arendt (eds), *Illuminations*, London: Cape.
Bennett, Tony (ed.) (1986) *Culture, Ideology and Social Process: A Reader*, London: Batsford/Open University Press.
—— (1998) *Culture: A Reformer's Science*, London: Sage.
Benton, Ted (ed.) (1996) *The Greening of Marxism*, London: Guilford Press.
Berlin, Isaiah (2000) *The Roots of Romanticism*, London: Pimlico.
Berman, Marshall (1983) *All That is Solid Melts Into Air*, London: Verso.
Bourdieu, Pierre (1976) 'Marriage Strategies as Strategies of Social Reproduction', in Robert Forster and Orest Ranum (eds), *Family and Society: Selections from the Annales – Economies, Societies, Civilisations*, Baltimore: Johns Hopkins University Press.
—— (1977) *Outline of a Theory of Practice*, Cambridge: Cambridge University Press.
—— (1987) 'The Force of Law: Toward a Sociology of the Juridical Field', *Hastings Law Journal*, 38, 5: 814–53.
—— (1988a) *Homo Academicus*, Cambridge: Polity.
—— (1988b) 'Vive La Crise! For Heterodoxy in Social Science', *Theory and Society*, 17: 773–87.
—— (1990a) *In Other Words*, Cambridge: Polity.
—— (1990b) *Photography: A Middle-brow Art*, Cambridge: Polity.
—— (1991a) *Language and Symbolic Power*, Cambridge: Polity.
—— (1991b) 'Genesis and Structure of the Religious Field', *Comparative Social Research*, 13: 1–44.
—— (1992a) *Distinction: A Social Critique of the Judgement of Taste*, London: Routledge.
—— (1992b) *The Logic of Practice*, Cambridge: Polity.
—— (1993a) *The Field of Cultural Production*, Cambridge: Polity.
—— (1993b) *Sociology in Question*, London: Sage.
—— (1996) *The Rules of Art: Genesis and Structure of the Literary Field*, Cambridge: Polity.
—— (1998a) *Acts of Resistance*, New York: The New Press.
—— (1998b) *On Television and Journalism*, London: Pluto Press.
—— (1998c) *Practical Reason: On the Theory of Action*, Cambridge: Polity.
—— (1998d) *The State Nobility*, Cambridge: Polity.

—— (1999) *The Weight of the World*, Cambridge: Polity.

—— (2000) *Pascalian Meditations*, Cambridge: Polity.

Bourdieu, Pierre and Darbel, Alain (1991) *The Love of Art*, Cambridge: Polity.

Bourdieu, Pierre and Haacke, Hans (1995) *Free Exchange*, Cambridge: Polity.

Bourdieu, Pierre and Passeron, Jean-Claude (1979) *The Inheritors*, Chicago: University of Chicago Press.

—— (1990 [1970]) *Reproduction in Education, Society and Culture*, London: Sage.

Bourdieu, Pierre and Wacquant, Loic J. D. (1992) *An Invitation to Reflexive Sociology*, Cambridge: Polity.

Bourdieu, Pierre, Chamboredon, Jean-Claude and Passeron, Jean-Claude (1991) *The Craft of Sociology*, Berlin and New York: Walter de Gruyter.

Brooker, Peter and Brooker, Will (eds) (1997) *Postmodern After-images: A Reader in Film, Television and Video*, London: Arnold.

Brubaker, Rogers (1985) 'Rethinking Classical Theory: The Sociological Vision of Pierre Bourdieu', *Theory and Society*, 14: 745–75.

Brunkhorst, Hauke (1999) *Adorno and Critical Theory*, Cardiff: University of Wales Press.

Buck-Morss, Susan (1977) *The Origin of Negative Dialectics*, Hassocks, Sussex: The Harvester Press.

Bulmer, Martin (1985) *The Chicago School of Sociology: Institutionalization, Diversity and the Rise of Sociological Research*, Chicago: University of Chicago Press.

Caesar, Michael (1999) *Umberto Eco*, Cambridge: Polity.

Callinicos, Alex (1989) *Against Postmodernism: A Marxist Critique*, Cambridge: Polity.

Cantor, M. G. (1971) *The Hollywood TV Producer: His Work and his Audience*, New York: Basic Books.

Carey, John (1992) *The Intellectuals and the Masses*, London: Faber and Faber.

de Certeau, Michel (1984) *The Practice of Everyday Life*, vol. I, Berkeley: University of California Press.

Chambers, Iain (1986) *Popular Culture: The Metropolitan Experience*, London: Methuen.

Clark, Katarina and Holquist, Michael (1984) *Mikhail Bakhtin*, Cambridge, MA: Harvard University Press.

Clarke, John, Hall, Stuart, Jefferson, Tony and Roberts, Brian (1976) 'Subcultures, Cultures and Class', in Stuart Hall and Tony Jefferson (eds) (1976) *Resistance through Rituals: Youth Subcultures in Post-war Britain*, London: Hutchinson.

Cohen, Albert K. (1955) *Delinquent Boys*, Chicago: Free Press.

Cohen, Phil (1980) 'Subcultural Conflict and Working Class Community', in Stuart Hall (ed.), *Culture, Media, Language: Working Papers in Cultural Studies, 1972–79*, London: Hutchinson.

Collins, Randall (1986) *Max Weber: A Skeleton Key*, London: Sage.

Coser, Lewis (1978) 'Editor's Introduction', *Social Research*, 45, 2.

Crane, Diana (1979) 'The Gate-keepers of Science: Some Factors Affecting the Selection of Articles for Scientific Journals', in James E. Curtis and John W. Petras (eds), *The Sociology of Knowledge: A Reader*, London: Gerald Duckworth.

—— (1992) *The Production of Culture; Media and the Urban Arts*, Newbury Park: Sage.

Dahrendorf, Ralf (1959) *Class and Class Conflict in an Industrial Society*, London: Routledge.

Dawe, Alan (1970) 'The Two Sociologies', *British Journal of Sociology*, 21: 207–18.

Dentith, Simon (1995) 'An Overview of the Writings of Bakhtin and His Circle', in *Bakhtinian Thought: An Introductory Reader*, London: Routledge.

Derrida, Jacques (1978) *Writing and Difference*, London: Routledge.

Dimaggio, Paul (1986) 'Cultural Entrepreneurship in Nineteenth Century Boston: The Creation of an Organisational Base for High Culture in America', in Richard Collins, Philip Schlesinger, James Curran, Paddy Scannell and Nicholas Garnham (eds), *Media, Culture and Society: A Critical Reader*, London: Sage.

Docker, John (1994) *Postmodernism and Popular Culture: A Cultural History*, Cambridge: Cambridge University Press.

Dominick, J. R. (1987) 'Film Economic and Film Content: 1964–1983', in B. Austin (ed.), *Current Research in Film: Audiences, Economics, and Law*, vol. 3, Norwood, NJ: Ablex.

Durkheim, Emile (1952 [1897]) *Suicide*, London: Routledge.

—— (1972) *Emile Durkheim: Selected Writings*, ed. and trans. Anthony Giddens, Cambridge: Cambridge University Press.

—— (1982 [1895]) *The Rules of Sociological Method*, Basingstoke: Macmillan.

—— (1984 [1893]) *The Division of Labour in Society*, Basingstoke: Macmillan.

—— (2001 [1912]) *The Elementary Forms of the Religious Life*, Oxford: Oxford University Press.

Durkheim, Emile and Mauss, Marcel (1969 [1903]) *Primitive Classification*, London: Cohen and West.

Eagleton, Terry (1976) *Criticism and Ideology*, London: New Left Books.

—— (1991) *Ideology: An Introduction*, London: Verso.

Eco, Umberto (1987 [1967]) 'Towards a Semiological Guerrilla Warfare', in *Travels in Hyper-Reality*, London: Picador.

Elias, Norbert (1995 [1939]) *The Civilizing Process*, Oxford: Blackwell.

Eliot, T. S. (1939) *The Idea of a Christian Society*, London: Faber and Faber.

—— (1954 [1948]) *Notes Towards a Definition of Culture*, London: Faber and Faber.

Engels, Friedrich (1968 [1890]) 'Letter to Bloch, September 21, 1890', in *Marx/Engels: Selected Works*, London: Lawrence and Wishart.

Erlmann, V. (1996) 'The Aesthetics of the Global Imagination: Reflections on World Music in the 1990s', *Public Culture*, 8, 3 (Spring).

Faulkner, R. (1983) *Music On Demand*, New Brunswick, NJ: Transaction.

Faulkner, R. and Anderson, A. B. (1987) 'Short-term Projects and Emergent Careers: Evidence from Hollywood', *American Journal of Sociology*, 92.

Featherstone, Mike (1991) *Consumer Culture and Postmodernism*, London: Sage.

Febvre, Lucion (1998) '*Civilisation*: Evolution of a Word and a Group of Ideas', in John Rundell and Stephen Mennell (eds), *Classical Readings in Civilization and Culture*, London: Routledge.

Fiedler, Leslie (1957) 'The Middle Aganist Both Ends', in B. Rosenberg and D. Manning White (eds), *Mass Culture: The Popular Arts in America*, New York: Free Press.

Fiske, John (1989a) *Reading the Popular*, Boston: Unwin Hyman.

—— (1989b) *Understanding Popular Culture*, Boston: Unwin Hyman.

Fowler, Bridget (1997) *Pierre Bourdieu and Cultural Theory*, London: Sage.

Frankel, Charles (1969) *The Faith of Reason: The Idea of Progress in the French Enlightenment*, New York: Octagon.

Friedberg, Harris (2001) ' "Hang Up My Rock and Roll Shoes": The Cultural Production of Rock and Roll', in C. Lee Harrington and Denise Bielby (eds), *Popular Culture: Production and Consumption*, Oxford: Blackwell.

Frisby, David and Featherstone, Mike (1997) *Simmel on Culture: Selected Writings*, London: Sage.

Fromm, Erich (1971 [1932]) 'Psychoanalytic Characterology and Its Contribution to Sociology', in *The Crisis in Psychoanalysis*, London: Cape.

Frow, John (1987) 'Accounting for Tastes: Some Problems in Bourdieu's Sociology of Culture', *Cultural Studies*, 1, 1: 59–73.

Game, Ann (1991) *Undoing the Social: Towards a Deconstructive Sociology*, Milton Keynes: Open University Press.

Gans, Herbert J. (1962) *The Urban Villagers: Group and Class in the Life of Italian-Americans*, New York: Free Press.

—— (1974) *Popular Culture and High Culture: An Analysis and Elevation of Taste*, New York: Basic Books.

—— (1978 [1966]) 'Popular Culture in America: Social Problem in a Mass Society or Social Asset in a Pluralist Society', in Peter Davison, Rolf Meyersohn and Edward Shils (eds), *Literary Taste, Culture, and Mass Communication*, vol. I, Teaneck, NJ: Chadwyck-Healey.

Garnham, Nicholas (1986) 'Extended Review: Bourdieu's *Distinction*', *Sociological Review*, 34, 2: 423–33.

Garnham, Nicholas and Williams, Raymond (1980) 'Pierre Bourdieu and the Sociology of Culture: an Introduction', *Media, Culture and Society*, 2, 3: 209–23.

Giddens, Anthony (1984) *The Constitution of Society: Outline of the Theory of Structuration*, Cambridge: Polity.

—— (1990) *The Consequences of Modernity*, Cambridge: Polity.

—— (1991) *Modernity and Self-Identity*, Cambridge: Polity.

Glasgow University Media Group (1976) *Bad News*, London: Routledge.

Gottdiener, M. (1995) *Postmodern Semiotics: Material Culture and the Forms of Postmodern Life*, Oxford: Blackwell.

Gramsci, Antonio (1971) *Selections from the Prison Notebooks*, London: Lawrence and Wishart.

Greenberg, Clement (1986 [1939]) 'Avant-garde and Kitsch', in John O'Brian (ed.), *Clement Greenberg: The Collected Essays and Criticism. Vol. I: Perceptions and Judgments 1939–1944*, Chicago: University of Chicago Press.

—— (1999) *Homemade Esthetics: Observations on Art and Taste*, New York: Oxford University Press.

Greenlee, Douglas (1973) *Peirce's Concept of Sign*, The Hague: Mouton.

Griller, Robin (1996) 'The Return of the Subject? The Methodology of Pierre Bourdieu', *Critical Sociology*, 22, 1: 3–28.

Habermas, Jürgen (1984) *The Theory of Communicative Action*, vol. I, London: Heinemann.

Halfpenny, Peter (1982) *Positivism and Sociology: Explaining Social Life*, London: Allen and Unwin.

Hall, Stuart (1981) 'Cultural Studies: Two Paradigms', in T. Bennett, G. Martin, C. Mercer and J. Woollacott (eds), *Culture, Ideology and Social Process: A Reader*, London: Open University Press.

—— (1993 [1980]) 'Encoding, Decoding', in Simon During (ed.), *The Cultural Studies Reader*, London: Routledge.

Hall, Stuart and du Gay, Paul (1996) *Questions of Cultural Identity*, London: Sage.

Hall, Stuart and Whannell, Paddy (1964) *The Popular Arts*, London: Hutchinson Educational.

Harland, Richard (1987) *Superstructuralism*, London: Routledge.

Harris, David (1992) *From Class Struggle to the Politics of Pleasure: The Effects of Gramscianism on Cultural Studies*, London: Routledge.

Harvey, David (1989) *The Condition of Postmodernity: An Inquiry into the Origins of Cultural Change*, Oxford: Blackwell.

Hassan, Ihab (1985) 'The Culture of Postmodernism', *Theory, Culture and Society*, 2, 3.

Hawthorn, Geoffrey (1976) *Enlightenment and Despair*, Cambridge: Cambridge University Press.

Hebdige, Dick (1988 [1979]) *Subculture: The Meaning of Style*, London: Routledge.

Heelas, Paul (1996) *The New Age Movement: The Celebration of the Self and the Sacralization of Modernity*, Oxford: Blackwell.

Hegel, Georg W. F. (1975) *Lectures on the Philosophy of World History: Introduction: Reason in History*, Cambridge: Cambridge University Press.

Held, David (1980) *Introduction to Critical Theory*, Cambridge: Polity.

Hirsch, Paul (1972) 'Processing Fads and Fashion: An Organisation Set Analysis of the Cultural Industry System', *American Journal of Sociology*, 77: 639–59.

—— (1978) 'Production and Distribution Roles Among Cultural Organisations: On the Division of Labour Across Intellectual Disciplines', *Social Research*, 45, 2: 315–30.

Hodge, Robert and Kress, Gunther (1988) *Social Semiotics*, Cambridge: Polity.

Hoggart, Richard (1962 [1957]) *The Uses of Literacy: Aspects of Working-class Life with Special Reference to Publications and Entertainment*, Harmondsworth: Penguin.

—— (1970a) 'Literature and Society', in *Speaking to Each Other*. Vol. II: *About Literature*, Harmondsworth: Penguin.

—— (1970b) 'Schools of English', in *Speaking to Each Other*. Vol. II: *About Literature*, Harmondsworth: Penguin.

—— (1970c) 'The Literary Imagination and the Sociological Imagination', in *Speaking to Each Other*. Vol. II: *About Literature*, Harmondsworth: Penguin.

—— (1973a) 'On Cultural Analysis', in *Speaking to Each Other*. Vol. I: *About Society*, Harmondsworth: Penguin.

—— (1982) 'Humanistic Studies and Mass Culture', in *An English Temper: Essays on Education, Culture, and Communications*, London: Chatto and Windus.

—— (1996) *The Way We Live Now*, London: Pimlico.

Honneth, Axel (1986) 'The Fragmented World of Symbolic Forms: Reflections on Pierre Bourdieu's Sociology of Culture', *Theory, Culture and Society*, 3, 3: 55–67.

Honneth, Axel, Kocyba, Hermann and Schwibs, Bernd (1986) 'The Struggle for Symbolic Order: An Interview with Pierre Bourdieu', *Theory, Culture and Society*, 3, 3: 35–51.

Horkheimer, Max (1972a) 'Art and Mass Culture', in *Critical Theory: Selected Essays*, New York: Herder and Herder.

—— (1972b) 'Materialism and Metaphysics', in *Critical Theory: Selected Essays*, New York: Herder and Herder.

—— (1972c) 'The Social Function of Philosophy', in *Critical Theory: Selected Essays*, New York: Herder and Herder.

—— (1972d) 'Traditional and Critical Theory', in *Critical Theory: Selected Essays*, New York: Herder and Herder.

Huyssen, Andreas (1984) 'Mapping the Postmodern', in Linda Nicholson (ed.), *Feminism/Postmodernism*, New York: Routledge.

Inglis, David and Holmes, Mary (2003) 'Highland and Other Haunts: Ghosts in Scottish Tourism', *Annals of Tourism Research*, 30, 1.

Inglis, David, Stockman, Norman and Surridge, Paula (2000) 'Bourdieu and Methodological Polytheism: Taking Sociology into the 21st Century', in John Eldridge, John MacInnes, Sue Scott, Chris Warhurst and Anne Witz (eds), *For Sociology: Legacies and Prospects*, Durham: Sociology Press.

Jameson, Frederic (1972) *The Prison-House of Language: A Critical Account of Structuralism and Russian Formalism*, Princeton, NJ: Princeton University Press.

—— (1992) *Postmodernism: or, the Cultural Logic of Late Capitalism*, London: Verso.

Jarvis, Simon (1998) *Adorno: A Critical Introduction*, Cambridge: Polity.

Jay, Martin (1974) *The Dialectical Imagination*, London: Heinemann.

—— (1984) *Marxism and Totality: The Adventures of a Concept from Lukács to Habermas*, Cambridge: Polity.

Jencks, Charles (1984) *The Language of Postmodern Architecture*, New York: Rizzoli.

—— (1986) *What Is Postmodernism?*, London: Academy Editions.

Johnson, Lesley (1979) *The Cultural Critics: From Matthew Arnold to Raymond Williams*, London: Routledge and Kegan Paul.

Johnson, Richard (1986/7) 'What is Cultural Studies Anyway?', *Social Text*, 16 (Winter).

Kellner, Douglas (1989) *Jean Baudrillard: From Marxism to Postmodernism and Beyond*, Cambridge: Polity.

Klein, Naomi (2001) *No Logo*, London: Flamingo.

Kolakowski, Leszek (1978) *Main Currents of Marxism*, vol. III, Oxford: Clarendon Press.

Kroeber, A. L. and Kluckhohn, Clyde (1963 [1952]) *Culture: A Critical Review of Concepts and Definitions*, New York: Random House.

Kuper, Adam (1999) *Culture: The Anthropologists' Account*, Cambridge, MA: Harvard University Press.

Lamont, Michele and Fournier, Marcel (1992) *Cultivating Differences: Symbolic Boundaries and the Making of Inequality*, Chicago: University of Chicago Press.

Lane, Jeremy (2000) *Pierre Bourdieu: A Critical Introduction*, London: Pluto.

Lasch, Christopher (1991 [1979]) *The Culture of Narcissism: American Life in an Age of Diminishing Expectations*, New York: W.W. Norton.

—— (1996) *Revolt of the Elites and the Betrayal of Democracy*, New York: W.W. Norton.

Lash, Scott (1990) *Sociology of Postmodernism*, London: Routledge.

Latouche, Serge (1996) *The Westernization of the World: The Significance, Scope and Limits of the Drive Towards Global Uniformity*, Cambridge: Polity.

Lazarsfeld, Paul (1984) 'Critical Theory and Dialectics', in Judith Marcus and Zoltan Tar (eds), *Foundations of the Frankfurt School of Social Research*, New Brunswick: Transaction Books.

Le Corbusier (1986) *Towards A New Architecture*, New York: Dover.

Leavis, F. R. (1962a) 'Literature and Society', in *The Common Pursuit*, London: Penguin.

—— (1962b) 'Sociology and Literature', in *The Common Pursuit*, London: Penguin.

—— (1986) 'Marxism and Cultural Continuity', in *Valuation in Criticism and Other Essays*, Cambridge: Cambridge University Press.

—— (1993 [1948]) *The Great Tradition*, Harmondsworth: Penguin.

Leavis, Q. D. (1990 [1932]) *Fiction and the Reading Public*, London: Bellew Publishing Company.

Lévi-Strauss, Claude (1986 [1963]) *Structural Anthropology*, vol. I, Harmondsworth: Penguin.

—— (1987 [1973]) *Structural Anthropology*, vol. II, Harmondsworth: Penguin.

Liebersohn, Harry (1988) *Fate and Utopia in German Sociology, 1870–1923*, Cambridge, MA: MIT Press.

Liszka, James Jakob (1996) *A General Introduction to the Semeiotic of Charles Sanders Peirce*, Bloomington: Indiana University Press.

Long, Elizabeth (ed.) (1997) *From Sociology to Cultural Studies*, Oxford: Blackwell.

Lowenthal, Leo (1957) *Literature and the Image of Man*, Boston: The Beacon Press.

—— (1961) *Literature, Popular Culture and Society*, Englewood Cliffs, NJ: Prentice-Hall.

—— (1984) *Literature and Mass Culture*, New Brunswick: Transaction Books.

Lukács, Georg (1971 [1923]) *History and Class Consciousness*, London: Merlin.

Lukes, Steven (1973) *Emile Durkheim: His Life and Work: A Historical and Critical Study*, London: Allen Lane.

Lynd, Robert S. and Lynd, Helen M. (1957 [1929]) *Middletown: A Study in Modern American Culture*, New York: Harcourt Brace.

Lyotard, Jean-François (1984) *The Postmodern Condition: A Report on Knowledge*, Manchester: Manchester University Press.

McCann, Graham (1994) 'Introduction', in Theodor W. Adorno and Hanns Eisler, *Composing for the Films*, London: The Athlone Press [1947].

MacCannell, Dean (1973) 'Staged Authenticity: Arrangements of Social Space in Tourist Settings', *American Journal of Sociology*, 79, 3.

Macdonald, Dwight (1978 [1953]) 'A Theory of Mass Culture', in Peter Davison, Rolf Meyersohn and Edward Shils (eds), *Literary Taste, Culture, and Mass Communication*, vol. I, Teaneck, NJ: Chadwyck-Healey.

—— (1962) 'Masscult and Midcult', in *Against the Grain: Essays on the Effects of Mass Culture*, New York: Vintage.

McGuigan, Jim (1992) *Cultural Populism*, London: Routledge.

McLellan, David (1984) *The Thought of Karl Marx*, Basingstoke: Macmillan.

McLennan, Gregor (1998) 'Sociology and Cultural Studies: Rhetorics of Disciplinary Identity', *History of the Human Sciences*, 11, 3: 1–17.

McRobbie, Angela (1994 [1989]) 'Second-Hand Dresses and the Role of the Ragmarket', in *Postmodernism and Popular Culture*, London: Routledge.

Maffesoli, Michel (1996) *The Time of the Tribes*, London: Sage.

Maier, Joseph B. (1984) 'Contribution to a Critique of Critical Theory', in Judith Marcus and Zoltan Tar (eds), *Foundations of the Frankfurt School of Social Research*, New Brunswick: Transaction Books.

Makkreel, Rudolf A. (1975) *Dilthey: Philosopher of the Human Studies*, Princeton: Princeton University Press.

Mannheim, Karl (1956) *Essays on the Sociology of Culture*, London: Routledge.

—— (1985 [1936]) *Ideology and Utopia*, Orlando: Harcourt, Brace, Jovanovich.

Marcuse, Herbert (1974 [1964]) *One-Dimensional Man*, Boston: Beacon Press.

Martin, Bill and Szelenyi, Ivan (1987) 'Beyond Cultural Capital: Toward a Theory of Symbolic Domination', in Ron Eyerman, Lennart G. Svenson and Thomas Sonderqvist (eds), *Intellectuals, Universities and the State in Western Modern Societies*, Berkeley: University of California Press.

Martorella, Rosanne (1977) 'The Relationship Between Box Office and Repertoire: A Case Study of Opera', *Sociological Quarterly*, 18 (Summer).

Marx, Karl (1977 [1859]) *A Contribution to the Critique of Political Economy*, Moscow: Progress Publishers.

—— (1981 [1844]) *Economic and Philosophic Manuscripts of 1844*, London: Lawrence and Wishart.

—— (1983 [1848]) 'Manifesto of the Communist Party', in Eugene Kamenka (ed.), *The Portable Karl Marx*, Harmondsworth: Penguin.

—— (1988 [1867]) *Capital*, vol. I, Harmondsworth: Penguin.

—— (1991 [1845–6]) *The German Ideology*, ed. Arthur, C. J., London: Lawrence and Wishart.

Matza, David and Sykes, G. M. (1961) 'Juvenile Delinquency and Subterranean Values', *American Sociological Review*, 26, 5.

Merrell, Floyd (1986) 'Structuralism and Beyond: A Critique of Presuppositions', in John Deely, Brooke Williams and Felicia E. Kruse (eds), *Frontiers in Semiotics*, Bloomington: Indiana University Press.

Merton, Robert (1965 [1938]) 'Anomie and Social Structure', in *Social Theory and Social Structure*, New York: Free Press.

Mills, C. Wright (1959) *The Sociological Imagination*, New York: Oxford University Press.

Milner, Andrew (1993) *Cultural Materialism*, Melbourne: Melbourne University Press.

Minh-Ha, Trinh T. (1989) *Woman, Native, Other: Writing, Postcoloniality and Feminism*, Bloomington: Indiana University Press.

Morley, David (1980) *The 'Nationwide' Audience: Structure and Decoding*, London: British Film Institute.

—— (1992) *Television, Audiences and Cultural Studies*, London: Routledge.

Mouzelis, Nicos (1995) *Sociological Theory: What Went Wrong?*, London: Routledge.

Mukerji, Chandra and Schudson, Michael (1991) 'Introduction: Rethinking Popular Culture', in C. Mukerji and M. Schudson (eds), *Rethinking Popular Culture: Contemporary Perspectives in Cultural Studies*, Berkeley: University of California Press.

Ortega y Gasset, José (1993 [1930]) *The Revolt of the Masses*, New York: W.W. Norton.

Owen, David (1997) 'The Postmodern Challenge to Sociology', in D. Owen (ed.), *Sociology after Postmodernism*, London: Sage.

Park, Robert (1952) *Human Communities: The City and Human Ecology*, New York: Free Press.

Parsons, Talcott (1937) *The Structure of Social Action*, New York: Free Press.
—— (1951) *The Social System*, New York: The Free Press.
—— (1961) 'Introduction – Part Four – Culture and the Social System', in Talcott Parsons, Edward Shils, Kaspar D. Naegele and Jesse R. Pitts (eds), *Theories of Society*, vol. II, Glencoe: Free Press.
—— (1977) *The Evolution of Societies*, Englewood Cliffs, NJ: Prentice Hall.
Peterson, Richard (ed.) (1976) *The Production of Culture*, London: Sage.
—— (1978) 'The Production of Cultural Change: The Case of Contemporary Country Music', *Social Research*, 45, 2: 292–314.
—— (1990) 'Why 1955? Explaining the Advent of Rock Music', *Popular Music*, 9.
—— (1994) 'Culture Studies Through the Production Perspective: Progress and Prospects', in D. Cranc (cd.), *The Sociology of Culture: Emerging Theoretical Perspectives*, Oxford: Blackwell.
—— (1997) *Creating Country Music: Fabricating Authenticity*, Chicago: University of Chicago Press.
Popper, Karl (1966) *The Open Society and Its Enemies*. Vol. 2: *The High Tide of Prophecy: Hegel, Marx, and the Aftermath*, London: Routledge.
Powell, Walter (1978) 'Publishers' Decision-Making: What Criteria do they use in Deciding Which Books to Publish?', *Social Research*, 45, 2.
Pryluck, C. (1986) 'Industrialization of Entertainment in the United States', in B. A. Austin (ed.), *Current Research in Film: Audiences, Economics and Law*, vol. 2, Norwood, NJ: Ablex.
Readings, Bill (1991) *Introducing Lyotard: Art and Politics*, London: Routledge.
Rickman, H. P. (1988) *Dilthey Today: A Critical Appraisal of the Contemporary Relevance of his Work*, New York: Greenwood.
Ritzer, George (1992) *The McDonaldization of Society: An Investigation into the Changing Character of Contemporary Social Life*, Thousand Oaks: Pine Forge.
Robertson, Roland (1992) *Globalization: Social Theory and Global Culture*, London: Sage.
Roe, Frederick William (1936) *The Social Philosophy of Carlyle and Ruskin*, New York: Peter Smith.
Rojek, Chris (1995) *Decentring Leisure: Rethinking Leisure Theory*, London: Sage.
Rojek, Chris and Turner, Bryan, S. (2000) 'Decorative Sociology: Towards a Critique of the Cultural Turn', *Sociological Review*, 48, 4: 629–48.
Rose, Gillian (1978) *The Melancholy Science*, Basingstoke: Macmillan.
Rosenberg, Bernard (1957) 'Mass Culture in America', in B. Rosenberg and D. Manning White (eds), *Mass Culture: The Popular Arts in America*, New York: Free Press.
Ross, Andrew (1989) *No Respect: Intellectuals and Popular Culture*, London: Routledge.
Roth, Guenther (1979) *Max Weber's Vision of History*, Berkeley: University of California Press.

Rylance, Rick (1994) *Roland Barthes*, London: Harvester Wheatsheaf.

Saussure, Ferdinand (1959 [1906–11]) *Course in General Linguistics*, ed. Charles Bally and Albert Sechehaye, New York: Philosophical Library.

Scheler, Max (1980 [1924]) *Problems of a Sociology of Knowledge*, London: Routledge.

Schlesinger Jr., Arthur M. (1991) *The Disuniting of America*, Knoxville, TN: Whittle Direct Books.

Schroeder, Ralph (1992) *Max Weber and the Sociology of Culture*, London: Sage.

Scott, James (1985) *Weapons of the Weak*, New Haven: Yale University Press.

Sennett, Richard (1999) *The Corrosion of Character*, New York: W.W. Norton.

Shils, Edward (1978 [1961]) 'Mass Society and Its Culture', in Peter Davison, Rolf Meyersohn and Edward Shils (eds), *Literary Taste, Culture, and Mass Communication*, vol. I, Teaneck, NJ: Chadwyck-Healey.

Simmel, Georg (1997) 'On the Concept and Tragedy of Culture', in David Frisby and Mike Featherstone (eds), *Simmel on Culture: Selected Writings*, London: Sage.

Spencer, Herbert (1961 [1897]) 'The Factors of Social Phenomena', in Talcott Parsons, Edward Shils, Kaspar D. Naegele and Jesse R. Pitts (eds), *Theories of Society*, vol. II, Glencoe: Free Press.

Stallabrass, Julian (1996) *Gargantua: Manufactured Mass Culture*, London: Verso.

Strong, Phil M. (1979) 'Sociological Imperialism and the Profession of Medicine', *Social Science and Medicine*, 13A: 199–215.

Swingewood, Alan (1977) *The Myth of Mass Culture*, London: Macmillan.

Sztompka, Piotr (1993) *The Sociology of Social Change*, Oxford: Blackwell.

Taylor, Charles (1975) *Hegel*, Cambridge: Cambridge University Press.

—— (1992) *Multiculturalism and 'The Politics of Recognition'*, Princeton: Princeton University Press.

Taylor, Timothy D. (1997) *Global Pop: World Music, World Markets*, London: Routledge.

Thomas, W. I. and Znaniecki, Florian (1984 [1918–1920]) *The Polish Peasant in Europe and America*, Urbana: University of Illinois Press.

Thompson, E. P. (1976 [1963]) *The Making of the English Working Class*, Harmondsworth: Penguin.

Thornton, Sarah (1995) *Club Cultures: Music, Media and Sub-cultural Capital*, Cambridge: Polity.

Tocqueville, Alexis de (1952 [1835]) *Democracy in America*, ed. Henry Steele Commager, London: Oxford University Press.

Tonnies, Ferdinand (1955 [1877]) *Community and Association*, London: Routledge.

Tuchman, Gaye (1978) 'The News Net', *Social Research*, 45, 2.

Turner, Bryan (1996) *For Weber: Essays on the Sociology of Fate*, London: Sage.

Twitchell, James (1992) *Carnival Culture: The Trashing of Taste in America*, New York: Columbia University Press.

Urry, John (1990) *The Tourist Gaze: Leisure and Travel in Contemporary Societies*, London: Sage.

—— (2000) *Sociology Beyond Societies: Mobilities for the Twenty-first Century*, London: Routledge.

Veblen, Thorstein (1994 [1899]) *The Theory of the Leisure Class*, New York: Dover.

Venturi, Robert (1966) *Complexity and Contradiction in Architecture*, New York: Museum of Modern Art.

Venturi, Robert, Scott Brown, Denise and Izenour, Steven (1977 [1972]) *Learning from Las Vegas: The Forgotten Symbolism of Architectural Form*, Cambridge, MA: MIT Press.

Verdes-Leroux, Jeannine (2001) *Deconstructing Pierre Bourdieu: Against Sociological Terrorism from the Left*, New York: Algora.

Voloshinov, V. N. (1973 [1929]) *Marxism and the Philosophy of Language*, Cambridge, MA: Harvard University Press.

Wacquant, Loic J. D. (2000) 'Durkheim and Bourdieu: The Common Plinth and its Cracks', in Bridget Fowler (ed.), *Reading Bourdieu on Society and Culture*, Oxford: Blackwell/The Sociological Review.

Warde, Alan, Martens, Lydia and Olsen, Wendy (1999) 'Consumption and the Problem of Variety: Cultural Omnivorousness, Social Distinction and Dining Out', *Sociology*, 33, 1 (February): 105–27.

Waters, Malcolm (1995) *Globalization*, London: Routledge.

Weber, Alfred (1998 [1920–1]) 'Fundamentals of Culture-Sociology: Social Process, Civilizational Process and Culture-Movement', in John Rundell and Stephen Mennell (eds), *Classical Readings in Civilization and Culture*, London: Routledge.

Weber, Max (1930 [1905–6]) *The Protestant Ethic and the Spirit of Capitalism*, London: Methuen.

—— (1966) *The Sociology of Religion*, London: Methuen.

—— (1982) 'Class, Status, Party', in Hans H. Gerth and Charles W. Mills (eds), *From Max Weber*, London: Routledge.

—— (1989) *Max Weber's 'Science as a Vocation'*, ed. Peter Lassman, Irving Velody and Herminio Martins, London: Unwin Hyman.

Werbner, Pnina (1997) 'Introduction: The Dialectics of Cultural Hybridity', in Pnina Werbner and Toriq Modood (eds), *Debating Cultural Hybridity: Multi-cultural Identities and the Politics of Anti-racism*, London: Zed.

West, Cornel (1990) 'The New Cultural Politics of Difference', in Russell Ferguson, Martha Gever, Trinh T. Minh-ha and Cornel West (eds), *Out There: Marginalization and Contemporary Cultures*, Cambridge, MA: MIT Press.

Wiggershaus, Rolf (1995) *The Frankfurt School*, Cambridge: Polity.

Williams, Raymond (1958) *Culture and Society 1780–1950*, London: Chatto and Windus.

—— (1976) *Keywords: A Vocabulary of Culture and Society*, Glasgow: Fontana.

—— (1977) *Marxism and Literature*, Oxford: Oxford University Press.

—— (1980 [1961]) *The Long Revolution*, Harmondsworth: Penguin.

—— (1981) *Culture*, Glasgow: Fontana.

—— (1989 [1958]) 'Culture is Ordinary', in *Resources of Hope: Culture, Democracy, Socialism*, London: Verso.

—— (1989 [1961]) 'Communications and Community', in *Resources of Hope: Culture, Democracy, Socialism*, London: Verso.

—— (1989 [1968]) 'The Idea of a Common Culture', in *Resources of Hope: Culture, Democracy, Socialism*, London: Verso.

—— (1989 [1975]) 'You're a Marxist, Aren't You?', in *Resources of Hope: Culture, Democracy, Socialism*, London: Verso.

—— (1997a) 'Literature and Sociology', in *Problems in Materialism and Culture*, London: Verso.

—— (1997b) 'Base and Superstructure in Marxist Cultural Theory', in *Problems in Materialism and Culture*, London: Verso.

—— (1997c) 'Means of Communication as Means of Production', in *Problems in Materialism and Culture*, London: Verso.

Willis, Paul (1977) *Learning to Labour: How Working Class Kids get Working Class Jobs*, Aldershot: Gower.

—— (1990) *Common Culture: Symbolic Work at Play in the Cultural Activities of Young People*, Milton Keynes: Open University Press.

Winner, Irene Portis (1986) 'Semiotics of Culture', in John Deely, Brooke Williams and Felicia E. Kruse (eds), *Frontiers in Semiotics*, Bloomington: Indiana University Press.

Wolff, Janet (1999) 'Cultural Studies and the Sociology of Culture', *Contemporary Sociology*, 28, 5 (September).

Wrong, Dennis (1980 [1961]) 'The Oversocialized Conception of Man in Modern Sociology', in Robert Bocock (ed.), *An Introduction to Sociology: A Reader*, Glasgow: Fontana.

Index

action, patterns of 5–6, 26, 32–4; theory 164; *see also* structure/action problem

Adorno, Theodor 39, 41–62, 100, 159, 197; *Dialectic of Enlightenment* 45–52; mass culture studies 45–54, 70, 72, 105, 201, 204, 205

advertising 105, 188, 192, 209; as exploitation 47, 48–9; semiotics of 124–6, 147

Afro-American philosophy 85

agnosticism, sociological 28–9, 224

Alexander, Jeffrey C. 11, 185

alienation 73–4; Adorno and Horkheimer on 46–7, 51–2; Marxist 23–4; in modern culture 63; postmodern 148–9; Simmel on 30–1; and solidarity 216–19; *see also* anomie

America: cultural disaster 67–71; defining 65–7; Middle 79–82; pulse of 82–4

'American Dream' 74, 83–4, 150–2, 208

American Revolution (1776) 66

anarchy 89, 90–1

anomie 32, 93

anthropology 72–3, 93–4, 97, 121

arbitrariness of signs 6, 116–18, 119, 120, 146–7, 167–8; *see also* cultural arbitrary (Bourdieu)

architecture 222; postmodern 143–4

aristocracy 16–17; and religion 30

Arnold, Matthew, *Culture and Anarchy* 90–1, 99, 107

art 18–19; autonomous (Adorno) 52–3, 57, 227; collective production of 193–4, 198–9; as compensation 52–4; fetishization of 59; and mass culture 144; modern 183; photography as 181; politics and 89–90

artists, as cultural workers 193–4, 198–9

audience: as discerning 55–7, 59, 61–2, 132–3, 221–2; the mass 49–52, 71, 132, 154; postmodern 155–7; social contexts 75–6

authenticity 191, 210–12

autonomy: of art 52–3, 57, 227; of culture 25–6

avant garde 52, 69–70, 72, 204

Barthes, Roland 113, 121–30, 136, 145, 167, 226; *The Fashion System* 127–8; *Mythologies* 124–5, 128, 135; and semiotics of popular culture 121–3, 147, 155, 178

base and superstructure (Marx) 21–2, 24–5, 43–4, 135; Critical Theory's rejection of 43–5; postmodernism and 158–9, 185; Williams on 108–9